Eric-Emman

Play

Don Juan on Tri
Enigma Variations, Between

Eric-Emmanuel Schmitt was born in Lyon in 1960, and graduated in philosophy from the Ecole Normale Supérieure in 1983. His first play, *La Nuit de Valognes*, opened in 1991. In 1993, his next play, *Le Visiteur*, won three Molières, and has since been produced all over the world. His other plays include *Golden Joe* (1994), *Variations énigmatiques* (1996), which first starred Alain Delon, *Milarepa* (1996), *Le Libertin* (1997), *Frederick* (1998) and *Hôtel des deux mondes* (1999). Schmitt has also written two books, *La Secte des égoïstes* (1994) and *Diderot, ou la philosophie de la seduction* (1997), and translated *Le Nozze di Figaro* for Opéra de Compiègne (1997), and *The Merchant of Venice* for the Maison de la Culture de Loire Atlantique (1994).

Jeremy Sams's work as a director includes *Schippel the Plumber* (Greenwich), *Passion* (West End), *Neville's Island* (Nottingham and West End), *Wild Oats* and *Marat/Sade* (National Theatre), *Enter the Guardsman* (Donmar Warehouse), *Maria Friedman – by Special Arrangement* (Donmar Warehouse and West End), *The Wind in the Willows* (Old Vic), *Two Pianos Four Hands* (Birmingham Rep), *Spend Spend Spend* (West End) and *Noises Off* (National Theatre and West End). His translations include *Les Parents Terribles*, *The Miser* and *Mary Stuart* (National Theatre), *The Rehearsal* (Almeida and West End), *Becket* (West End), *A Fool and His Money* (Nottingham and Birmingham Rep), *Figaro's Wedding*, *La Bohème*, *The Magic Flute*, the *Ring* cycle (ENO) and *The Merry Widow* (Covent Garden). He has written, arranged and directed music for over fifty shows for theatre, TV and radio, including *The Wind in the Willows* and *Arcadia* (National Theatre), *The Merry Wives of Windsor* (RSC), *Have Your Cake and Eat It* (Initial Films) and Jane Austen's *Persuasion* (BBC), for which he won a BAFTA.

John Clifford was born in 1950 and educated at the University of St Andrew's. He is a poet, playwright, journalist, critic, broadcaster and translator, and has also written for TV, radio and film. His plays, which include *Losing Venice* (Traverse Theatre, Edinburgh, 1985), *Playing with Fire* (Traverse, 1987), *Light in the Village* (Traverse, 1991) and *Dreaming* (Edinburgh Puppet Company, 1994), have been translated into several languages and performed all over the world. He has received numerous awards, has led writers' workshops in Scotland, India, Singapore and Spain, is Vice-Chairperson of the Scottish Society of Playwrights, and on the board of the Scottish theatre company Suspect Culture. He is also a lecturer in the Acting and Drama Department of Queen Margaret College, Edinburgh.

ERIC-EMMANUEL SCHMITT

Plays: 1

Don Juan on Trial
The Visitor
Enigma Variations
Between Worlds

introduced by David Bradby

Methuen Drama

METHUEN DRAMA CONTEMPORARY DRAMATISTS

1 3 5 7 9 10 8 6 4 2

This collection first published in Great Britain in 2002 by
Methuen Publishing Limited

Copyright © Eric-Emmanuel Schmitt, 1991, 1993, 1996, 1999; copyright in the English translations of *La Nuit de Valognes* (*Don Juan on Trial*), *Le Visiteur* (*The Visitor*) and *Variations énigmatiques* (*Enigma Variations*) © Jeremy Sams, 1996, 2002; copyright in the English translation of *Hôtel des deux mondes* (*Between Worlds*) © John Clifford, 2002.

Eric-Emmanuel Schmitt, Jeremy Sams and John Clifford have asserted their rights under the Copyright, Designs and Patents Act, 1988, to be identified as the author and translators of these works.

Introduction copyright © David Bradby 2002

A CIP catalogue record for this book is available from the British Library

ISBN 0 413 76020 0

Typeset by Deltatype, Birkenhead, Merseyside
Printed and bound in Great Britain by
Cox and Wyman Ltd, Reading, Berkshire

Caution

All rights in these plays are strictly reserved. Application for performances in English should be made before rehearsals begin to Alan Brodie Representation Ltd, 211 Piccadilly, London W1V 9LD; for US rights for *Don Juan on Trial* and *Enigma Variations* to Dramatic Publishing, 311 Washington Street, Woodstock, IL60098; and for performances in other languages, and for all other translations, to Agence Drama, 24 rue Feydeau, 75002 Paris. No performance may be given unless a licence has been obtained.

This book is sold subject to the condition that it shall not, by way of trade or otherwise, be lent, resold, hired out, or otherwise circulated in any form of binding or cover other than that in which it is published and without a similar condition, including this condition, being imposed on the subsequent purchaser.

Contents

Eric-Emmanuel Schmitt: A Chronology

1991 — *La Nuit de Valognes* (*Don Juan on Trial*). Co-production between Maison de la Culture de Loire Atlantique, Nantes and Comédie des Champs-Elysées, Paris. Subsequently produced in the USA and UK (RSC, 1996) and throughout the world.
Translated *Sarcophagus* by Vladimir Goubariev.

1993 — *Le Visiteur*. Petit Théâtre de Paris. Ran for over two seasons, Paris and French tour. Won three Molières: Best Play, Best Playwright and Most Promising New Work.

1994 — *Golden Joe*. CADO d'Orléans and Théâtre de la Porte St Martin, Paris.
Novel *La Secte des égoïstes*.
Translated *The Merchant of Venice* for the Maison de la Culture de Loire Atlantique.

1996 — *Variations énigmatiques*. Théâtre Marigny, Paris (revived 1998, Théâtre de Paris). Subsequently produced all over the world.
Milarepa (first part of trilogy). Théâtre Vidy, Lausanne, Switzerland. (Revived at the 1997 Avignon Festival and opened in Paris, 1999.)

1997 — *Le Libertin*, Théâtre Montparnasse. (Later adapted for the screen.)
Diderot, ou la philosophie de la séduction (essay).
Translated libretto of *Le Nozze di Figaro* for Opéra de Compiègne (revived for tour and Casino de Paris).
Adapted musical *Nine* by Maury Yeston and Arthur Kopit for the Folies Bergère.

1998 — *Frédérick, ou le boulevard du crime*. Théâtre Marigny, Paris.
Revival of *Le Visiteur*, Théâtre Marigny, Salle Popesco, Paris.

1999	*Hôtel des deux mondes*. Théâtre Marigny, Salle Popesco, Paris. Nominated for seven Molières. *Monsieur Ibrahim et les fleurs du Coran* (monologue section of trilogy, following *Milarepa*). Théâtre La Piscine, Châtenay Malabry. Revived at the 2001 Avignon Festival.
2000	Novel *L'évangile selon Pilate*. Won the Grand Prix des Lectriccs de *Elle* and nominated for the Prix de l'Académie Française and the Prix Interallié. *Le Visiteur* adapted as an opera, with music by Stavros Xarhakos, Théâtre Impérial, Compiègne.
2001	Novel *La Part de l'autre*. Nominated for the Prix de l'Académie Française. Received the Prix du Théâtre de l'Academie Française for his entire theatrical *œuvre* (to date). Screenplay of *Volpone*. Screenplay of *King Lear*. Screenplay of *Les Liaisons dangereuses*. Television adaptation of Aragon's *Aurelien*.
2002	Revival of *Monsieur Ibrahim et les fleurs du Coran*, Studio des Champs-Elysées, Paris.
2003	*Oscar et la dame Rose* (part three of the trilogy) due to open outside Paris and subsequently at the Théâtre des Mathurins, Paris.

Introduction

Eric-Emmanuel Schmitt was born in 1960. His first play was written when he was twenty-nine and since then he has written a dozen more (eight full-length and four short pieces), all of which have enjoyed long runs on the Parisian stage. Schmitt is highly prized for his success in reviving a type of play that many had thought dead and buried: the witty play of ideas. It is a form that has never gone into eclipse in the English theatre, as the continuity of work from George Bernard Shaw to Tom Stoppard and Christopher Hampton demonstrates, but in France it disappeared between Sartre and Schmitt. During the early years of the twentieth century, it was a staple of many Paris theatres. Jean Giraudoux and Jean Anouilh were the most prominent playwrights of this kind, but many others, including Armand Salacrou, Henri-René Lenormand and André Obey were the life-blood of the Paris theatres until the Theatre of the Absurd burst on to the stage in the aftermath of the Second World War and swept all before it. Sartre is one of the reference points for Schmitt when situating his own work (Schmitt quotes Sartre in his interview, published in *Mise en scène: French Theatre Now*, Methuen, 1997), and there is another reason why he often refers back to the 1940s and 1950s: this was the last time when playwrights did not have to be writers for the stage alone, but when dramatic works were accepted naturally alongside novels, essays, philosophy, politics, even poetry, each contributing to building up the profile of the author as a writer with something to say to the nation at large, not just to theatre-goers.

Schmitt did not originally plan to be a dramatist. He first studied Music at the conservatoire of his home town, Lyon, before going to the Ecole Normale Supérieure in Paris, where he took the *agrégation* exam in philosophy and went on to complete a doctoral thesis on Diderot and metaphysics. His beginnings as a writer were in the genres of literary and philosophical criticism rather than as a playwright. His novel, *La Secte des égoïstes* (Editions Albin Michel, 1994) won the prize awarded for best first novel of the year, and he has gone on to publish two further novels as well as a book-length essay (*Diderot ou la philosophie de la séduction*, Editions Albin Michel, 1997) and his twelve plays. Each of the plays in this volume is prompted by an intellectual rather than a theatrical idea. This does not mean that Schmitt cannot display a mastery of stage-craft. Each of these plays shows that he can. But the form is there to serve the debate rather than the other way round. He is not primarily interested in dramatic experiment but in exploring all the different ideas that may follow from a given proposition. The ideas that concern him are universal ones, accessible on many levels and not restricted to those with an interest in philosophy. In fact he has said that, 'When I write a play, I want it to appeal to my grandmother as well as to my intellectual friends' (*Mise en scène*, p. 170). The four plays in this volume turn around two major preoccupations of human beings everywhere: the nature of love and the existence of God.

In *Don Juan on Trial*, Schmitt imagines a situation in which some of the women who have been seduced and abandoned by Don Juan gather together to put him on trial. They are in no doubt about the outcome of the trial, and have already prepared his sentence: he will be obliged to marry the young Angélique, who is infatuated with him even though he has treated her cruelly, and has even killed her brother in a duel. The opening of the play establishes the characters of each of the women: one is a romantic, another is a cynic, a third has taken refuge in religion, etc. Schmitt here demonstrates his mastery of dramatic dialogue. Each woman thinks she is articulating a clear condemnation of Don Juan's behaviour while in fact revealing her own profound weaknesses. The tone is light and witty but also manages to touch on profound truths. For Schmitt, dramatic construction necessarily entails a complex interplay of character and situation: 'the opening up of space in psychological, intellectual and temporal terms, with complex relationships between people; with the exchange of different ideas with a situation which unfurls in a certain time period and which seeks a solution. It's created by tensions and oppositions, and it's the force of these tensions which gives life to a performance. There should be no immobility, no anonymity, but there should be characters, contradictions and often lies' (*Mise en scène*, p. 173). In this play, half of the fun for the audience comes from detecting the lies of the various characters and watching the process through which each character separates the lies from the truth in the others' behaviour.

When Don Juan enters, he is not the handsome young seducer of tradition: he is a raddled, exhausted old debauchee. But it is not simply old age that has caused his despair. He is still able to turn heads, as the infatuation of the young Angélique demonstrates. Rather, it is the disturbing experience he has had with her brother that has changed him. As the action unfolds, it centres on the nature of the fascination that may draw one human being to another and the attachment that one may feel for another person. There is a highly polished passage of extended dialogue between Don Juan and Angélique in Act Two, in which she is drawn into speaking with intense passion of the devotion he has inspired in her, and through this she defines the power of love. In the third and final act, Don Juan recounts exactly what happened in the duel with her brother and we realise that the brother was equally attached to him, and engineered his own death because he understood that the Don would never reciprocate his love. It is this that has so profoundly affected Don Juan. Belatedly, he has realised that sex and love are not necessarily connected, and that his frenetic pursuit of sex throughout his life as a seducer has blinded him to the far more powerful force of love.

Schmitt has commented that 'in the versions of the seventeenth and eighteenth centuries, Don Juan is punished by the Commander. Rather than a God of vengeance, drawn from the Old Testament, I have sketched a Son who is more loving, too much so, a figure both Christ-like and perverse' (website). So the play turns out not to deal with the topics of lust, seduction and sexual conquest, but rather with the power of sacrifice, devotion, loss of self in the other and submission to others that adds up to the definition of love offered by the New Testament rather than the possessive, jealous, all-conquering love of the Old Testament. *Don Juan on Trial* [*La Nuit de Valognes*] was first performed in 1991, in a co-production between the Maison de la Culture de Loire Atlantique, Nantes and the Comédie des Champs-Elysées, Paris, directed by Jean-Luc Tardieu. The translation published here was commissioned by the Royal Shakespeare Company for a production at The Other Place in Stratford in 1996.

Schmitt's first play was followed by *The Visitor* [*Le Visiteur*] in 1993, which had an enormous commercial success. Not only did it run for over two seasons (in Paris and on tour) with a very successful revival in 1998–9, it also sold over 40,000 copies, more than any other contemporary French play. The fact that it enjoyed such sales is significant. It justifies Schmitt's claim to be seen as a writer, whose work, for all its success with theatre audiences, also extends beyond the world of the stage. His plays can be enjoyed for their literary qualities as much as for their effectiveness on stage.

For his second play, Schmitt chose as his central character not a mythical archetype such as Don Juan, but an historical figure: Sigmund Freud. The play is set in Vienna, in the brief period between the *Anschluss* of March 1938, when Hitler annexed Austria as part of the greater German *Reich* and June of the same year, when Freud went into exile. Against this grim background, Schmitt develops a rather whimsical dialogue, as a character (named simply 'The Stranger' [*L'inconnu*] in the list of characters) appears in Freud's flat, claiming to be God. Freud, who is in a nervous state, vacillates between believing him and dismissing him as an escaped lunatic on the run from the Gestapo. However, the identity of the mysterious visitor (never resolved) is less important than the substance of the debate that follows between him and Freud. This is the play's backbone. Even more than *Don Juan on Trial*, it develops into a philosophical drama of ideas dealing with the problem of how it is possible to believe in a God of Love as the creator of a world that includes such horrors as the Nazi death camps. The question becomes more than just a theoretical debate because of its insertion into a real historical context. Freud, as a confirmed atheist, must deny the existence of God. But when placed in a situation of extreme danger, he realises that the human heart may be capable of horrors that even he cannot account for, and vacillates briefly in his belief that everything is subject to rational explanation.

Schmitt has given the following account of how the idea for the play came to him. One evening, watching the news on television, he was overcome by a sense of depression ('it was no worse than any other day, just the usual hash of crime and injustice') and the idea occurred to him, 'How discouraged God must be as he watches the evening news!' He went on to wonder what God does when he goes into depression. Is there anyone to whom he can talk about it? 'Immediately the idea hit me: God on Freud's couch. And then the counter-image: Freud on God's couch.' He felt that God and Freud would have an enormous amount to say to one another, and that it would be a huge challenge to write their dialogue, 'given that neither believes in the other' (website). The fundamental question of how it is possible to believe in God in the face of the problem of evil is in the background of the lengthy dialogues between Freud and his mysterious Stranger, but what might have become an abstract discussion is given force and immediacy by the circumstances. Anna, Freud's daughter, has been taken off to the Gestapo headquarters for questioning. No one knows what is happening to her there, nor whether she will emerge alive. Moreover, Freud himself is faced with an extremely difficult moral choice: the Nazis will give him a safe passage out of Vienna to the destination of his choice, but only if he will sign a paper to say that the regime has treated him with respect. As a doctor and a rationalist, he cannot bear to put his name to a false document. This dilemma, and the occasional interruptions of a Nazi officer trying to squeeze money out of Freud, break up the dialogue between Freud and the Stranger and help to create a sense of movement through the play as Freud's most basic ideas are challenged, one by one, and his certainties dismantled. The play has one uninterrupted act and the action is intended to take the same time as the duration of the play itself.

Enigma Variations [*Variations énigmatiques*] again takes place in a single scene and takes the form of a dramatic dialogue for only two characters. It was written for Alain Delon, and was staged in 1996 at the Théâtre Marigny; the first London production was at the Savoy Theatre in 2000, directed by Anthony Page, with Donald Sutherland in the role of Znorko, following a successful run at the Mark Taper Forum, Los Angeles, the Royal Alexandra Theater, Toronto and the Malvern Festival. This time, Schmitt has pared his cast down to only the two protagonists. The first is a reclusive writer, Abel Znorko (played by Delon/Sutherland), who lives on a remote island in the Norwegian Sea. The second, Eric Larsen (played in the first production by Francis Huster), turns out to be something of an enigma, not unlike the Stranger of Schmitt's second play. A third character, Helen Metternach, who is of crucial importance to them both, and to their unfolding relationship, is already dead when the play opens, though the full truth about her does not emerge until the very end of the play. In life she was both the wife of one and the former lover of the other, but her precise meaning to each of the men shifts back and forth in the course of the afternoon and evening during which their first meeting takes place.

Eric Larsen has posed as a journalist, coming for an interview with the famous writer Znorko, who has just had his greatest success yet with an epistolary novel chronicling a great love affair. In fact, as it emerges, Larsen is a music teacher who married Helen Metternach and nursed her as she died of a chronic illness. A major part of this play's fascination lies in the gradual revelation of the triangular relationship between its three characters, and so it would be unfair to summarise the plot any further, but it retains its surprises until the very end. In his own note on the play, published on his website, Schmitt calls it 'no doubt the most autobiographical of my plays'. He goes on to explain that there is much of himself in both Znorko and Larsen:

'Like Znorko, I have known betrayal, suffered from lies and loneliness, and have found a refuge in writing. Like Larsen, I have known that love, simple, undemanding, that accompanies a loved one, day by day, through illness to death. [. . .] Znorko and Larsen embody two different ways of loving' (website). But the gulf between the reality of our lives and the mendacious image we construct for ourselves of that reality is explored with great wit and sensitivity. Schmitt has made it clear that this theme is very dear to him: 'The conflict between thought and reality is perhaps the single subject of all my plays.'

Between Worlds [*Hôtel des Deux Mondes*] is the most recent of the plays in this volume: it had its first performance at the Théâtre Marigny in 1999. It is set in a hotel lobby with a lift in a way that resembles the first few minutes of Sartre's play *Huis Clos*. The audience shares the characters' uncertainty about precisely where they are, but they come to understand that the hotel is, literally, between two worlds. It is a place where people find themselves in a state of limbo when they have suffered a near-fatal injury and are in a coma. While their real bodies are in intensive care, their astral bodies wait around here until the teams of medical staff attending to them back on earth manage to restore them to consciousness, or, alternatively, decide to switch off their support machines. They then take the lift – if it goes up, they have died, but if it goes down, it means that they will recover and live again. The 'hotel' is presided over by a mysterious figure named simply Doctor S. Her job is to go through the record of each person's life and, in this way, the audience finds out about them. The central character is Colin (Julien in the original), a forty-year old who has been drinking too much and has crashed his car into a tree. Schmitt describes him as 'the man of our times: pessimistic, materialistic, unhappy, he drives too fast, falls in and out of love too fast, thinks too fast. He exhibits all the prejudices of off-the-peg contemporary thought with its negative certainties. He is stifled by the ideological weight of this, it prevents him from truly living, keeps him at a distance from things, makes him uncommitted' (website).

The other characters offer a cross section of different

social types. The Chairman is a self-important businessman perpetually preoccupied with his belief that the only way he can get away is if he can get a private interview with the doctor and explain how well connected he is. The Magus is a fairground fortune-teller who has a detached, rather sardonic view of the others but with an underlying warmth and affection. Jessie is a cleaning woman whose life on earth has never been easy or comfortable, and who is amazed to find herself being so well cared for. Laura arrives half-way through the play and changes Colin's whole attitude. In real life, Laura is a paraplegic, confined to bed or wheelchair and unable do anything for herself. But here in the 'hotel', she has a normal healthy body and Colin feels instantly drawn to her. But because of her experience, she is unlike any girl he has previously met. Instead of simply wanting to seduce her, he finds himself experiencing a new emotion for the first time: 'A certain trust, and I want to be able to have hope in something I do not understand' (p. 274). He has discovered what it is to really love someone else for the first time and begs the doctor not to separate him and Laura from one another. The Magus observes this, and feels moved to persuade the Doctor to let him help them. Taken as a whole, the play can be seen as a meditation on love and on what it means to escape from the narrow limits of concern with self, and lay oneself open to the attraction of the other. It is also attempting to say something about the acceptance of death and the way in which this may lead to a new appreciation of life. The tone of the dialogue reminds one of Anouilh – it is witty and fast-moving, but also hints at deeper truths.

The commercial success enjoyed by Schmitt's plays can be attributed to several factors. They avoid alienating Modernist devices that might be seen as 'difficult' by audiences. The plays all tell an intriguing story, involving characters with whom the audience can sympathise. These characters may be taken from history or literature, but always emerge in a surprising new light. Schmitt has said that 'Theatre permits form to triumph over chaos and sense over nonsense' (*Mise en scène*, p. 173), deliberately echoing similar statements by earlier authors such as Oscar Wilde or Jean Anouilh. The dialogue in his plays sparkles with wit and intelligence, and if he may sometimes be guilty of scoring points in order to flatter his audiences by persuading them of their own cleverness, he nevertheless succeeds in developing thought-provoking discussions on the place of European cultural traditions in the world of today.

David Bradby
London, May 2002

References

Mise en scène: French Theatre Now, by David Bradby and Annie Sparks, London: Methuen, 1997.

Website: www.eric-emmanuel-schmitt.net

Don Juan on Trial

translated by Jeremy Sams

La Nuit de Valognes was first performed at the Maison de la Culture de Loire Atlantique, Nantes on 17 September 1991. The cast was as follows:

Don Juan	Mathieu Carrière
Duchess de Vaubricourt	Micheline Presle
Angelique	Florence Darel
Chevalier de Chiffreville	Dominique Guillo
Comtesse de la Roche-Piquet	Danièle Lebrun
Mademoiselle de la Frotte	Delphine Rich
Madame Cassin	Nathalie Juvet
Sganarelle	André Gille
Marion	Friedericke Laval
Hortense de Hauteclaire	Marie-Christine Rousseau

Directed by Jean-Luc Tardieu
Designed by Dominique Arel
Lighting by Jacques Rouveyrollis

Characters

Don Juan, *ageless*
Duchess de Vaubricourt, *a beautiful older lady*
Angelique, *a young girl*
Chevalier de Chiffreville, *her brother*
Comtesse de la Roche Piquet, *a libertine, in her middle years*
Mademoiselle de la Frotte, *a writer of romantic novels*
Madame Cassin, *a bourgeoise*
Sganarelle, *Don Juan's valet*
Marion, *a young, pretty servant*
Hortense de Hauteclaire, *a nun*

Setting

The salon of a provincial chateau in France in the mid-eighteenth century.

Act One

Scene One

Setting: An eighteenth-century chateau. Abandoned. Old furniture.

At rise: Night. **Countess** *enters – in red – preceded by* **Marion**, *the serving maid. Looks around disapprovingly.*

Countess Are you quite sure I'm in the right place, my girl? I am the Countess de la Roche-Piquet.

Marion I will inform Madame of your arrival.

Countess I always knew the Duchess was eccentric, but I never thought she would go so far as to receive guests in the lumber room. I mean, asking me to drop everything, to leave Paris, without so much as a word to my husband or even to my lovers – I begrudge her none of this, I owe it to her in the name of friendship. But to ask me here, to the middle of nowhere, to the wild wastes of Normandy . . . well! These godforsaken plains, these stunted trees, these stunted houses. Why in God's name did they put the countryside so far away from Paris? What a journey. (*She fingers the dust.*) Are you sure these aren't the servants' quarters or something?

Marion No, Madame. If they were, you'd think you were in the cellars or in the storerooms.

Countess I would not. I don't think I've ever seen the storerooms –

Marion Madame La Duchesse has not lived in this house for thirty years –

Countess I don't blame her.

Marion – and three days ago she decided to return here.

Countess Then I do blame her. The smell, my child, the smell.

Marion It's all been locked up. Stuffy.

Countess Yes, it's odd, that. Why should stone, wood, and bits of cloth – why should they smell? You associate smells with human beings, at least I do, but inanimate objects . . . well, I suppose anything will sweat or melt or something if you leave it long enough. Look at this place. God, our forefathers must have been so bored. The past always seems so unfriendly, so severe, don't you think?

Marion Excuse me, Madame, but I hear a carriage.

Countess Really? Are there to be more of us? (**Marion** *exits. The* **Countess** *goes to the mantelpiece – sees the portrait, hidden from us.*) Good God – that portrait . . . (*Briefly panicked – she goes slowly up to it, looking at it maliciously. She whistles through her teeth.*) Oh, I see! (*Distant thunder – a storm is brewing.*)

Scene Two

Enter a **Nun,** *shivering.* **Marion** *follows.*

Nun Let me get to the fire, yes, here by the fire. I've had enough – I'm completely destroyed. Oh, I'm terribly sorry, Madame, I didn't see you. Hortense de Hauteclaire, or rather by God's grace, Sister Bertille of the Flagellation of Christ.

Countess Countess de la Roche-Piquet.

Nun Delighted to meet you. I'm sorry – my mind's all over the place. I've never been away before. You're extremely beautiful. I should try to be calm, but how can one be after being jostled about and shaken to bits. I'm sure I look awful.

Countess Would it matter if you did?

Nun God who made us women, made us vain. It's so hard to forget one's own face.

Countess I think if I were you I'd manage.

Nun (*genuinely admiring*) And, yes, of course, how right you are. Excess of humility is inverted pride. And merely an excuse to talk about oneself. I'm a vain silly thing, I know, but I can't get used to any of this, it's all so extraordinary. First the letter from the Duchess of Vaubricourt – to me – and I've never had a letter in my life, then the Reverend Mother calling me in the dead of night, the stagecoach at the back door, the watchman dressed in black, all my sisters sleeping soundly, no idea where I am . . .

Countess Sounds to me like an elopement.

Nun (*without thinking*) Yes, doesn't it just? (*Worried.*) Sorry, you must think me dreadfully frivolous.

Countess Not at all – it is your right – I'm sure it perks up your dreary seclusion. Anyway, frivolity sits well upon a woman: I've devoted myself to it – almost religiously.

Nun I should not let you say these things.

Countess Then don't listen.

Nun (*sees portrait.*) Ah! My God!

Countess (*not understanding*) I'm sorry – did I upset you?

Nun There – there – the portrait.

Countess Oh, I see. (*Brusquely.*) Do you know this man?

Nun I've – I've never seen him in my life.

Countess But you cried out!

Nun Never seen him, never, it doesn't even look like him, no, sorry I don't know him. I'm sorry, it's the cold, the heat, the journey. I shouldn't be . . . I should never have left the convent – I'm going back – it's cold, I'll catch my death here.

Countess (*gently*) He must have really hurt you.

Nun Oh, yes, so much. What have you made me say? Help me, I must go back; you'll have to make my excuses to the Duchess, tell her the coach has been called back.

Scene Three

Marion *enters with* **Mademoiselle de la Frotte**. *Seeing the* **Nun** *on the point of leaving,* **Marion** *firmly grabs her luggage – takes it upstairs. The* **Nun** *is too astonished to react.*

La Frotte Madame. Sister.

Countess Madame.

Nun Madame.

La Frotte We've all been asked here, haven't we, by Madame de Vaubricourt?

Countess We have. And we don't know why.

La Frotte Well, nor do I. Countess, I think we've met before.

Countess Yes, I do believe we have. You were to be heard speaking, I recall, in certain salons I once deigned to frequent, Mademoiselle de la Frotte.

Nun Mademoiselle de la Frotte? No, not *the* Mademoiselle de la Frotte? – not the author of *Diana and Phoebus*, of *The Trials of Destiny* and of *Star-Crossed Lovers*?

Countess Indeed – no less.

La Frotte Indeed and indeed. And, Sister, I'm delighted to hear my books are popular even behind the convent walls.

Nun Some do slip in, Mademoiselle – smuggled in under the cassock, so to speak, for they are love stories and so we are not allowed to read them. I've only read *Star-Crossed Lovers*, myself – and Sister Blanche was caught with *Diane and Phoebus* under the bedclothes. Never to be seen again. *Diane and Phoebus* I mean, of course, not Sister Blanche, she's still very much around. And it was so beautiful, so poetic, written in such a high tone.

Countess Miles too high for earthly love. For real love. All the crazy constancy nonsense. And all those pointless obstacles tossed in willy-nilly. So we're left with not one kiss, not one embrace. Your stories manage to make love sound every bit as dull as virtue. Which is quite an achievement. Mademoiselle never so much as mentions the blind urgency of lovers thrown together – the animal heat of body on body, the pain of separation, the thrill of reunion. She betrays a complete lack of imagination . . . or possibly of experience. Hard to tell, I've never actually been able to finish one of her books.

La Frotte Oh, I didn't know you could actually read.

Countess I seldom have time, my dear. Because you know, for me, true romance is not to be found sitting at one's desk.

La Frotte Yes, I can see. Your love affairs have been printed on your skin.

Countess They have, and by some first-rate engravers.

La Frotte And look, we can read every line.

Nun Please, ladies, ladies. Decency, decorum, I beg of you. We sound like poor women in the street. We should be trying to find out why the Duchess has ordered us here. It must be something serious – my note said 'It's a matter of life and death.' What about yours?

La Frotte 'It concerns a woman's honour.' I came as quickly as I could.

Nun And yours, Countess?

Countess It merely says 'Do drop round tonight, there's a matter of some importance' – but the Duchess and I are very close – she has no need to frighten me to attract my attention. By the way, Mademoiselle, did you notice this portrait? (**La Frotte** *puts on her spectacles – examines it calmly.*) Well?

La Frotte I'm sorry – I'm really no expert – of course I dabble a bit in watercolours, not entirely unsuccessfully, or so I've been told, but I think I can safely say that this specimen has no merit whatsoever.

Countess You mean unfaithful – to life?

La Frotte Oh, I can hardly comment on the likeness – I mean purely aesthetically. The features are unfocused. The whole composition would benefit from being completely rearranged. (*She turns away.*) No – sorry – it's a dreadful old mess. (*Offhand.*) Do you know the subject?

Countess All too well. Yourself?

La Frotte No, no, not at all.

Countess (*looking*) Well, I'm unlikely to forget him.

Thunderstorm. **La Frotte** *and the* **Nun** *hide their emotions.*

Scene Four

Marion *enters, leading* **Madame Cassin**.

Marion Please, Madame, do come in. Now you've all arrived the Duchess will be down shortly.

Cassin (*timidly*) Mesdames . . . (*Sees the portrait.*) Ah! (*She swoons – the* **Nun** *catches her – helps her to a chair.*) Him – it's him.

Countess (*to* **La Frotte**) Now there's a woman who appreciates a good painting.

La Frotte I insist it is bad.

Countess And I disagree!

Nun (*to* **Cassin**) Please, Madame, no cause for alarm, you are among friends here. Here, a glass of water, that will calm you down.

Cassin My ladies, do excuse me, it's the journey, the exhaustion.

Countess Yes, yes, of course – you recognised him, didn't you?

Cassin (*ignoring her*) I'm sorry, look at me, I'm so exhausted, I'm forgetting my manners. I'm sorry – allow me – I am Madame Cassin.

Countess I'm sorry, Madame de who?

Cassin Merely Madame Cassin – wife to Monsieur Cassin, of the Rue Royale in Paris – goldsmith to the King.

Countess Goldsmith. Heavens, I had no idea the Duchess wanted to set up a workshop in her living-room. But this is the country, they probably do things differently here.

Nun Allow me to make the introductions. Madame la Comtesse de Roche-Piquet, Mademoiselle de la Frotte, the celebrated novelist, myself, Hortense de Hauteclaire, now sister Bertille of the Flagellation of Christ by the grace of our Lord. Do you know why you're here? We have not yet worked it out ourselves.

Cassin I have no explanations to offer. I had a note from the Duchess asking me to see her this evening. That's all.

Countess Quite right – women of her class require no explanations. One snaps one's finger, they arrive.

La Frotte You do seem to keep a tight grip on your privileges, Countess.

Countess I was born to them. I have no need to toil and sweat to justify my existence. Why should I pretend I need to work?

La Frotte Just as well, I suppose. There are names for women who get paid for what you do.

Countess Now that I will not permit.

Nun Ladies, ladies, decorum, dignity, please, let us be worthy of the Duchess's attentions. Let us try to work out why we are here. What do we have in common?

Countess We are all women.

La Frotte So? (*To* **Countess**.) Be that as it may, you and I still have nothing in common. I do not spend all day primping and painting myself.

Countess A pity. Perhaps you should.

La Frotte Nor do I dream at night of sacrificing my dignity on the altar of a man's bed.

Countess Yes, clearly you have sacrificed very little.

La Frotte I've dedicated my life to art and inteligence.

Countess *Faute de mieux.*

La Frotte I have written fourteen novels.

Countess Or rather one novel, fourteen times.

La Frotte As I say, fourteen novels, a classical Greek grammar, and a new translation of Herodotus.

Countess Quite right, you stick to the classics, my dear, dead authors, dead men, nothing living or thrusting nothing to threaten your virtue.

La Frotte I have no need to fight for my virtue.

Countess Indeed no, vice would take one look at you and give up completely.

La Frotte Whereas when he takes one look at you. . .

Countess Yes, exactly – he goes all hot and red . . . and . . .

Nun Ladies, ladies, please. What would the Duchess think?

Scene Five

Duchess *appears at the head of the stairs.*

Duchess The Duchess is terribly broad-minded she'd forgive anyone anything. Or to put it more precisely she's lost all her illusions – which comes to more or less the same thing. Ladies, good evening. (*She descends – they bow to her.*) Oh, but you're all so charming – all these Paris blooms transplanted to the country; how fresh, how pungent, a real urban bouquet. All this health, all this life within these sad old walls – and it only makes them look older and more crumbly. A bit like their owner, I fear.

Nun Now, Duchess. Really . . .

Duchess Pick up your cues, Sister, pick up your cues.

La Frotte Come, come, Duchess. We all know that physical beauty is only of fleeting importance.

Duchess Never, ever say that, someone might believe you. (*Charm itself.*) Please, ladies, be seated. (*They sit – except for the* **Countess** *who paces nervously.*) Shocking weather, isn't it?

Nun (*joining in*) Certainly is!

Duchess (*to the* **Countess**) The weather is in fact a topic of supreme indifference to me. But I'm told that in society it is polite to complain about it. (*Back to the* **Nun**.) Shocking weather, isn't it?

Nun (*automatically*) Rather.

Countess These reflections on life and art, profound as they may seem, can hardly be the reason, dear Duchess, that you have summoned us hither. Explain, please – now.

Duchess My dear, sweet, Agatha, you never change – always direct, frank and to the point; swift to chide and slow to bless. But indeed, I do owe you an explanation. (*The* **Countess** *does not sit. A pause.*) Well, then. It's my peacock. He's dying.

Nun Your what?

Duchess My peacock. You know, the bird thing responsible for all those gorgeous feathers . . . they don't grow out of vases, you know, or hats. Anyway, it always amazes me that women wish to adorn their heads with something extracted from a bird's bottom.

Countess Sooner that than vice versa.

Duchess Indeed. (*Thinks.*) Indeed.

La Frotte Sorry, you said your peacock was dying.

Duchess He is.

Cassin Were you very, very fond of him?

Duchess We've known each other since childhood.

Nun (*innocently*) I didn't know peacocks lived that long.

Duchess Well, thank you very much. (*She pretends to be annoyed, then continues in a new tone.*) It is a tradition in my family that a child is born at the same time as a peacock. It has always been the case. We were born here, my peacock and I. He somewhere in the grounds, and myself in a state room in the west wing. And yes, I admit I neglected him as our lives went on. But once, fifteen years ago, I came back here, almost by chance – and there he was – still here, but in a shocking old state: fat, lame, half his feathers missing, rheumatic in the joints – his plumage broken and bent like a discarded umbrella; so we were reunited in mutual self-pity. For to tell the truth, we had both grown old. The days of our glory dead and gone. For I have to say, without any false modesty, that he was a particularly handsome peacock. Everybody thought so. Said so. So anyway, I took him back to Paris with me, where he's lived in my garden ever since. But this last week has been very trying for him. His condition has deteriorated – he can hardly breathe, he's more and more lethargic. He cannot walk, he cannot even sing.

Nun Oh, do peacocks sing?

Duchess (*ebulliently*) Oh yes. Unforgettable. The first time I went to the opera, I was convinced he'd followed me in and got shut in the orchestra pit.

Nun (*not getting it*) Oh, the poor thing!

Duchess Poor thing, indeed. I'm not worried for myself, though. My father outlived his peacock by five years, which did seem unfair at the time, my father being such a dreary old bore and his peacock being so absolutely gorgeous. (*Changing tone suddenly.*) He only has a few hours left to live.

Countess Well, that of course is jolly sad, but what can we do? I'm not a veterinarian so my knowledge of peacock husbandry is sadly limited, I'm afraid.

Duchess (*charmingly*) No, indeed, and that is entirely as it should be. But the fact of the matter is that it is the hour of reckoning – when we must examine and evaluate our lives. I mean all of us. The fact that my peacock is in his death throes tells me that it is time for me, for you, for all of us to put our affairs in order. And I am here to help.

La Frotte But what has any of this to do with us?

Countess Yes, what on earth are you talking about?

Duchess He will come – he must – this very evening. (*Storm outside.*)

Countess (*thinks she's understood – hopefully*) But – do you really mean . . . ?

Duchess The man over there, in the portrait which you all spotted as you came in, which you've studiously avoided looking at ever since – the man you've all been thinking about as I've been wittering on. Don Juan.

Countess Don Juan.

Cassin My God.

Nun But, Your Grace . . .

Duchess And that, as the clever old Countess saw straight away, is why we are all here. There you all are, the women I've called together – the victims of Don Juan,

La Frotte
Nun
Cassin } (*together*) What? Excuse me! What are you talking about? This is simply shameful. I have no connection whatsoever with . . . what did you say his . . .

Duchess Do stop prattling – of course it's only human nature that you feel you have to deny it for a while, but do make it a short while, won't you, we haven't got all night. Right. Good. Thank you. Don Juan is coming here this evening. He suspects nothing. He thinks he's going to a ball – but we five are waiting for him. Five women he has defiled, damaged, unpicked. Five women whose minds he still stalks like a malignant ghost, whose past life tortures them to this day. Five women who will judge him and who will condemn him. Tonight, Don Juan will stand trial.

Nun Are we going to judge him?

Cassin And condemn him?

Countess To what?

Duchess Reparation.

Countess How?

Duchess He must marry one of his victims, remain faithful to her and make her happy.

Countess That's absurd! He'd never agree to that . . .

Duchess He will.

Countess You must be dreaming.

Duchess I have a royal warrant here – signed but still blank, which, let's face it, is the least His Majesty could do for me, considering everything I've done for him – I have only to append his name. We will offer him the choice: reparation or incarceration.

Countess Well, bravo, Duchess, very nice work. And whom should he marry? I'd imagine you've organised that as well . . .

Duchess Not one of us, you can rest assured.

Nun (*hypocritically*) Thank God for that. I'd sooner die.

Duchess As I thought. We are his former victims – all true love has died in us – only hate remains alive. And kicking. Upstairs, above our very heads, there is a young girl. Twenty years old. Who longs to die. It's only at twenty that you have the strength to want to die, you need firm flesh for that: good muscles, strong bones. As you grow older, the flesh falls, the body shrinks and one can glimpse the corpse that is to come – That's when you hang on to life, however much you may have cursed it when you had it in abundance. She is twenty, and her story . . . well, some may find it shocking, we'd find it banal. She knew

Don Juan, he seduced her, he abandoned her – just like all the others. She is my god-daughter and he will marry her.

Nun (*drily*) So she will have the chance we never had.

Duchess Yes, Sister Bertille, I know that it's a painful business – having to give what one would rather receive. Charity is hard. (*Pained.*) As for us, we're past saving – but my little girl can still be saved, and he can still be saved. Two birds with one stone. And my bird won't have died in vain. (*Authoritatively.*) You all accept?

Countess/Nun/Cassin We do, we accept. (**La Frotte** *remains silent. They look at her.*)

Duchess You will not join us, Mademoiselle?

La Frotte I really don't think I can.

Countess For what reason?

La Frotte For the very good reason that I have neither had the good fortune of knowing this Don Juan – nor the misfortune of being known by him.

Duchess You think not . . .

La Frotte I more than think, Madame, I am most certain.

Countess But tell us, dear Duchess, how could you possibly have known that we'd all once been seduced and abandoned by the selfsame man? I mean, in my case, fair enough, my name, if not my person, has been publicly connected with practically anything male that moves – with the possible exception of your peacock – so, law of averages, why not Don Juan? But what about these ladies?

Duchess The notebook.

La Frotte Well, as far as I'm concerned, I . . .

Duchess (*ignoring her*) Sganarelle, the Don's valet, has the utterly disgraceful, but in this case quite convenient, habit of entering his master's many conquests in a little green leather-bound notebook. You like figures? Sganarelle does. Don Juan probably too, though they'd make even his head spin. Italy – 640; Germany – 231; 100 in France. In Turkey, 91, but in Spain . . .

Countess How many did you say in France?

Duchess A hundred. Yes, I was a bit surprised. It's a lot, of course, but compared to other countries . . . only a hundred French women against (*Checks book.*) 1,003 swarthy, wide-hipped, moustachioed *señoritas* – I mean, it is a little galling. I took it up with Sganarelle. I said, 'Why so few of our compatriots? Are we a nation of misshapes; rejects, of hobgoblins and rank offences against nature, eh?' You know what he said? 'Madame, the French are indeed fair, none fairer, but, on the whole, a bit of a pushover. My master requires a challenge. If the French attract him less than others it is because they set more store by pleasure than by virtue. Whereas the Spanish . . .' Well. I was shocked. I was hardly a pushover.

Nun Nor was I.

Cassin Nor was I.

Countess And nor was I, till later.

Duchess (*ironic*) Well, it seems that man was our reward for our virtue. But here you all are, ladies, and it was here that I found you – your various undoings are meticulously chronicled.

La Frotte Still, I very much doubt if I . . .

Enter **Marion**.

Marion Madame, Monsieur Don Juan has arrived.

Cassin Oh my God!

Nun I must leave at once.

La Frotte (*spluttering*) I have no place here.

Duchess Very good, Marion, show him in. And you take care what he says to you.

Marion Come, come, Madame, he seems perfectly harmless.

Duchess Perfectly harmless? Then yes, it's him.

Cassin (*fixing her hair*) Oh my God, oh my God.

Nun (*straightening her habit*) I've got to go, got to go. I mustn't miss the Angelus. (*The* **Countess** *and* **La Frotte** *are also adjusting their toilette.*)

Duchess Ladies, please, shame on you. Pull yourselves together. What are you doing? Primping and crimping yourselves. You still wish to please him.

Nun (*without thinking*) It's all very well for you, you've had all day to get ready – some of us spent all evening in a stagecoach. And you, at your age!

Duchess Sister, please! Please. Now, we must be careful. Keep an eye on each other – and not hesitate to denounce publicly any one of us who tries to beat Don Juan at his own game, that is to say, seduction. We must be firm and solid. And ready to call out any simpering or backsliding – publicly. Agreed? Ah, here he is. (*And, unconsciously, the* **Duchess** *also adjusts her toilette.*)

Scene Six

Don Juan, *the others. Lightning, followed by thunder.*

Don Juan I've just been getting to know your forefathers, Duchess. Funny-looking bunch. (*Melancholy.*) I came up via your cemetery. The moon was up, but black as death. Silence, deafening silence. When I eased open the iron gate, the owls shrieked at the intruder, all the rats scuttled into the graves, the glow-worms all glimmered at once – I don't think they're used to visitors. A thousand eyes turned on me in the darkness. It's teeming with life – I mean for a graveyard. It set me thinking. (*Pause.*) It's strange – the soil, the very soil we plough and sow is compounded of nothing but rotting humanity. Hearts that used to beat and break are merely clods of earth – and all that flesh and blood and belly and spleen and sperm has all returned to dust. And thence back to life. An odd journey. Makes one rather question the power of death. (*To the* **Duchess**.) I bumped into the statue of your great-great-grandfather, the Comte de Lamolle – wild stare, stern brow, hand on his sword. Couple of birds nesting in his eyes – sweet – so he's done something useful at last. (*Brusquely*.) But I'm spoiling the party with these morbid reflections.

Duchess On the contrary. You're giving it tone. Well, Don Juan, what is your disguise – what have you come as?

Don Juan As the vile seducer.

Duchess Well, it's superb. And if one removed the mask?

Don Juan What's behind it is even more life-like.

Duchess Splendid. Most conscientious. You've excelled yourself. We shall rely on you to thoroughly deceive us.

Don Juan I will do my very best. But you must excuse me, ladies, what is your disguise? I can't work it out.

Duchess We have come, all of us, as your former victims.

Don Juan Oh, that's a very nice touch – you always were the most attentive of hostesses.

Countess Yes, Don Juan, your victims. Is the disguise not life-like?

Don Juan (*to the* **Duchess**) Is Madame also one of my victims? (*She nods*.) She seems a little aggressive for a victim.

Countess Well, Don Juan, answer the question, do we seem to be what we claim to be?

Don Juan Hard to say. As a rule I don't see my victims. A general's role is to win battles – it's someone else's job to clear up the corpses.

Duchess But you recognise these faces?

Don Juan These masks? Let's examine them. (*Does so*.) Now what should it look like – the face of a victim? Hard, full of hate – the mouth pinched into a rictus of bitter memories, the jaw set for vengeance . . . and I see nothing like that here. Quite the contrary.

Duchess What do you see?

Don Juan I see – which of course is very flattering – nostalgia, rather than bitterness – cheeks blushing with shame, not red with anger. I see women, trembling, coquettish – their breasts peering out over the balcony to get a better view – or to give one. (*Brusquely to the* **Nun**.) Are you sure you're disguised as a victim?

Nun Don Juan, don't you recognise me?

Countess Sister, that's a foul – trying to attract attention.

Nun But . . .

Countess A definite foul.

Nun (*sulky*) You're just jealous because he recognised me.

Duchess We have bantered long enough, Don Juan. Let us speak seriously. It is now many years since . . . our paths crossed . . . and yet, not a day has gone by when I haven't . . .

Don Juan The years have been kind to you – Duchess – you are just as beautiful as ever you were.

Duchess That will do. You know that it is not true, however much I like to hear it. You are flattering me. You have not changed either. You are still the same. Dark, slender . . .

Countess Foul!

Duchess You're quite right. His compliment went straight to my head. It's the shock. When you haven't had a drink for years – half a glass of wine and your skirts are up round your waist. No, you haven't changed, Don Juan – arrogant eyes, greedy mouth – the manners of a man who expects everything. The Devil chose you as his minister on earth.

Countess Foul!

Duchess Foul? But I'm not . . .

Countess Foul. He enjoys being attacked. You're flattering his perverted pride.

Duchess My God, it's hard to forget one is a woman.

Countess I can do it. Let me talk to him.

Nun Foul!

Countess What?

Nun Foul! Butting in all the time, she's only trying to make herself more interesting. Just like Sister Emmanuelle, who's always got more sins than anybody else. She's unbearable. You're only crying 'foul' so you can take charge yourself.

Don Juan So. The psychology of the convent – must come from all that rampant vice behind closed doors.

Duchess Don Juan, I would like to refresh your memory. Do you recognise nobody here?

Don Juan (*looking at* **Madame Cassin**) I recognise the beauty in some of these faces.

Countess You don't recognise me, you traitor?

Don Juan No, Madame.

Nun Nor me?

Don Juan No, Madame.

Cassin Nor me?

Don Juan No.

Duchess Total amnesia. Odd. Must go with total irresponsibility.

Countess You can't have forgotten . . .

Nun Those unique and perfect moments . . .

Cassin I remember everything. (*The light shifts. The three women tell their tales, almost religiously, lost in the past.*)

Countess My father was giving a reception. A Sunday lunch – long and dull and sad. Oh, the endless afternoons of my endless youth.

Nun You entered. No one had asked you, no one expected you, you simply appeared. You bowed, you smiled ... who to?

Cassin My father said – 'Do please join us, Don Juan. Never let it be said that I have neglected as famous and generous a host as yourself...'

Countess You were just as you are today, different, elegant, cynical, a shining black diamond. I looked elsewhere, anywhere, but saw only you.

Nun And you were pretending not to look at me. I say pretending because everyone could see you, assiduously avoiding me. And every time you let your gaze slide round me, past me, over me, I felt more and more desirable.

Cassin Also at the table there was my fiancé. I looked at him and for the first time, saw him as he was. And he seemed coarse. Everything about him, the way he ate, his hands, his overstated gestures. They all belonged to a ridiculous, gross peasant with ideas above his station.

Countess It was only at that moment, when despair was gnawing at my heart, when self-pity was beginning to engulf me, it was only then that you looked at me...

Nun How can I describe your eyes? They burned into my breast, they ripped open my dress – I was becoming a woman. How could anyone fail to notice – that the air was becoming heavy, clotted – all the other faces disappeared, an unfocused blur – only you and I were left alive on the earth...

Cassin At the end of the meal you stood up. You might have seemed to have been having various conversations, passing the odd compliment, but that was only to edge your way, subtly, round to me. And when you were close by, so close that we nearly bumped into each other – you slipped me a note...

Countess It's hard to say what troubled me more – the note or the touch of your hands. But in any case, now we shared a secret. We were accomplices. I withdrew to read what you had written . . .

Nun It was brief, as urgent as your desire. 'Be by the shrubbery at ten o'clock this evening – or I will no longer be of this world . . .'

Cassin A rendezvous . . .

Countess A forbidden meeting . . .

Nun By moonlight . . .

Cassin Of course I decided immediately that I would not go.

Countess My head said no . . .

Nun But my heart said yes.

Cassin But then I had to wait. Oh the long slow eternity which now stood between me and the appointed hour, the hour I would not be going to meet you.

Countess And then how you wooed me. 'The loveliest eyes . . .'

Nun 'The sweetest mouth . . .'

Cassin 'The smallest hand in the world . . .'

Countess I let you continue. I listened, my eyes widening, breathing in your compliments. But when you became impetuous I recoiled. You insisted. I could feel your male desire, butting and pressing against me, demanding ingress, but I'd been well taught, and taught to say no . . .

Nun So then I must have run away. It was the only way to resist. I locked myself in my room. I shut the door and I burst into tears.

Cassin Long, long minutes passed. Then I heard a faint scratching at the door.

Countess 'Who is it?'

Nun 'Your fiancé.'

Cassin What happened? I should have recognised your voice – I did – I should have seen through your plan – I did – and yet – and yet I opened my door.

Countess 'Snuff out your candles, my dear, I would not offend your sense of shame.'

Nun So you said, before you entered.

Countess Then . . .

Nun Then . . . you kissed me and you pressed yourself against me – I couldn't breathe, we tumbled on to the bed . . . we . . . (*She can't seem to speak, but thinks with a mixture of pleasure and horror.*)

Cassin We . . .

Countess We . . . (*They all stay transfixed – frozen in the same thoughts.*)

Duchess It all sounds terribly repetitive. (*They return to reality – the lights change.*) I had credited you with a little more imagination.

Don Juan Why should the wolf bother to change if the lambs remain the same?

La Frotte Really! Shining eyes – moonlit trysts. How banal.

Nun No more so than your novels, Mademoiselle de la Frotte, which is why I love to read them.

La Frotte But can't you see how he's manipulating you? The more you torture yourself, the more he crows. Stop it now, that's enough. He won't remember any of you and that's that.

Don Juan Not true. (*Troubled.*) You. I recognise you.

La Frotte (*compulsively*) Impossible – quite impossible and anyway you said you didn't remember. And you've had so many, many women, why should you remember this one or that one or anyone at all. Nobody should remember my misfortune – it is mine and mine alone. The past has been wiped out.

Don Juan (*tells his tale – almost nostalgically*) There was a spring, a freshwater spring set in a cool shady wood. And a young girl sitting, singing, surrounded by local lads, drawn to her, how could they help it, but she didn't see them, she was waiting for her handsome prince to come, the one in her story books, for you see, her habit began young. There were two or three young fellows at her feet ready to die of love for her – but they were too . . . down to earth. I mean imagine, they had real hands and eyes and legs and fingers and ate and slept and sweated at night. Strange creatures, men . . . I saw her, I wanted her. A very special soul in a delectable body, what a dish for a jaded palate. And I was so careful not to hurry her, not to bruise her, not to brush her butterfly wings.

La Frotte (*sadly*) That isn't true, Don Juan – that isn't me – I mean, look at me – the fairest of the fair? The most graceful? I'm always bumping into things.

Don Juan It is you, Mademoiselle de la Frotte. Would you have written your stupid books if you hadn't been that girl.

La Frotte What do you mean? My books are not stupid.

Don Juan They are stupid, Mademoiselle, and pretentious. I haven't actually read any myself – but when I see the people who like them, I know they are stupid.

La Frotte (*almost weeping*) I hate you.

Don Juan I played the perfect lover to perfection, gratefully received your scarves and ribbons and flowers in lieu of kisses. And I was patient, very patient. It was a siege – I starved you out. You weakened and I attacked. I asked for your hand. And got it, naturally. But it was not what I wanted. What I wanted was for you, only you, for all your virtue, and your airy-fairy-head-in-the-clouds-aren't-I-a-clever-little-girlishness, to give me your body before marriage. And you did.

La Frotte Then you do remember. You too. Don Juan, you remember everything. My little dog, Cabon, d'you remember when we were in bed, he used to . . .

Don Juan No. Not at all.

La Frotte But you must . . . he used to . . .

Don Juan Don't press the point or you'll find out the truth.

La Frotte What truth, what do you mean?

Don Juan The truth that that was all a fairy story based on your face, your spectacles, your cantankerous manner, and that I haven't the slightest recollection of you. I can always guess people's souls from their faces – how did I do? Any of that hit home? (**La Frotte** *weeps.*)

Duchess You are disgusting.

Don Juan Thank you.

Countess No. You're very good. Very clever. Very careful to only tell the things we do not wish to hear – for you know that it is hate that holds us together, love which breaks us apart. But you are royally found out, Don Juan, we'll know how to parry your thrusts from now on. Speak, Duchess.

Duchess Well, Don Juan, this is not a ball, however much you seem to be amusing yourself. It is a trial.

Don Juan Oh yes? And who's to be tried?

Duchess You are.

Don Juan And the judge and the jury?

Duchess Ourselves.

Don Juan Hence the gowns, I suppose, and the wigs. Not sure about the petticoats. And the plaintiff, the victim?

Duchess The victims are many, too many to cram in here, so we had to present a small selection.

Don Juan (*kisses her hand, delighted*) My dear Duchess, there is not a hostess in the land to equal you – I thank you from the bottom of my heart.

Duchess The trial will be held tonight.

Don Juan And the execution at dawn?

Duchess No, that will last longer than you can imagine.

Don Juan Torture? My favourite!

Countess Believe me, in a few hours' time, none of this will seem quite so amusing.

Don Juan And how sweet to have invited such a picturesque selection . . . how do you find them?

Nun How dare you – Her Grace's peacock is dying!

Don Juan Her in particular. Priceless. Where did you dig her up from?

Duchess Laugh while you can, Don Juan, I am resolute. Chiffreville, the family Chiffreville, does that ring any bells? Chiffreville – oh, look, he's stopped laughing. (*He goes pale.*) He goes pale. (*He sits down nervously.*) He sits down nervously. (*He wipes his brow uneasily.*) He wipes his brow uneasily. Well, he's read the stage directions, and we appreciate the performance, don't we, ladies? – a touch over the top perhaps. Little Angelique is here, upstairs. And since you seduced her, abandoned her, then killed her brother, yes I know the duel was legitimate and I know he forgave you as he died – she is sick, Don Juan, sick at heart – doctors don't know the disease – but women do – the despair of love. You will marry her.

Countess And be faithful to her.

La Frotte And never leave her.

Nun And give her children.

Cassin And make her happy.

Duchess Or – this warrant will do its worst – I will subscribe your name, Don Juan, and the forces of law will be at your heels, and you'll end your days in the peace and quiet of the Bastille.

Countess So, marriage or prison, the choice is yours.

La Frotte I doubt if even you will be able to charm the gaolers there.

Countess Some mouse might fall for you.

La Frotte No, there're only rats.

Countess Only vermin.

La Frotte Nothing in a skirt.

Nun No sun.

Cassin No freedom.

Nun Nothing. Only God.

La Frotte And you will beg him for forgiveness.

Countess And since you don't even believe in him, he'll get bored and fractious.

Duchess Ladies, please. We will hold this trial and you will marry this girl.

Don Juan I accept.

Duchess I'm sorry?

Don Juan I accept. I will do what you say.

La Frotte You'll marry her?

Don Juan Yes

Cassin And not try to run away?

Don Juan No.

Nun But . . .

Don Juan No – I accept unconditionally. (*He suppresses an emotion. Then seeks to lighten the situation.*) Being rather mean with the refreshments, aren't we?

Duchess (*reflex action*) Marion, champagne.

Don Juan For the condemned man. (*He takes his drink, then retires upstage to sulk. The women gather together, whispering urgently and with astonishment.*)

Nun He agrees.

Cassin Without discussing it.

Nun It's . . . it's . . .

La Frotte Unbelievable.

Duchess (*darkly*) Precisely. Unbelievable. (*Beat.*)

Countess (*slowly*) Duchess?

Duchess Yes?

Countess He wouldn't really be in love with the girl, would he?

Duchess (*laughs*) No. (*More thoughtful.*) No.

La Frotte No.

Nun No.

Cassin No. (*Silence. They think.*)

Countess What's she like? (**Duchess** *shrugs.*) Physically?

Duchess (*bored*) Oh, you know, blonde, gorgeous, lovely skin, lots of hair.

Countess Morally?

Duchess Beyond reproach. Charming character, good-hearted, very intelligent.

Countess Her education?

Duchess Perfect manners – reserved, graceful.

Countess Any fortune?

Duchess More than most.

Countess So there's nothing particularly special about her.

Duchess Nothing at all.

Countess Completely insignificant, then?

Duchess Completely. (*Meanwhile, in the background,* **Don Juan** *has written a note on a piece of paper – he beckons* **Marion** *to him, unseen by the women.*) But on the other hand, she is twenty.

La Frotte Well?

Countess That doesn't make her the first.

Cassin Nor the last.

Nun Par for the course.

Duchess No, you're right, it's not that either.

Countess Well then, it's a trick. Yet another trick. He is the Prince of broken promises.

Duchess No – that's too vulgar – too obvious. Plus, the Normandy officers are most conscientious, he knows that they'll track him down. No, ladies, we must not back down now – he must be tried – he must be punished. (*They don't seem to relish the thought. She turns.*) Don Juan? (*Just before they turn to him,* **Don Juan** *passes the note to* **Marion**, *whispering in her ear. She hides it in her corsage.*) Come this way please – the hearing will commence.

Don Juan (*charmingly*) Of course – should I lead the way or should you?

Countess Your charm is wearing ever so slightly thin . . .

Don Juan *leads, they follow.*

Scene Seven

Duchess *is left alone but for* **Marion**.

Duchess Marion!

Marion Madame?

Duchess You must tell me the truth and not be afraid. When you were with Don Juan just now did he use his charm, did he try to seduce you?

Marion No, he sat in the darkest corner and waited in silence.

Duchess I see. But, not a word, a gesture, a look which could . . .

Marion No, Madame.

Duchess Marion, stand there. No, back a bit. Tell me, are you considered pretty?

Marion (*blushing*) Most girls are so plain.

Duchess And are you much admired?

Marion Most men are such fools.

Duchess And he made no advances, no promises?

Marion No, Madame.

Duchess It's all very rum, very rum . . . Bring us refreshments, Marion – Russian liqueurs, something bracing – it promises to be a long night. (*She leaves the room.* **Marion,** *left alone, removes the note from her cleavage, waves it in the air.*)

Marion (*shouting, happy*) Mademoiselle Angelique, Mademoiselle Angelique. (*She rushes off.*)

Blackout.

Act Two

Scene One

Setting: The same.

At rise: A few hours later. Candles. **Sganarelle** *sits in the room, smoking a pipe, while the women continue the trial next door. Raised voices are heard. Suddenly the* **Countess** *bursts out of the trial room pushing* **Don Juan** *in front of her. The other women follow angrily.* **Don Juan** *is amused.*

Countess No – I promise you it's much better if he isn't here.

Nun But why? We must listen to his testimony.

Countess Listen? Excuse me, you've done nothing but stare at him. Don Juan, I insist that the hearing should continue – without you, otherwise we'll never finish. Thanks to you these women have lost not only their virtue but also their objectivity. It's quite impossible.

Cassin But he has the right to explain himself.

La Frotte I insist we hear his evidence in its entirety.

Countess No. He speaks too well – as he opens his mouth, he's got you. Women are like rabbits – you catch them by the ears. Back, back, come on. And you (*To* **Don Juan**.) – wait till you're called. (**Don Juan** *is left with* **Sganarelle**.)

Scene Two

Don Juan What are you doing?

Sganarelle Dreaming. Pipe dreams. The smoke rises up to the ceiling – and there, if only we could read it, we could tell our fortune.

Don Juan Well?

Sganarelle (*tries to read*) The future seems turbulent, Monsieur.

Don Juan Well, there's a draft in the room.

Sganarelle (*as if receiving messages*) Oh, ah, really? No! Well . . .

Don Juan You never get bored, do you, Sganarelle.

Sganarelle How could I, the life we lead?

Don Juan What about when you're alone?

Sganarelle I sleep.

Don Juan Sleep. Yes. Have you ever wondered where we go when we sleep? When we come back our eyes are bloodshot, our hair all over the place and we're tireder than we were before. What've we been up to? I don't know which is worse – sleeping or waking. Sleeping, because I don't know who I am, or waking because I do. To be endlessly meeting oneself and knowing better than anyone one's desires, one's limitations, but still to be endlessly wondering who one is . . . to be stuck with this intimate stranger . . . do you not sometimes wonder who you are, Sganarelle?

Sganarelle Who I am? Now don't be silly, Monsieur, I have no problem about that one.

Don Juan Well then, I'm all ears.

Sganarelle Well, I'm me and that's fine, and when I examine myself I've every cause to be content. Which is to say that nature has on occasion come up with more delicate features, more elegant frames, but has given me a face which inspires confidence and a body which inspires affection. As for intelligence, I know enough to be a valet, but not enough to bemoan my condition. I am a complete stranger to none of the mysteries of the human condition, but I lose no sleep by peering into the unknown and the unknowable, as you do: when my brain has been thoroughly exerted, I switch it off and rest, instead of exhausting it beyond repair by forcing it into further fruitless investigations which are more likely to lead to permanent damage than lasting satisfaction.

Don Juan In short, you're fine.

Sganarelle Couldn't be better.

Don Juan In that case I'm bewildered. Why have you allied yourself to such a master? To the greatest villain unhung, a madman, a rakehell, a cur, a devil, a heretic.

Sganarelle Heaven sent me to teach you a little common sense.

Don Juan Heaven's done little else for me.

Sganarelle Be grateful. A complete and independent conscience on tap is very handy. Particularly when it's not your own – then you can shut it up with a smart kick in the pants – as indeed you do – and it works!

Don Juan My conscience? Monsieur Sganarelle, you seem quite thrilled with my evil deeds; not only do you do nothing to obstruct them, you lap them up and catalogue them all.

Sganarelle I don't know what you mean.

Don Juan Come, come, your notebook. I've been told all about it. You give readings. And by advertising my exploits so exhaustively, you've done more for my reputation than I could ever do. You have served me better than I could have hoped. It's true.

Sganarelle (*delighted*) Well, perhaps I'm more complex than I thought – full of hidden depths and contradictions, well, maybe I've misjudged myself.

Don Juan (*good-humoured*) You may not know yourself but at least you like yourself – whoever you may be.

Sganarelle Well, who would be his own enemy – what would be the point?

Don Juan (*more darkly*) No point at all. It is not something one chooses.

Sganarelle I'm still right though. It's pleasant to be able to debate like this – one's a bit starved of intellectual stimulation in the kitchens or the stables. But I must return to my prognostications, sir. We are disturbing the vibrations. (*He returns to 'smoke-reading'.*)

Don Juan What do you see, Sganarelle?

Sganarelle Women. Many, many astonished women. And then I see you alone. Then me alone. Both alone together.

Don Juan Your smoke's mistaken. Hasn't it heard that I am to be married, to hang up my ravisher's disguise and retire.

Sganarelle It doesn't believe it.

Don Juan Do you?

Sganarelle Oh, me, you know . . .

Don Juan Well?

Sganarelle It frightens me.

Don Juan You don't want it?

Sganarelle It frightens me.

Don Juan You think it's a trick?

Sganarelle That was my first reaction – but in your case one's first reaction is never right. So I feel you will marry her.

Don Juan You should be pleased.

Sganarelle I should.

Don Juan Well then.

Sganarelle I can't manage it. It's what I've always wished for – even predicted – 'Youth must have its fling,' I'd say. 'Let him get it out of his system. He's only sowing his wild oats, he'll settle down . . .' and other such hackneyed sentiments. But here you are, really marrying a girl, and I'm uneasy. I'm wondering if it's really her you're marrying.

Don Juan Well, who else?

Sganarelle Well, for the last few weeks I've been wondering if you would end up marrying someone. I could feel this sort of nuptial wind in my bones. So, we chose her. Fine. But I don't think it's this girl you want to marry. You're just getting married, that's all.

Don Juan You're going mad, Sganarelle.

Sganarelle I don't think so. If I were, you wouldn't be taking me so seriously.

Don Juan I have my reasons for marrying her.

Sganarelle Come off it, sir, we both know that for several months now, Don Juan hasn't exactly been Don Juan.

Don Juan That will do.

Sganarelle No, you'll hear me out. That's what I'm for – I'm the conscience that God forgot to give you. Look, for months now I haven't had a single new name to write in my notebook.

Don Juan So you admit you have one?

Sganarelle Now I do, now that it's no longer being used. No new names, virtue reigns, libertinage is dead and Don Juan's asleep.

Don Juan Well, you know about me and French women.

Sganarelle Hasn't stopped you in the past. We've seen girls, ugly or hairy or toothless, ghastly enough to cool the ardour of an eighteen-year-old virgin – and yet nothing about them would stop you when there was mischief to be done.

Don Juan Come on, Sganarelle, recently there's been . . . I mean, what about the Guerin girl, Madame Dumeslee, and Champetrie and that chambermaid at the Foxes, who . . .

Sganarelle Wrong, wrong. Ineligible. You told everyone

you know that you'd had them, but nothing actually happened. I know. I'm a proper chronicler – I do my research. And you didn't go the whole hog with any of these ladies – not because they put up a struggle, on the contrary, they were among your easier victims, but because you ran away at the last minute – just ran away. There were complaints – honestly. They all thought they were too ugly or smelly, poor loves. The whole world's gone mad.

Don Juan But . . .

Sganarelle So let me ask you your own favourite question. Why? Why run away? And why pretend that it's business as usual? Why lie? To me? Don Juan pretending to his valet – well, now I've seen it all.

Don Juan Shut up. Can't you hear someone's coming? Is it her? Did she get my note?

Sganarelle Yes. Here she comes – your latest non-conquest.

Don Juan Go – quickly.

Sganarelle *exits.* **Don Juan** *is left alone for a moment.*

Scene Three

Angelique *enters, barefoot, in a nightgown.* **Don Juan** *is still facing us.*

Angelique Don Juan?

Don Juan Yes.

Angelique No, don't turn round. Stay where you are. I'm . . . I'm in my nightgown.

Don Juan Doesn't bother me.

Angelique No, don't move. Stay there. Don't look. Not yet. I've got so pale, I've got so thin.

Don Juan How long do I have to wait. Are you planning to get a tan or put on weight in the near future?

Angelique Don Juan?

Don Juan Yes.

Angelique Don't look, or you'll lose me. I'm Eurydice. You've come to fetch me from the underworld. Now I'm being reborn – coming up to the light – let me get used to it. We're coming up to the surface.

Don Juan Fine! Let's be superficial, that'll make things easier. Can I turn round?

Angelique Please don't. If you die, I'll die – I'll die a second time, but this time for good and all. And we won't be able to love one another any more.

Don Juan So be it. But what's the good of loving back to back?

Angelique Your back – it's not stiff as before, less confident – you've suffered too. Your back speaks volumes. (**Don Juan** *turns around suddenly*. **Angelique** *hides her face.*) I'm horrible.

Don Juan If you were, you wouldn't say so. Let me see you. No, you're not horrible. No more so than before.

Angelique Thank you. (*He turns away again.*) Don Juan?

Don Juan Yes.

Angelique Is it really you?

Don Juan Has your eyesight gone as well? Being in the underworld for so long has taken its toll. And yes, it is me. I still look like me. Especially from the back.

Angelique But which you? The one who loved me, or the one who left me?

Don Juan They're the same, for God's sake! You women – such arrogance. Someone flatters you, says he loves you? He's telling the truth. He leaves you, goes away, he doesn't love you any more? Then he's mistaken! And does it never occur to you the seducer is after one thing, and that he gets it when you idiots let him seduce you. After which, why stay? when you're dead meat.

Angelique If he sets off again, off on his endless wandering, ricocheting from woman to woman – surely it's because he hasn't found what he was looking for – because he himself doesn't know what he's looking for.

Don Juan And what could he be looking for that he could never find?

Angelique Don't be silly. Why love, of course.

Don Juan Oh well, yes, that word – had to come. Says it all: love. At sixty you say 'God' and at twenty you say 'Love', and they're both said with the same bright eyes, the same faith, the same enthusiasm. There's a woman speaking.

Angelique And there's a man protesting too much. To admit to having a heart, a frustrated heart, a broken heart: how shaming! Does the fact that you pee standing up make you immune to all feeling?

Don Juan Is this a secondary symptom of your mysterious illness, talking like a demented school-marm?

Angelique What do you mean? I'm not ill.

Don Juan Oh, I've been misinformed – I was told you were feverish, in your death agony . . .

Angelique That's not illness – that's good sense. I had no reason to stay alive.

Don Juan Then you should have embraced death with enthusiasm. Not this half-hearted flirtation.

Angelique I haven't enough self-confidence to . . . Oh, Don Juan, you came. It's really you. (*She embraces him. He lets her.*)

Don Juan That's odd . . .

Angelique What?

Don Juan There's something almost virile in your eyes – like your brother.

The **Duchess** *– unseen – looks in the room – crosses the stage in silence.*

Angelique Oh, Don Juan, the Duchess taught me what to say and do but I can't keep it up. Is it true that we're to be married?

Don Juan You're right not to ask me to propose. I've done it so often. And lied so often.

Angelique But this is a real proposal?

Don Juan Real enough.

Angelique You'll never leave me.

Don Juan I never will.

Angelique Oh. When you were away, I thought all kinds of things. You promised, you said, 'I'll come back,' and at first I believed you, then the doubts came, then I thought I'd die, then I thought I'd deceive you, for revenge, then the hope returned, which was worse than the pain, and I believed you all over again. You see, I don't know how to wait – that's my illness. I knew I was right – I knew you loved me.

Don Juan Don't be stupid. I don't love you, not in the least. I'll marry you – that's quite enough.

Angelique You . . .

Don Juan No.

Angelique You don't get married if you're not in love.

Don Juan You do!

Angelique You don't.

Don Juan Me above all. Oh, but excuse me. I'd quite forgotten you're an expert on my personality – you certainly know more about it than I do myself, about what I do, and what is to happen to me. You've created me, like a fictional character, you're the author of my misfortunes. So carry on, believe anything if it cheers you up. Don Juan is in love. Fine. I'll try and believe it too. One has to have some faith in one's future wife after all . . . you look pale.

Angelique You don't love me.

Don Juan No, no, I do, anything you say.

Angelique You'd marry me, without loving me?

Don Juan What's the difference, ultimately?

Angelique ... but if you don't love me – I'll refuse to marry you. There. Then I'll kill myself.

Don Juan You see! Who's making a big silly fuss now, eh? Listen, little girl, I'll tell you why you have to marry me. If you refuse, they'll put you on trial too. (**Angelique** *doesn't understand.*) They will, they're unstoppable. Mine's on at the moment. But it's a foregone conclusion. I'm guilty. And you know what they're going to sentence me to? To you. I'm lucky – it could have been a lot worse.

Angelique A trial, a sentence? What are you talking about? My godmother told me ...

Don Juan Your godmother, my love, is quite a considerable woman. And quite a blackmailer. It's you or the Bastille. (*Silence. Suddenly sweeter.*) Don't say she didn't tell you? No? Really not? So you thought I ... you poor little love. No, really that's shocking of her ...

Angelique But she said you'd agree unconditionally, after ...

Don Juan I called her bluff and agreed at once.

Angelique But why? To gain time before escaping?

Don Juan Why care why? The outcome's the same. I'm marrying you. You can't alter facts.

Angelique Forget facts, feelings! Why? (*Horrified.*) I've got it. Don Juan, I see your game. You've pretended to accept to appease these women, and now you're trying to seem appalling in my eyes, to force me to refuse you. Brilliant. The marriage is called off and it's all my fault. Bravo. (*Suddenly broken by grief.*) Aren't you satisfied? Why do you want to destroy me all over again? What are you looking for?

Don Juan Why should you imagine I'm looking for anything? I don't look. I take, I pluck the apples from the bough and crunch them with my teeth. And then, when I'm hungry, I grab some more. That's hardly a quest, is it? Hardly a search. Merely appetite. My mouth wants to savour every kind of fruit. Every kind of mouth. Fat ones, juicy ones, tender ones, and hard ones, closed, open, the narrow mouth of the prude, the sunken lips of the sensualist, the astonished pout of the schoolgirl, I want them all. Men, my love, men envy me, because I do what they wouldn't dare to do – and women resent me because I give pleasure to all of them. All of them.

Angelique Nonsense. The men hate you because you steal their wives and their sisters, and the women hate you because you promise them the moon, then desert them. You're not a saint, not a hero, don't flatter yourself, you're a crook, a petty thief of love.

Don Juan Now that is nonsense. You're all afraid of pleasure and you're right to be. Only the strong know how to channel it. Imagine if the edict went out to the whole world: 'Put down your pickaxes, and your needles and thread. Our new currency is pleasure. Take some, take lots, here, now, without shame.' What'd happen? No one would be there to work, to sweat, to fight. Idle men, devoted entirely to pleasure. No children would be legitimate or illegitimate – just a vast babble of brats with thirty-six mothers, and 120 fathers. No more property, or inheritance or blood privileges, because blood would be generally spread about, like sperm, flowing everywhere. Life would be one big happy bordello. With nothing but whores – no customers, and no pimps. Can you imagine the wonderful unholy mess? What would happen to trade, industry, families, fortune. No more money, no more poverty, because pleasure would be the only wealth, and in that regard we are all equally gifted. So tell me things I've heard a thousand times, this nonsense about quests, searches. One only seeks what one has not found. Only the frustrated and the hopeless search – the happy man doesn't bother. I've never had to look far for pleasure, and that's all I've ever wished for.

Angelique Human beings are not apples to be plucked. And when you bite them, it hurts. Now if you were faithful . . .

Don Juan Faithful! Freedom in a little cage. That's all fidelity is.

Angelique And what is freedom but your right to betray!

Don Juan 'Betrayal', always 'betrayal', women's mad mouths always flecked with the same foam. But it's you who are the most false. You insist on being promised a lifetime of fidelity for five minutes of pleasure. It's only a form of words, you know that, everyone knows that. Certain words pay for certain pleasures. That's not betrayal, that's a transaction. The true traitor is the one who feigns ignorance of the fact.

Angelique You profane everything. Don Juan, women, words, everything. You're only good at doing ill.

Don Juan So why do you love me? If you're really so 'good', so 'kind'. You should have made a better choice.

Angelique (*suddenly vicious*) I'm not good. I'm not kind. And I never have been.

Don Juan You're just a little child.

Angelique That's right, and the principle characteristic of children is their selfishness. And what if I was the same as you? What if I had a taste for conquest? Do you think it's only men who like collecting scalps? Of course I could exhaust myself by possessing every man I met, but why bother? I'd rather catch one big fish than a handful of minnows. And imagine: Don Juan, the man who always gets away, and I have him in my net. You will be my triumph, my badge of honour. Everyone'll say, 'That's the girl who tied Don Juan down.' What publicity. Of course people will hate me, you can't be successful without a certain amount of resentment.

Don Juan And with what weapons are you to conquer

me? Women's weapons – tears, sickness, groans, waiting . . .

Angelique To each his own. How would you rather I fought – with trumpets and cannons, men's weapons? Well . . . when you described my godmother as considerable, you misjudged her. She is a kindly old lady, with a sentimental weakness for believing ideas which others put into her head. She may have a will of iron but she's none the less malleable for that.

Don Juan What are you saying?

Angelique I'm saying, Don Juan, that by feigning illness and delirium, it was easy enough for me to insinuate certain vague ideas of vengeance, which she knew how to put into practice, brilliantly, I'll give her credit where it's due. So do not criticise my 'tactics', for they have worked, for you will marry me. (*Silence.*) You will, won't you?

Don Juan (*troubled*) Yes.

Angelique There we are. I have made my official proposal, everything is as it should be.

Don Juan Don't attempt to look tougher than you really are.

Angelique Male pride again. 'The weaker sex.' Wrong, Don Juan. 'Weakness' as you would call it is one of our greatest strengths. The secret weapon which no man suspects. You are far too coarse and stupid to notice it being deployed.

Don Juan You're explaining much too much, which means you're lying.

Angelique You'll marry me, Don Juan. And what will I do? I'll leave the next morning – you'll find a note: 'Thanks, but I have things to do elsewhere.' By the afternoon, you'll find me with some rough stable boy. My double victory, first to marry Don Juan, then to deceive him.

Don Juan That would only be a victory if it hurt me. Neither your running away, or your sleeping around would concern me in the least. You will of course be quite free.

Angelique What?

Don Juan Yes, yes, let us make a pre-nuptial contract, if you wish. You have the right to sleep with whomsoever you wish – you won't hear a peep out of me.

Angelique Oh, I see – cunning – you'll force me to reciprocate.

Don Juan Not at all. For my part I'll conjoin never to sleep with any woman but you.

Angelique Madness. Won't you be jealous?

Don Juan It's not in my nature.

Angelique You will be shamed, the whole of Europe will know about it.

Don Juan Even if I believed in honour, I'd place it somewhere a bit safer than in a woman's drawers. But what's wrong? Changed your tune? Does my being a model husband take the edge off your victory? Well, I'm terribly sorry. I'll never leave you, or deceive you, and everyone will think it's a love match made in heaven. So there!

Angelique I hate you, I hate you.

Don Juan Nice try, but I fear you were overambitious.

Angelique But why? Why? Why promise me marriage and fidelity without love?

Don Juan Let's call it the end of an era. Pleasure bores me, conquest too. Let's see if goodness is as good as it's cracked up to be. With the softness of a gently rotting fruit.

Angelique You can go now.

Don Juan Don't cry.

Angelique Leave me alone – it's just my eyes, just a reflex, just an irritation. My soul is intact.

Don Juan You really do love me, don't you?

Angelique Yes, Don Juan, I love you. And I wish I

didn't, for this love makes me miserable, and it may last for ever.

Don Juan But . . .

Angelique You have it in your power to love me, but I do not have it in mine not to love you. I couldn't summon it up. I hoped . . .

Don Juan What?

Angelique I hoped you might love me and not know it – and that you wouldn't consent.

Don Juan (*kindly*) I don't understand.

Angelique You see, I understood you from the first. You do evil to prevent it being done to you. You strike first. Out of fear. And if you ever really love, then you would almost die for love, and so I thought you might be afraid of me.

Don Juan Afraid of a little girl?

Angelique You say little girl, but I know more of the human heart than you. My misery has allowed me access to many places hidden to you.

Don Juan But your heart hasn't seen half of what mine has.

Angelique Your heart has been muzzled for so long. If one loosened the straps it would scream with pent-up pain.

Don Juan Better leave it alone then.

Angelique By now the straps are biting into the flesh, it's bleeding away, in spite of you. And it will bleed to death.

Don Juan I know.

Angelique I have powers of healing, my touch can save it. (*Childlike.*) But I have to believe you love me a teeny bit – or I'm not going to play.

Don Juan How can I know if I love you if I don't know what love is?

Angelique You don't need to know it in order to recognise it. Have you ever seen a fish?

Don Juan Yes . . .

Angelique And birds . . .

Don Juan Yes.

Angelique The one you love seems like a fish in water or a bird in the air. He takes up no space, the world slips around him. He doesn't lie down, he luxuriates. At once out of his element and in it.

Don Juan And then?

Angelique He's also made a pact, or so it seems, with the whole of creation – they're agreed that the universe should always show him the utmost beauty, and that he, uniquely, knows how to make its splendours clear to all. So when you are near him the world is in holiday humour, the sun is never too hot, the rain never too cold, the gardens always smell sweet, and stone benches always seem soft as eiderdown. Nature loves him, and attends him.

Don Juan And then . . .

Angelique His face isn't like others' faces. Another mystery. Faces one does not love, Don Juan, are easily seen for what they are, you read the architecture of the bone and cartilage. Beneath the hair and the flesh, you see the folds, the blotches, the flabbiness, the blackheads, it's almost disgusting. But his is not that stuff, it's made of something else, not flesh or clay, but something from a dream.

Don Juan And then?

Angelique You always feel ill, or ugly and tired before you see him, and quite alive when he's there, it's always fresh morning.

Don Juan And then?

Angelique He drives all clocks to distraction. For time creeps when you're waiting for him, and races when he's there.

Don Juan And then . . .

Angelique You lead a double life. Once for you, once for him. Even as things happen, you're thinking, 'How shall I tell this to him?' You become a sort of poet.

Don Juan And then . . .

Angelique You are no longer alone. Something links you, umbilically with the world. There is no more independence – only slavery. But these are chains which will set you free.

Don Juan And then . . .

Angelique All questions end.

Don Juan And then?

Angelique Especially 'and then'. There is no 'then' or now or next or is or was. No hope, no nostalgia – everything merely is what it is. There and in its place. It's a faith.

Don Juan Is it at all like believing in God?

Angelique It's what believing in God means. A world replete with meaning and warmth.

Don Juan You are a good teacher.

Angelique Everything I know, I've learned from you. Have you ever felt it, Don Juan?

Don Juan Yes. (*She moves to him.*) And if you touch me I won't say another word.

Angelique Have you felt it for anyone but me?

Don Juan What a question . . . someone very like you.

Angelique In this country?

Don Juan In this country.

Angelique A few months ago?

Don Juan A few months ago.

Angelique How many?

Don Juan Five months and fifteen days.

Angelique We've known each other for five months and fifteen days.

Don Juan (*sadly*) You've counted them as well?

Angelique (*happily*) Of course!

Don Juan Then poor you.

Angelique No. I have nothing to complain of any more. God has forgiven my sins. The heavens have opened. (*She approaches him, he isn't interested.*) You reject me?

Don Juan I'm so unhappy, Angelique.

Angelique I know, Don Juan, I know what you mean. (*As she continues, he leaves quietly – she doesn't know.*) At first, sudden happiness is like pain, it tears you apart and hurts, and hurts. It is a blow to one's pride to see how much one has depended on someone else. You have to let go to be able to love. Good night, Don Juan. I will dream of you. (*Exits.*)

Scene Four

We hear knocks. Then louder. **Marion** *enters, works a lever which operates a secret door, revealing a secret passage and the* **Duchess** *in the darkness. She enters, cupping her hands.*

Duchess Caught, trapped and . . . (*She claps her hands together.*) . . . done for, Marion.

Marion Who? Mademoiselle Angelique?

Duchess No, Marion, this spider. It mistook me for a wall while I was hiding back there. We stared at each other for quite a while, and then, once it had run up and down me to introduce itself, it decided to build a web on me. And I couldn't budge an inch, I couldn't make a sound.

Marion But, Your Grace, you're terrified of spiders.

Duchess I was, Marion, not any more. Spiders are like people, you're only afraid of them when you don't know them, but once you've seen them for what they are, honest, and hard-working, one is reassured. Marion, it's taken me many years to say it, but say it I can. I'm not afraid of spiders any more.

Marion You still killed it though.

Duchess That's for all the ones who did frighten me.

Scene Five

Madame Cassin *puts her head round the door.*

Cassin She's in here.

Countess *appears, nervous.*

Countess But, Duchess, where on earth did you get to?

Nun *stumbles in.*

Nun What's going on? Where is Don Juan?

La Frotte *enters.*

La Frotte Madame, we have deferred the proceedings long enough, we must complete our depositions and begin the trial.

Duchess Ladies, everything has changed. My ears have brought me new intelligence – there are disturbing new factors which must completely alter the course of our proceedings. I'm afraid we may well have made a serious mistake.

The women sit together, facing upstage – the **Duchess** *begins to explain. Sudden blackout.*

Act Three

Scene One

Setting: Same place.

At rise: It is not yet dawn. The seven women are still there, in candlelight. Remnants of breakfast which **Marion** *is clearing up – she then exits.*

Countess So when did he die?

Duchess During the night.

Countess Who found him?

Duchess The guard – came across the body just now while he was doing his rounds.

Cassin Where was he?

Duchess Lying on the path, under the windows of the west wing. I went at once – it was ghastly – he was so beautiful – broken, bruised, unmade – the blood had already started to coagulate at his temples.

Countess But how can it possibly have happened?

Duchess I don't know – he must have jumped from his window – and been crushed by the impact. (*She weeps.*)

Cassin Did you love him that much?

Duchess I hadn't realised how much. But, well, he had a good life, and after all, he didn't know how to fly . . .

Nun He couldn't fly!

Duchess No, Madame. Peacocks cannot fly, and no more could he. Poor things. They're doomed to be for purely decorative purposes, walking ornaments for our parks. But he might not have realised his limitations – and – in the folly of age – made a belated attempt at flight. Or else it was suicide.

Countess Come, come, Duchess – don't let's

overdramatise. No one lives for ever, least of all a bird.

Scene Two

Enter **Angelique**.

Angelique Has Don Juan come down yet?

Countess You seem particularly perky for an invalid.

Angelique I'm terribly sorry, Countess. So, where is he?

Duchess You're right – I suppose we should call him. So my peacock won't have died for nothing . . . (*She weeps.*)

Nun Your Grace, Your Grace. (*Weeps with her.*)

Countess Duchess, quite frankly, you're a considerable woman – and full of surprises, but still I fail to see any connection between what we're doing here and your peacock.

Duchess Don't bother looking, there is none. None at all. Just me wittering on. Pure self-indulgence on my part. Sheer bloody-mindedness. I have now, I thank God, arrived at an age where I can, with impunity, witter on remorselessly, and not give a damn what people think. I've been so bored for so many years . . . At ten years old you can say what you will, nobody bats an eyelid, precocity is applauded; at twenty, if you're still talking away – provided you have a pretty enough face, you're considered bright, witty even. But after thirty you're muzzled – pretty much for good. Impunity only returns with incipient decrepitude. They say, 'That old lady goes on a bit . . .' but nobody really minds. Sometimes they go further, 'Marvellous for her age, don't you think?' They paint me even older than I am. Then the more polite among them, having awarded me an extra twenty years, exclaim that I hardly look like them, and aren't I well preserved. So I witter on and on and on, any old nonsense. Really I should have been a writer.

La Frotte Speaking as a writer, I object . . .

Duchess You speak only for yourself, Mademoiselle de la Frotte.

Angelique Godmother, sorry, but don't you think that Don Juan . . .

Duchess Besides, you're wrong to object. I've nothing but admiration for those who choose to witter on and on on a professional basis. For is that not what a young writer is? A premature old bore? (**La Frotte** *makes to object. Thunder. The women wheel round.*)

Women Don Juan!

Scene Three

Sganarelle *enters, astonished, followed by* **Don Juan**, *looking older and tireder.*

Angelique (*rushing to him*) Don Juan, what's the matter?

Don Juan (*surprised*) Nothing. (*He tries to look at her, it hurts him.*)

Angelique But really, is this 'trial' absolutely necessary?

Duchess Absolutely.

Angelique But since Don Juan loves me . . .

Countess (*correcting her*) . . . is to marry you . . .

Angelique Loves me and is to marry me, can't we dispense with all this rigmarole?

La Frotte First of all, what on earth makes you think he loves you?

Angelique He told me so himself.

Nun And whom has he not told?

Countess He says 'I love you' like a duellist says '*en garde*' – it's the prelude to an assassination.

Duchess Moreover, if he does love you, this trial becomes essential.

Angelique But you will cause him pain.

Countess We fervently hope so.

Angelique But how can you be so horrid. Do you care nothing for our happiness?

Countess Frankly I care as little for your happiness as I do for a gnat's orgasm. This trial was not arranged for you, it is for us.

Duchess Even so, Agatha, Angelique's happiness has to be . . .

Countess Happiness, Duchess? Happiness? What a ludicrous, newfangled notion. Do we expect happiness – any of us? She's betrothed to God above, she's devoted herself to literature and I'm wedded to vice.

Cassin I'm happy.

Countess Well, of course you are. Happiness seems perfectly appropriate at the back of the shop along with the beef stew and carpet slippers.

Cassin No, I am happy and have no rancour against Don Juan. None at all. I am responsible for my feelings and my behaviour. He took me, yes, but only because I gave myself. I believed in his words of love as he spoke them, but at that moment, I'm certain, so did he. There was a sort of shared hope, an outstretched hand, an empty space to be bridged, and how we waited and how we trembled in anticipation. But what happened in bed unlocked our heart's desires, so that when he fled, he left me the best part of him – the only part I could have – his memory.

Countess Be quiet, will you. If you can keep memories it means you have no memory. Memory is a thing not of the past, but of now. With him, he might have left me twenty years ago, but yesterday, this morning even, my body was still exhausted, my sheets still warm.

Duchess The trial has had a set-back, Don Juan. We gathered here to judge and to silence a man who is iniquity incarnate . . .

Don Juan Well?

Duchess This was our wish. It is still our wish. But it is no longer possible.

Don Juan Why?

Duchess (*pointing*) This man is not Don Juan. He is an impostor. (**Don Juan** *smiles, as if relieved.* **Angelique**, **Sganarelle**, **Marion**, *are all amazed.*)

Sganarelle Madame, you are mistaken. It is my master, it is Don Juan.

Duchess Excuse me, you must be blind. Take a good look – is this your master? His shoulders are bowed and bent with the weight of . . . well what? Nothing ever weighed on your master. Look at his eyes – lost in thought – nostalgic. Impossible, Don Juan has no memory. And look here, time has just begun to weave its web – these little creases running from his eyes to his ears and here – from his ears to his lips.

Sganarelle He's getting older, that's all, just like . . .

Duchess Like the rest of us . . . ?

Sganarelle Like the rest of us.

Duchess Exactly – he's never grown older before. He's beyond the reach of time.

Don Juan No. You're right. I have changed.

Nun How dare you change.

Duchess Thus our trial must also change. There's no point in stringing up a man already dead. Previously, you were being . . .

Angelique No, no, stop. You do not understand. He wants to be with me.

Duchess Poor child.

Angelique How dare you pity me. (*To* **Don Juan**.) Well, go on, tell them. Otherwise they won't believe me. Say it.

Duchess Don Juan, are you in love with Angelique?

Don Juan (*sadly to* **Angelique**) No. (*She is struck dumb.*) No, don't cry. I'll try – if that's what you'd like.

Countess 'I'll try'! This has become a nightmare!

Duchess Don Juan. Stand up and solemnly swear to tell us the truth.

Don Juan I'll tell you whatever you wish.

Duchess Not your truth – real truth.

Don Juan I promise.

Cassin Duchess – I think we may have gone far enough. In a secret world, mystery is better than truth.

Duchess I want to know.

Cassin I mean that when we blow away the cobwebs, lighten the darkness – you, we, may lose him altogether.

Nun Then the only true seducer will be God – for we will never know what He is thinking.

Duchess Sganarelle, you are our first witness, how long has he not been himself?

Sganarelle Don't worry, sir, I'll stick up for you – I'll prove that you're every bit as evil as you always were.

Don Juan Sganarelle . . .

Sganarelle I know all your villainy – I know how polluted your heart is – the cesspit of your soul. He is, ladies, what he always was.

Don Juan Sganarelle, that will do, I will answer for myself.

Duchess Sganarelle, you are our witness. What exactly happened five months and fifteen days ago?

Angelique But . . .

Duchess Look in your book.

Angelique Godmother!

Duchess Try to remember what happened – before – or after. (**Don Juan** *tries to speak.*) Not yet. All in good time.

Sganarelle Yes, I do remember. It was last autumn. An evening – a night rather – in Valognes. The town was asleep. (*The light starts to change.*) We were on the way back from some scrape or other – a virgin or widow, married woman, can't remember, it'll be in here somewhere, anyway, an average evening, merrily leaving tears and misery behind us. When, suddenly . . . (*The flashback is complete. A shadowy figure is approaching.*) My God, look! A ghost.

Don Juan Not another one.

Sganarelle Look, pointing at us – nemesis. It's vengance.

Don Juan Oh, yes, what's it look like this time – angel or devil?

Sganarelle Look, look, you're not looking. It's a statue.

Don Juan That's new.

Sganarelle It's moving.

Don Juan It must have got bored up there. Actually, it's refreshing to know statues can move. I've always felt very sorry for them – when you're standing still you have terrible urges – to scratch, or blow your nose, or shift your balls an inch to the left. Good heavens, you're right – he's reaching out to me.

Sganarelle Don't touch it.

Don Juan It would be rude not to, he's offering me his hand.

Sganarelle It'll burn you.

Don Juan Nonsense.

He takes the young man's hand. It is the **Chevalier de Chiffreville**. *He's slightly drunk, bursts out laughing.*

Chevalier Bravo – you are hard to frighten.

Don Juan And it speaks too. I like this statue more and more.

Sganarelle Well, as I see it, a statue which moves and speaks is not a statue.

Don Juan Well, what is it?

Sganarelle It's more like a man.

Don Juan Are you a man?

Chevalier I'm not sure what I am.

Don Juan Then you are.

Chevalier I'm sorry, my friends – I wasn't being a demon or a supernatural beast, merely an automaton.

Sganarelle What's that when it's at home?

Chevalier Well, it rarely is. It walks abroad – and inside it's all fake – there's no heart, no blood, no brain, no innards, no bowels or bits – merely cogs, pistons and pulleys. It drinks only oil and thinks not at all. It's entirely mechanical.

Sganarelle Diabolical.

Don Juan My man has rather simplistic theology. He thought you were sent from heaven a minute ago. And I'm Don Juan.

Chavlier Chevalier de Chiffreville – and my cogs are oiled only by wine, rather well oiled tonight I fear. Hence my excursions into the metaphysical. I'm a little too fond of wine, I fear.

Don Juan No matter. To be fond is to be too fond by definition. Excess is *de rigueur*. And what are you doing here?

Chevalier Running away. My hobby.

Sganarelle From the police?

Chevalier No, no, from someone a little nearer home: me. But I can never quite shake myself off. Wine helps – I lose the track, quite often. But come morning, here I am again – forced to remain myself all day.

Sganarelle I knew a man like you once – he was afraid of his shadow.

Chevalier It's not that. Your shadow isn't you – merely jump in the air and you've shaken it off – briefly – live in the dark and you lose it for good. I do neither – I drink – which has a similar effect – initially elevating, ultimately unenlightening.

Don Juan What is it in you that you hate so much?

Chevalier That would be telling – but I feel another dose of uplift and oblivion coming on, won't you join me?

Don Juan *takes his hand. Back to the previous scene.*

Scene Four

Countess So that was it? Just Mademoiselle's brother?

La Frotte Well, nothing odd about that.

Duchess Sganarelle, continue your story.

Sganarelle Well – that evening my master, who hated nothing more than the company of men, unless it led to some other advantage, some other seduction – went drinking with this young cavalier. Actually my master didn't drink – he doesn't much, he's too wary. He sat, he listened – and at dawn we delivered him to his sister.

Scene Five

A tavern – a table, bottles. **Don Juan** *waiting alone. We hear* **Angelique***'s voice from Act Two describe what it is to love. Over this we hear* **Sganarelle***'s voice.*

Sganarelle He came back . . . every night . . . and he would wait . . . as if nothing else mattered . . .

Don Juan *waits. Lights down.*

Scene Six

Nun (*naively*) What a touching friendship.

Sganarelle I assume you're joking. A few days later the Chevalier didn't turn up. What had my master said or done to cause such an absolute snub? What crime, what abomination? I never found out. The Chevalier was nowhere to be found. For days my master sought him, in his hotel, at the barracks: he'd become invisible. (*Again the lights change. We are back in memory.*) Then one evening we had a visitor. And yet again Don Juan plunged into sin, into debauchery.

Nun How horrible.

Countess Nonsense. You know you're excited.

Nun Please! How can you know what I'm thinking.

Scene Seven

A dark room with a large white-covered bed. **Don Juan** *sits on it – depressed. Enter* **Angelique**, *disguised in a cloak.*

Don Juan You?

Angelique Oh, Don Juan, help me – I beg of you. Only you can help. It's about my brother.

Don Juan Your brother?

Angelique Since you stopped seeing him, his extravagances have gone from bad to worse. Against all advice he is to marry a one-eyed noblewoman who lives nearby, but at the same time he parades around town with a dire creature on his arm – a flaming redhead, she always dangles a puppet from her hand . . .

Don Juan Fiametta. She's a whore.

Angelique She's half-naked. They mouth and maul each other in public and frequent hell holes which stink of wine and worse. Scandal pursues them everywhere. Oh, Don Juan, you're my only hope.

Don Juan Does he talk of me?

Angelique Never. And he used to talk of you so often, as I did.

Don Juan How could he do this to me? After I gave him my friendship, my time, my care. To give so much and yet . . .

Angelique (*simply*) Were you fond of him?

Don Juan (*changes mood, rises sarcastically*) Why should I bother to be fond of your brother? What good would it do me? What's he done to deserve it?

Angelique You seemed to be solicitous.

Don Juan A trick, my love, a simple trick. A means to an end. That's all your brother ever was to me.

Angelique To what end?

Don Juan To you. Men lead me only to women – to their wives, or their sisters – I've no taste for mothers – and you were my only goal, my only destination. I am in love – dying of love – but only for you.

Angelique I don't believe you. I see something in your eyes, it frightens me.

Don Juan What do you see?

Angelique It . . . it looks like hatred.

Don Juan No – it is desire – it is hot animal lust. Quick (*Points to bed.*) – let's wait here for your brother. Here.

Angelique No, I don't want to – I mean, I can wait for him at home.

Don Juan To hell with your brother – it's not him that I want, it's you, d'you hear? Now, quick, do it. (*They kiss.*)

Angelique My God, my God.

Don Juan Your God's abandoned you – he doesn't give a toss. Let the whole world rut like rabbits, he doesn't see – he's stuck there, rotting on his deathbed for all eternity, while bellies and innards thrust and plunge. So it's just men and women, you and me . . .

Blackout.

Sganarelle (*voice-over*) So with foam on his lips, rage in his heart, blood in his eyes – he had her, forced her love. But in the morning – force of habit, lack of sleep, whatever – he muttered some semi-affectionate words and she could believe that she'd just spent the loveliest night of her sad little life.

Scene Eight

An open plain. Dawn. **Chevalier** *and* **Don Juan** *appear.*

Chevalier Have your seconds arrived?

Don Juan Not yet.

Chevalier Nor have mine.

Don Juan Chevalier . . .

Chevalier Look, dawn. I've never seen it sober. It's rather lovely. Like a newly washed slate.

Don Juan We don't have to fight.

Chevalier You have dishonoured my sister.

Don Juan I'll make amends. I'll marry your sister.

Chevalier All the more reason to fight.

Don Juan Do you understand? I'll make amends – your sister loves me.

Chevalier Little fool!

Don Juan She loves me, she came to me, while you – you were in the arms of Fiametta.

Chevalier You don't love my sister.

Don Juan No, not at all.

Chevalier No. You wanted revenge.

Don Juan For what?

Chevalier *En garde*, Don Juan.

Don Juan Your seconds?

Chevalier I've sent them away. So have you. We're alone. *En garde.*

Don Juan *En garde.* (*They wait.*) Why did you stop coming to see me?

Chevalier Surely you got my message. I was too busy.

Don Juan What, with military life, in a one-horse garrison town?

Chevalier How would you know?

Don Juan Very well. But Fiametta, a guttersnipe slut whom you don't even like.

Chevalier (*sarcastic*) Perhaps she gave me something you couldn't for all your high-flown sentiments. Could you have taken her place, in my bed, a lovely, red-headed whore? Could you have gone that far – let me kiss your lips instead of hers? What do you say to that?

Don Juan Nothing.

Chevalier Well then. So what good are you? Long live Fiametta.

Don Juan You neither love nor desire her.

Chevalier I hate her.

Don Juan Then why?

Chevalier Why you and my sister? Why stain my name?

Don Juan I don't know. I thought I'd . . .

Chevalier What?

Don Juan I won't fight.

Chevalier You will, or I'll run you through.

Don Juan You wouldn't.

Chevalier Beware. I'm stone-cold sober. I'm capable of anything.

Don Juan I'm scared, now, of death – and for the first time. Not my own death, yours. It's so close . . . I won't fight.

Chevalier (*angrily*) *En garde.*

Don Juan Yes. Sorry. And don't pretend to be fiercer than you are.

Chevalier I hate you.

Don Juan I still don't believe you, Chevalier. It's not hatred I see in your eyes. It's sadness – and, God, yes, there, now, like a ray of hope, yes, a hope, I can see – Chevalier . . . (*Suddenly the* **Chevalier** *falls on* **Don Juan**'*s sword. He falls, mortally wounded.*) I . . . I didn't . . . I didn't do anything.

Chevalier I know. I would have had a drink, Dutch courage. But I was afraid of bungling it. I only hope I've done enough to die.

Don Juan Why?

Chevalier Dogs with mange have to be put down. And lepers. I've hurt you a lot these last few days – I could hurt you even more.

Don Juan You don't hate me, surely . . .

Chevalier My sister and I met a stray dog once, this is years ago. We were out with a servant, who was sentimental about animals and wanted to keep it. We weren't so sure as it was very ugly, scabrous, toothless and smelled awful. But so affectionate, tender, loving, its whole body wagged to see us. But we didn't care, he was horrible. He loved us, so we kicked him. He followed us, we spurned him. Only one day, suddenly, he bit my sister, then me, then the servants. Unrequited love, I suppose, had sent him mad, or rabid, so we had him killed anyway, he'd become dangerous.

Don Juan But I would have returned your affection.

Chevalier Yes, perhaps, but my love?

Don Juan Chevalier!

Chevalier Don't say anything. You'll only say something stupid. (*Pause.*) You know Fiametta – I bribed her to tell people, but I never touched her – to put people off the scent . . . you appreciate sex, I know, and now destiny sends you true love in a form you cannot desire! Punished . . . And I was put on earth to love, but not how or where I should. So punished again. Why? What have we done wrong? Is God wicked, or is mankind? But God does exist, Don Juan, I know he does. Because, what I feel for you, must be a part of him.

Don Juan If God is here, in you, in me, why die? All this bloodshed . . .

Chevalier I can't live by your side, and not . . . (*He moves to touch him, then stops.*) and if I didn't die, I wouldn't be able to tell you. And you'll tell me too, won't you, you can tell me too.

Don Juan Yes, I will.

Chevalier Yes, but not with words. You've spoken them too many times. Tell me with your eyes. (**Don Juan** *looks at him.*) Yes. That's beautiful. I can see you're not used to that. No. Slowly. Try again. Do it again. Yes. I can die now.

Blackout.

Scene Nine

We are back in the salon.

Don Juan You see, I knew about sex. And I knew about war. I hoped to know pleasure, all I ever knew was sheer excitement. I loved conquest – nothing more. When I took them, held them in my hands, between my thighs, when I entered them, there were a few seconds when I could feel them yield, then I was the conqueror. Thereafter it was the mere mechanics of pleasure. I made love mathematically, out of necessity, but I hated their growing enjoyment, stretched out, their cheeks red, their throats red, crying out, shaking, thrashing, faces matted with joy, ugly in their ecstasy, and me, flying like a shuttle, a spring, a machine, with infinitely more variety, obviously, but with the same intransigence. Inhuman, certainly. I felt nothing. And when they gave their final, piercing cry, I'd turned from master into slave. So I left them. I'd always longed for one of them to stop me, to hold me back. I'd look in their eyes and say to myself, 'I'm leaving.' And I could always leave.

Duchess And him . . .

Don Juan I didn't spot him – or rather, I'd expected to see love wearing petticoats. (*To* **Angelique**.) Angelique, may I marry you?

Countess Stop that at once.

Don Juan (*softly*) So he will have died for nothing.

Cassin You cannot marry your memories.

Don Juan He was the first to show me something outside myself. It would profane his memory if I was as stupid after his death as before. I want to love.

La Frotte Yes. But not her.

Don Juan She is suffering.

Countess Sainthood now! You do nothing by halves. Before you smelled of sulphur, now you stink of sanctity. Actually, a cassock might suit you.

Don Juan She needs me.

Angelique No.

Don Juan I want to make you happy.

Angelique And I don't want a man who wants to cheer me up. I want a selfish man, selfish and jealous and possessive enough to love me because he has to, for himself, to make himself happy, happy with me.

Don Juan But that is not love.

Angelique It's how I love. Selfishly. And that's how I wish to be loved in return. Leave us. I now know why you wish to marry me and your reasons are so lofty, they disgust me. I'd rather be unhappy – at least it's on my own terms.

Don Juan (*sadly*) Angelique. (*She turns.*) And I would have been able to love you . . . (*She exits, hiding her grief.*)

Nun God is a bastard.

Duchess Sister!

Nun A complete bloody bastard.

Duchess Sister, control yourself.

Nun Why? Look what He's done to us, to all of us, to him. Betrayal, deception, betrayal. No, God is a bastard, a fucking bastard.

Duchess Sister, control yourself.

Nun But look what He's done to us, to Don Juan. Lying, cheating, betrayal. God makes us fall in love with someone – then whisks the love away. The angler dangling a juicy maggot. We bite, we're trapped, we're hauled out of the water and left to gasp to death in a cold white world. Such fun. He must be wetting himself up there.

Don Juan Sister . . .

Nun Don't you call me sister, not you. Anyone but you. Let me say it out loud. He doesn't exist, God doesn't exist – or if he does, he's an invention of the devil. (*Exits.*)

La Frotte (*enraged*) So the next girl you meet, whoever it is, you're going to love them?

Don Juan Yes.

La Frotte Truly and absolutely?

Don Juan Yes.

La Frotte And for ever?

Don Juan Yes.

La Frotte Just like in my books?

Don Juan Yes.

La Frotte (*shouting*) You idiot. My books are stupid. (*She slaps him. He doesn't flinch.* **La Frotte** *withdraws,* **Cassin** *tries to console her.*)

Countess Ignore them, they don't understand you – they all think that they are victims. But I understand, and you have been my teacher. When you left, I didn't sit and sniffle and sulk, oh no, I thought and took stock, then I undertook to learn your catechism, item by item. I learned that love has nothing to do with love – merely with conquest, winners and losers and that victory is an end in itself, with no further consequences. I've learned that pleasure is insipid if it isn't laced with malice, that a caress is never far from a slap, that a kiss has the same shape as a bite. I've learned that you can catch a man by his cock but you bleed him dry by his heart – and all that I've learned thanks to you. It is my – fidelity. So come.

Don Juan No, it's too late. I'm cured.

Countess You'll come back, I know you will. A fish out of water will drown. (*She takes her cloak and starts to go.*) In the meantime, don't worry. I'll do enough for two. I'll break hearts, and lie and cheat, and pollute whatever innocence I can find. Until I arrive in glory, scabrous and syphilitic, to meet our master in Hell. And I'll see you there, Don Juan.

She exits, **La Frotte** *follows.*

Scene Ten

Duchess Marion, put out the candles.

Marion But, Madame, it's so dark.

Duchess Do as you're told. It's almost dawn. (*She does so. Darkness – then a slow dawn till the end.*) They say that newborn children are almost blind for their first few weeks on earth, everything is a blur of colours and shapes until one day, something, it might be a mother's smile, a father's touch, disperses this thick gauze around their cot and everything suddenly comes into focus. So perhaps later, in adult life, there is a man or a woman, or event, something, that has the same effect. Making one see things with new eyes, for the first time. That's what the Chevalier did for you, isn't it? Where will you go?

Don Juan I don't know. Beyond myself.

Duchess That doesn't have to be far.

Cassin Yes it does. Good luck, Don Juan. (**Marion** *opens the curtains.* **Don Juan** *is about to leave.*)

Don Juan Duchess, is there a word for this, after blood, tears and screams of pain – preparing to face the unknown, a new world?

Duchess Yes. Birth, I suppose.

Don Juan And how about for the fear of being blinded by the light, betrayed by every hand, buffeted by the world – terrified of merely existing, a speck of dust, lost in the universe? Is there a word for that?

Duchess Yes, courage. And I wish you lots of it. (**Don Juan** *exits into the growing light.*) Isn't it odd – the way the cold light of day blurs everything. By candlelight, our profiles were clear-cut, our feelings quite uncomplicated – our problems were knots either to be undone or sliced apart. But now Don Juan has to go and face the day. A man is born.

Cassin Just an ordinary man . . .

Duchess Well, yes, but what could be more ordinary than mankind?

The Visitor

translated and adapted by Jeremy Sams

Le Visiteur was first performed at the Petit Théâtre de Paris on 23 September 1993. The cast was as follows:

Sigmund Freud	Maurice Garrel
Anna Freud	Josiane Stoléru
Nazi Officer	Joel Barbouth
Stranger	Thierry Fortineau

Directed by Gérard Vergez
Designed by Carlo Tomasi
Costumes by Florence Emir
Lighting by André Diot
Music by Angélique and Jean-Claude Nachon

Characters

Sigmund Freud
Anna Freud, *his daughter*
Nazi Officer
Stranger
Two soldiers

Setting

Freud's consulting room, 19 Berggasse, Vienna, the evening of 7 April 1938.

The action takes place in one act, corresponding to actual time, on the evening of 22 April, 1938, that is, between the invasion of Austria by Hitler's troops (11 March) and **Freud***'s departure for Paris (4 June).*

The scene is Dr **Freud***'s consulting room, 19 Berggasse, Vienna. It is an austere room, its walls panelled with dark wood; there are gleaming bronzes and heavy, double curtains. Two pieces of furniture give structure to the room: the divan and the desk.*

However, abandoning this extreme realism, the décor fades away at the top; beyond the shelves of the bookcase, it rises up in a magnificent starry sky held up here and there by the outlines of the main buildings of the city of Vienna. It is a scholar's study, opening on to infinity.

Scene One

Freud *slowly putting his books away in the bookcase, books which have been thrown around with some violence. He is old but he has a lively look, sombre eyes. Throughout the night he will cough discreetly and make a few grimaces; his throat, consumed by cancer, is already making him suffer.* **Anna** *appears to be more exhausted than her father. Sitting on the sofa, she is holding a volume in her hands, yawning whilst thinking she is reading. She is a severe-looking woman, somewhat of a blue-stocking, one of the first prototypes of intellectual women at the beginning of the century; but she escapes from caricature through her childlike expressions and, visible on her face, her deep, very great love for her father.*

Freud Go to bed, Anna. (**Anna** *shakes her head.*) You must be sleepy.

Anna *denies this, suppressing a yawn. The singing of a group of passing Nazis is then heard a little more loudly than before, coming up through the open window.* **Freud** *instinctively walks away from the window. To himself:*

If only they sang a little worse . . .

Anna *has dropped off over her book. Walking behind the sofa,* **Freud** *gently puts his arms round her.*

My little girl's got to go to sleep.

Anna (*waking up, surprised*) Where was I?

Freud I don't know . . . dreaming . . .

Anna (*still surprised*) Where does one go when one sleeps? When everything fades away, and you're not even dreaming? Where do you wander off to? (*Quietly.*) Tell me, Papa, if we were to wake up from all this, from Vienna, your study, these walls and from them down there . . . and if we were to learn that all this too was only a dream . . . where would we have been in the meanwhile?

Freud Still a little girl. Children are instinctive philosophers; they ask questions.

Anna What are adults?

Freud Instinctive idiots: they answer them.

Anna *yawns again.*

Freud Go on, go to bed. (*He insists.*) You're grown up now.

Anna And you've grown out of it . . .

Freud Of what?

Anna (*smiling*) Being grown up.

Freud (*responding to her smile*) I am old, it's true.

Anna (*gently*) Yes, old and ill.

Freud (*echoing*) And ill. (*As if to himself.*) What does it signify – age? It's just abstract, just figures . . . Fifty, sixty, eighty-two. What does that mean? Eight and two? I've said, variously, four, seven, twenty, forty-three . . . And they're only numbers, random integers which don't have any flesh or any meaning, someone else's problem.

Anna Forget numbers, by all means . . . They won't forget you.

Freud One doesn't change, Anna, it's the world that changes. Other people start moving faster, and talking softer, winters are colder, summers more unbearable, staircases are steeper and longer, soup is blander, love less surprising, books written in smaller and smaller print . . . It's all a conspiracy organised by others because when push comes to shove we don't change at all. (*In sudden jest.*) You see, that's the thing about old age . . . it only affects young people! (**Anna** *yawns.*) Go to bed.

Anna (*irritated by the singing*) How is it that there are so many of them shouting in the streets?

Freud They're not Viennese. The Germans are bringing in partisans by the planeload and letting them loose on the streets. (*Obstinately.*) There aren't any real Nazis in Vienna. (*He coughs.* **Anna** *frowns.*)

Anna No, there aren't any real Nazis in Vienna. But I tell you I've seen much worse looting and humiliation here than in Germany. I saw the SA dragging an old couple on to the streets and forcing them to wipe off graffiti, pro-Schuschnigg stuff. 'That's the work for the Jews, at last some proper work for Jews,' the crowd was yelling. 'Let's thank the Führer who's giving the Jews some work that suits them!' Further on, they were beating up a shopkeeper, right in front of his wife and children . . . Further on, there were the crumpled bodies of Jews who had thrown themselves out of the window, hearing the soldiers coming up their staircase . . . No, Father, you're right, there aren't any real Nazis in Vienna . . . The term Nazi is too polite for them.

Freud *is seized by an even more painful coughing fit.*

Anna (*suddenly urgent*) Sign that paper, Papa, so that we can leave.

Freud It's too disgusting.

Anna You have the support you have abroad, we're lucky; we can leave Vienna, and do it officially. In a few weeks' time, we'll have to flee as refugees. What's the point in waiting? It'll be impossible.

Freud What about solidarity?

Anna Solidarity with the Nazis?

Freud With our brothers, our brothers here, who are being robbed, humiliated, obliterated. To be able to leave is a horrible privilege.

Anna Would you rather be a dead Jew or a living Jew? Your choice. Please, Papa, sign.

Freud We'll see. Go to bed.

Anna *shakes her head.*

You're a stubborn little girl.

Anna Wonder where I get that from?

Freud You're treating me like a condemned man.

Anna (*very quickly*) Papa . . .

Freud And you're right: we're all condemned to death and either way I'm leaving with the next transport. It's not the Nazis, not the destiny of Austria that makes you stay here every evening; you're clinging to me as if I was going to expire any minute; every time I cough, you start like a rabbit. You're holding a vigil over my body already. Please . . . don't be too gentle with me, too caring. Don't be too loving, not you nor your mother, otherwise I . . . I'm going . . . to get stuck . . . Don't make it too difficult for me to leave, Anna.

Anna Good night, Father, I am sleepy now.

She goes towards him and proffers her forehead. **Freud** *goes to kiss her.*

Scene Two

There is heavy knocking at the door. Sounds of boots behind it. Then, without waiting for a reply, the **Nazi Officer** *bursts in.*

Officer Gestapo! (*Speaking to his men behind him.*) Guard the doors front and back. (*The sound of boots is heard in the corridor.* **Freud**'*s eyes gleam with anger. The* **Nazi Officer** *walks around the owner, taking his time.*) Just a friendly little visit, Dr Freud . . . I see that we have begun to tidy up our books.

(*Supposing he is being subtle and ironic.*) Terribly sorry to get them in a bit of an old muddle last time . . .

He knocks some more down.

Freud (*in the same tone of voice*) That's quite all right: it's always a pleasure to deal with a fellow scholar.

The **Nazi Officer** *runs his eyes suspiciously over the shelves.*

Anna What did you do with them last time? Burned them, did you?

Freud In the Middle Ages, they would have burned me; now, they make do with burning my books. I suppose that's progress of a sort . . .

Officer (*muttering*) Never too late to do things properly.

Anna *instinctively makes a protective gesture towards her father.*

Freud (*still ironic, not allowing himself to be upset*) Have you found what you were looking for? Anti-Nazi documents, wasn't it? Nothing tucked into the volumes you took away? (*The* **Nazi Officer** *makes an impatient gesture.* **Freud** *adopts an understanding expression.*) I'll tell you a secret; actually you couldn't have found them there for . . . (*He lowers his voice.*) . . . the most virulent anti-Nazi documents are kept . . . well, shall I tell you? (*Interested, the* **Nazi Officer** *goes nearer.*) . . . Why not? (*Taking his time.*) . . . They are kept . . . (**Freud** *points to his head.*) . . . here!

Anna (*also points to her head*) And here!

The **Nazi Officer** *glares at them threateningly.*

Officer Sorry. A Jewish joke?

Freud (*continuing to be provocative*) Actually I had quite forgotten that I was a Jew, but it was the Nazis who reminded me. A timely reminder. And actually, if I hadn't already been one, I'd certainly have wanted to convert . . . One look at you lot and who wouldn't? You should be careful . . . You're going to create more than you destroy.

The **Nazi Officer** *is about to shout something when* **Freud**, *continuing to look at him without flinching, says rapidly and more coldly:*

Anna, go and get the money.

Officer (*suddenly relaxed, with a carnivorous smile*) Oh how well you know us, Dr Freud!

Freud You're not that opaque.

Anna But father, there isn't any more money.

Freud The safe.

He points to the back of the room. **Anna** *makes her way there, lifts up the picture and then opens the safe which is behind it.*

(*To the* **Nazi Officer** *in a very studiously polite voice.*) Hadn't you thought of that?

Officer Jewish dogs always have a tasty bone buried somewhere.

Freud Are you complaining?

Anna (*to her father*) Why give them more money?

Freud Why? For some peace.

Anna God, if this is peace, what's war like?

Freud Stick around, they'll show you.

Anna (*to the* **Nazi Officer**, *while putting the money on the table*) Take it.

Officer How much is there?

Freud Six thousand schillings.

Officer My goodness! (*Admiring whistle.*)

Freud Not bad, eh? You can be proud of yourself: I never earned that much myself – not in a single session.

Officer (*seizing the money*) What disgusts me about you Jews is that you do not even put up a fight.

Anna (*no longer able to contain her anger, bursts out*) Now that you've got your money, you can shut up and piss off.

Officer I beg your pardon?

Anna You heard. Piss off and tell your louts not to scrape their rifle butts over the parquet like last time. Emily spent three days polishing.

Officer Oy, Yid, who do you think you're talking to?

Anna I know exactly who I'm talking to! Don't you remember, lieutenant, that you've already been rapped on the knuckles for treating us with your customary elegance? Remember that we have support all over the world, that Roosevelt and even Mussolini have interceded with your Führer to defend us and demand that we be allowed to leave. You're only a pawn and a pawn who doesn't even understand the rules of the game.

The **Officer** *makes as if to strike* **Anna**.

Freud Anna!

Anna (*to her father*) Just because an idiot shoots his mouth off, do we therefore have to hold our tongues?

Freud Anna!

Anna Papa, have you seen his shiny boots? Like black marble. He must spend hours polishing his boots! (*To the* **Officer**.) Is that your idea of a good time? Out with the wax, on with the brush, then out with the duster. Rub a dub dub – the more you rub, the more they shine. Sad man, all on his own, rubbing away. When did you last make love? You're better at boots than women, aren't you?

Officer I'm taking her away!

Anna Are you now?

Officer To the Gestapo!

Anna Of course, so we can talk about you. You see he loves being discussed. Loves to be the topic of debate. You want me to tell you why you spend half an hour a day parting your hair precisely down the middle with a comb and a slide rule. Or why you love a tight crease in your trousers. Why you bite your nails. You want me to tell you why you loathe women and drink beer with men. Yes, take me away. I'll discuss you till you're laid quite bare. I think you may tire of it before I do!

Officer (*takes her by the arm*) To the Gestapo!

Freud Don't do that! Don't do that!

Anna Leave it, father! Why should I be afraid of a bunch of cowards?

Officer This is careless talk – it could cost you a lot . . .

Anna It costs me sod all.

The **Nazi Officer** *goes towards her with his hand up in order to hit her.*

Freud Little girl!

Officer To the Gestapo!

Anna That's right, go round us all up: you'll feel stronger.

Officer (*to* **Freud**) Take a good look at her one last time, Jew boy.

Anna Don't worry, Papa. They're only trying to scare you because it's too late and that's all they can do . . . They know we're leaving, the whole world knows that we shall leave Vienna in a few days.

Officer She's so ugly and she thinks she's so bright! Jewish girls, all the same.

He takes **Anna** *off, pulling her violently by the arm.*

Anna (*as she exits*) The paper, Papa, just sign the paper! And don't say anything to Mama, I'll be back tomorrow morning. But sign the paper, otherwise we'll never get the exit visa. (*Freeing herself from the* **Nazi Officer***'s grasp.*) Let me go! I'm coming . . .

They disappear. The **Nazi Officer** *bangs the door.*

Scene Three

Freud (*alarmed, repeating mechanically*) The paper, the paper! Anna! . . . Anna . . .

He makes a violent effort to calm himself. He wipes his forehead and goes up to the desk which is somewhat untidy. Still mechanically, but more peacefully:

The paper . . .

Then he has an idea. He picks up the telephone and without hesitating, dials a number.

Hello, is that the American Embassy? It's Professor Freud speaking. Can you put me on to Mr Wiley? Freud! It's urgent! (*Pause.*) Hello, is that the ambassador? It's Freud here. They've just taken Anna away . . . my daughter . . . Gestapo of course! Do something, please do something . . . Yes, yes I promise you, I'll sign that paper . . . Yes, call me back!

He hangs up, very distressed. Then, too late, he says to the receiver which has been replaced:

Thank you.

Then he remembers what **Anna** *and the ambassador have asked him to do . . .*

The paper . . . the paper . . .

He finds the letter in question and sits down at his desk. He re-reads before signing.

'I the undersigned, Professor Freud, confirm that after the Anschluss of Austria with the great German Reich, I have been treated by the German authorities and in particular by the Gestapo, with all the respect and consideration due to my scientific reputation, that I have been able to live and work in complete freedom, that I have been able to continue to pursue my activities in the way that I desire, and that I do not have the slightest cause for complaint.'

With a sigh, he is about to sign when he has a sudden inspiration. Dipping his pen in the ink again, he adds:

'PS. I can cordially recommend the Gestapo to everyone.'

He is about to sign. He takes his pen, but at the last minute he cries out:

No!

In despair, he clutches his head in his hands.

Scene Four

The **Stranger** *pushes back the double curtains and appears abruptly. He has not been seen crossing the window-sill. His coming must seem both natural and mysterious. He is elegant, even a little too elegant: tail-coat, gloves, cape, walking-stick with knob on end: he's like a dandy coming out of the opera. He looks at* **Freud** *sympathetically.* **Freud**, *feeling that he is being observed, turns around.*

Stranger (*very naturally*) Good evening.

Freud *stands up suddenly, leaning on the desk.*

Freud Who are you?

Silence.

What do you want?

The **Stranger** *smiles but still does not answer.*

How did you get in?

The **Stranger** *remains amiable and silent.*

What are you after? There's no more money, you've come too late.

Stranger (*pulling a face*) I preferred you when you were asking questions.

Freud Who are you?

The **Stranger** *smiles, disinclined to reply.* **Freud**, *containing himself no longer, then opens the drawer of his desk and takes out a revolver. But, at the moment of pointing towards the* **Stranger**, *he feels a little ridiculous and keeps it in his hands.*

Who *are* you?

Stranger (*lightly*) You wouldn't believe me. And that toy won't help.

The **Stranger** *goes up to the sofa and drops on to it elegantly.*

Let's have a chat, shall we?

Freud (*putting the weapon down*) Sir, I will not speak to a man who breaks into my home and refuses to even introduce himself.

Stranger (*standing up*) Very well, since you insist . . .

He goes nimbly behind the curtain, disappears there for two seconds. He comes out again, breathless and with his clothes untidy. Seeing **Freud** *and seeming to catch sight of him suddenly, he rushes towards him and falls at his feet.*

Sir, sir, please, please save me! Save me, they're after me. (*He acts perfectly.*) They're there, behind me . . . (*He runs to the window and seems to catch sight of some men below.*) The Gestapo! They've seen me. They're coming into the building! (*He again throws himself at* **Freud***'s feet.*) Save me, don't say anything!

Freud (*taken in by the acting for a moment*) The Gestapo?

Stranger (*begging him too theatrically*) Hide me! Hide me!

Freud (*has come back to earth; pushing him away rather violently*) Leave me alone!

Stranger (*stopping his acting suddenly*) Don't you feel any pity for a victim of persecution?

Freud For a victim, yes; not for a fraud.

The **Stranger** *stands up.*

Stranger Then don't ask stupid questions.

Freud (*getting a grip on himself and speaking authoritatively*) Listen: I can postulate two hypotheses to explain why you burst in here: either you are a thief or you're ill. If you are a thief, you've come to the wrong house: your Gestapo colleagues have beaten you to it and not left you a crumb. If you are ill, you . . .

Stranger What would the third hypothesis be?

Freud You're not ill?

Stranger (*for whom this word is disagreeable*) 'Ill', it's a horrible word! Health walking hand in hand with death.

Freud Why would you come, otherwise?

Stranger (*lying*) Oh, many other reasons: you know, curiosity, admiration.

Freud (*shrugging his shoulders*) That's what all my patients say!

Stranger (*lying*) Perhaps I've come about a friend . . .

Freud (*ditto*) That's the other thing they always say.

Stranger (*irritated*) Right. Even so, say I have need of you, what do you suggest I do?

Freud Make an appointment! (*Pushing him towards the door.*) I'll see you soon, sir, at a time which suits us both . . . See you in a few days.

Stranger (*stopping him*) Impossible. Tomorrow I won't be here, and in eight weeks' time, you won't either.

Freud Pardon?

Stranger You'll be in Paris, with Princess Bonaparte . . . then in London, in Maresfield Gardens . . . if my memory serves me right . . .

Freud Maresfield Gardens? But . . . You can say what you like, I don't know anything about it . . . I haven't made any arrangements . . .

Stranger No, no, that's where you'll be. You'll like the London spring, you will be fêted, and you'll even manage to finish your book on Moses.

Freud I can see you read the scientific press.

Stranger What'll you call it? *Moses and Monotheism.* I'd rather not tell you what I think of it.

Freud (*interrupting him*) I haven't decided on a title yet! (*Repeating to himself, interested by the* **Stranger***'s suggestion.*) *Moses and Monotheism* . . . Why not? It trips off the tongue! Are you interested in psychoanalysis?

Stranger No, only in you.

Freud Who are you?

Stranger But the oddest thing is that you will miss Vienna.

Freud (*violently*) I will not.

Stranger It has a taste one can't forget. A forbidden fruit . . . and you're to be banished from paradise. Yes, you will miss Vienna . . . You are already missing it, must be, since you've been refusing to leave for a month.

Freud Pure optimism. I thought that the situation would improve.

Stranger Pure nostalgia. You played in the Prater in short trousers, you announced your first theories in the cafés, you walked arm in arm with your first love along the Danube, then you longed to die in its dull, bottle-green water . . . In Vienna, your youth will be left behind. In London, you will only be an old man. (*Very quickly, to himself.*) And yet how I envy you . . .

Freud Who are you?

Stranger You wouldn't believe me.

Freud (*in order to have done with uncertainty*) Then leave!

Stranger How tired of the world you must be to get rid of me so soon. I would have thought you would be more welcoming towards ill people, Dr Freud. You are throwing me out – is that the way to treat a psychotic? When you're my last resort? What if after leaving you, I were to go and throw myself under a car?

Freud, *genuinely surprised by his behaviour, sinks on to the sofa.*

Freud You've picked a bad evening, there is no longer a Dr Freud . . . I may cure others . . . Do you believe that caring for people prevents *me* from suffering? There are some evenings when I'm angry with them for having saved them and I'm left alone, all alone with my pain. And no one to turn to . . .

Stranger She will come back . . . (**Freud** *makes a questioning gesture.*) Anna. They won't keep her for long. They know they can't keep her. You'll hold her in your arms when she comes back and you'll embrace her with that familiar joy that is a close cousin to despair, with that feeling that life dangles only by a thread, and that that thread is, for the time being at least, taut again . . . The thread is fragile – that's why love has to be strong.

Freud Who are you?

Stranger I would so much like to tell you when I see you like that.

He makes a gesture to stroke his hair. **Freud**, *surprised, reacts by taking a decision. He stands up energetically. One can see that the practitioner in him is returning.*

Freud You need me to help you?

Stranger (*slightly surprised*) Yes. No. That is . . . I've been silly – I'd hoped so – I got rather lightheaded with the thought but actually – I don't think you can.

Freud Of course not. (*Jubilant.*) They all believe they are unique but science presupposes the contrary. But I will see you – I have to wait here tonight so I might as well . . . (*He looks up at the* **Stranger**.) Oddly, I don't feel like treating you with kindness.

Stranger Nor should you.

Freud (*rubbing his hands together*) Very well. Let's begin. (*He's cheering up.*) Very good, lie down there. (*He points to the sofa. The* **Stranger** *does so.*) What is your name?

Stranger Are you serious?

Freud It's the rule. (*Patiently.*) What is your name? Your father's name.

Stranger I have no father.

Freud Your first name.

Stranger No one addresses me by my first name.

Freud (*irritated*) Do you trust me?

Stranger Perfectly; you don't seem to trust me.

Freud Let's try another tactic. Tell me about a dream . . . your last dream.

Stranger I never dream.

Freud (*diagnosing*) Memory blockage – self-censorship. Serious. But not unheard of. Tell me a story.

Stranger Any story at all?

Freud Anything at all.

The **Stranger** *then stares at* **Freud**, *as if he were sounding his soul. For a moment, he seems to draw his strength from* **Freud**'*s gaze, then he begins to speak.*

Stranger I was five and up till then the sky had always been blue, the sun yellow and the housemaids sang songs from dawn to dusk . . . there was this heady aroma of musk and vanilla from between their breasts . . . Then one day I was all alone in the kitchen. It was a vast room in which all the furniture was slap bang against the walls, hanging on to them, as if hurled centrifugally from the immense empty space. Red and white tiles scudding across the floor. And it was my playground. I could always scamper about on all fours between the servants's legs, pick up bits of bacon, lick the plates . . . Why was everyone out that day? No idea – that's a grown-up's question. It was merely the case. I hadn't noticed, I was there, sitting on the burnt-umber and cream tiles. Each tile was a whole world; for adults, tiles are just these flat things on a floor; for a child, each tile has its own face and tells its own story. One was a dragon standing, with gaping jaws, at the back of a cave; another one showed a procession of pilgrims; another, a face peering out from behind a mud-spattered pane, another . . . anyway . . . the kitchen was a vast world where other worlds rose to the surface, floating up through the tiles. And then, suddenly, I called out. I don't know why. Perhaps to hear myself existing and to see someone coming. I called. There was only silence.

Freud *seems to be more and more struck by this story.*

The tiles became flat. They were silent. The stove had fallen asleep. The fireplace, where normally a pan was always humming, appeared to be dead.

Freud, *staring into memory, moves his lips at the same time as the* **Stranger**.

And I was calling. And my voice rose to the first floor, to the second, and echoed between the walls where there were no human ears to hear it.

Freud (*continuing, as if he knew the text*) And my voice rose and rose and echoed . . . and the echo made the silence more intense.

Stranger (*continuing without interruption*) The kitchen had become foreign, a juxtaposition of things and objects – a nice clean floor.

Freud The world and I were separated from then on. Then I thought . . .

Freud and **Stranger** (*the* **Stranger** *says the words with his lips at the same time as him*) 'I am Sigmund Freud, I am five, I exist; I shall have to remember this moment.'

Pause. **Freud** *turns slowly towards the* **Stranger**.

Stranger (*continuing in the same dreamy voice*) 'And the house will always be empty when I call, when I cry. No one to hear me. And the world is a vast, empty house where no one answers when you call.' (*Pause.*) I have come to tell you that is wrong. There *is* always someone who hears you. And who comes.

Freud *looks at the* **Stranger** *in alarm. Then he goes up to him and touches him. Feeling that he is real, he backs away.*

Freud It's impossible. Somebody has given you the

information. You have been to the Gestapo, you have read my papers.

Stranger Why? Have you ever written that?

Freud (*pause*) No. Nor even told it. (*Pause.*) You've just made it up!

The **Stranger** *does not reply. Nonplussed for a few moments, wanting to doubt,* **Freud** *has an idea.*

Freud Don't move. (*He picks his pendulum off the table.*) Lie down, yes, there, stretch out.

The **Stranger** *allows himself to do so.* **Freud** *places his pendulum in front of the* **Stranger**'*s face while shaking it slowly in a swinging movement.*

You are tired, you are letting go, you . . .

Stranger (*amused*) Hypnosis, Doctor? I thought that you abandoned that years ago.

Freud When the subject is too tense to interract, nothing does the trick like my trusty old pendulum. (*Continuing to manœuvre in a persuasive tone of voice.*) Your eyelids are becoming heavier and heavier . . . you must sleep . . . you try to raise your left arm but cannot . . . you are so tired, so very tired. You must sleep. Sleep, you m . . .

The **Stranger** *has fallen asleep. During the whole time of the hypnosis, a strange, very quiet, indefinable music will from now on bathe the scene in unreality. The* **Stranger**'*s own tone of voice becomes musical when he replies to* **Freud**'*s questions.*

Freud Who are you?

Stranger Labels? Labels are only useful to show what sort of thing one is. I am no sort of thing. I am one of a kind.

Freud Who are your parents?

Stranger I have no parents.

Freud Are they dead?

Stranger I was born an orphan.

Freud Have you no memory of them?

Stranger I have no memory.

Freud Why don't you want to have memories?

Stranger I would like to have memories. I have no memories.

Freud Why do you want to forget?

Stranger I never forget anything, but I have no memories.

Freud When did you meet Sigmund Freud?

Stranger The first time that he made himself known to me, he said: 'I am Sigmund Freud, I am five, I exist; I shall have to remember this moment.' I listened to that little frail tear-clogged voice rising up amid the racket of the world.

Freud But Sigmund Freud is older than you. How old are you?

Stranger I have no age.

Freud You could not have heard of Sigmund Freud, you were not yet born.

Stranger It's true: I was not born.

Freud Where were you when you heard his voice?

Stranger Nowhere. It is neither far nor near nor even elsewhere. It is . . . unimaginable, for one only imagines with pictures; there is nothing there, there is nothing any more, no meadows, no clouds, no expanses of blue, nothing . . . Where are you when you dream?

Freud I ask the questions. Where is man where you are?

Stranger There, in me, but nowhere, just as dreams are in them.

Freud Where are you, this evening?

Stranger In Vienna, in Austria, on the 22nd of April 1938, at 19 Berggasse, in Dr Freud's study.

Freud Who is Dr Freud?

Stranger A human being who has juggled many hypotheses, as many truths as lies; in short, a genius.

Freud Why him?

Stranger Seers have sightless eyes and soothsayers have cancer of the throat. He is very ill.

Freud Will he die soon?

Stranger Very soon.

Freud When?

Stranger On the 23rd of September . . . (*Suddenly opening his eyes.*) I'm terribly sorry, Doctor, I don't answer that kind of question.

The music has suddenly stopped.

Freud (*taken aback both by the sudden awakening and the* **Stranger***'s reply*) But . . . one does not come out of hypnosis like that . . . You . . .

Stranger If I answered your question, you might decide to snuff it on that day out of sheer politeness. I'd feel responsible.

He stands up and capers about the room.

Freud (*to himself*) I'm going mad.

Stranger The path of wisdom often consists of following one's madness rather than one's reason. (*He shakes his arms and legs.*) It's fun having a body, but how quickly one stiffens up! I had lost the knack. (*Looking at himself in the mirror.*) What do you think of me? This face is fun, isn't it? I've given myself the head of an actor, who'll be born after you die.

Freud (*spontaneously*) You're good-looking.

Stranger (*sincerely surprised, he leans towards the mirror*) Really? However, that has nothing to do with what I am.

Freud (*also going up to the mirror*) Do you think that I recognise me, myself, in the bearded old man who lurks in my mirror? I am getting used to it, but I do not recognise myself there . . .

Stranger You don't like what you see?

Freud Because the mouth moves when mine does and the hand echoes my hand, I think: 'it's me'. But that furrowed forehead, those pepper-and-salt eyebrows, those dry, stiff lips. They're not me. My forehead was smooth, I had brown hair; but then it was the same thing; that might not have been me either.

Stranger Funny, that's exactly how I feel every time I incarnate myself. I'm surprised it's the same for humans.

Freud (*still looking in the mirror*) Do forgive me – I can't quite believe it's really . . . you.

Stranger I know. You do not believe in me. Dr Freud is an atheist, a magnificent proselytising atheist.

Freud Why me? Why not go to a priest or to a rabbi?

Stranger (*lightly*) There is nothing more tiresome than talking to a fan. And then . . . Preaching to the converted! Also . . .

Freud Also what?

Stranger I am not sure that a priest would recognize me in the way I need. These people are so accustomed to speaking in my name, acting for me, advising on my behalf . . . I'd feel almost in the way.

There is the sound of boots and calls in the street.

Freud Why me? (*Pause.*) To convert me?

Stranger (*laughing*) What pride! No, it is too late. In a few months, you will publish your *Moses*, I will not have converted you.

Freud I can see you.

Stranger You can see a man and nothing else.

Freud You appeared suddenly.

Stranger I could have come in through the window.

Freud You knew that the Gestapo had taken Anna away.

Stranger The whole building knows.

Freud You're playacting. How could you have told me what I experienced when I was five?

Stranger Some people have the knack of telling stories which everyone thinks are unique to them. They're called writers. Perhaps I'm not . . . God . . . but only a good writer? No doubt you're not the only little chap who realised he existed one day when he was sitting with his legs apart on the kitchen tiles.

Freud (*brushing all these objections aside in a fit of bad temper*) I know where I stand!

Stranger (*going nearer*) Isn't it odd, my dear Freud, that at this moment, all of a sudden, you would love to believe . . . to wallow in certainty . . . (*Suddenly.*) How old were you when he died?

Freud Who?

Stranger Your father.

Freud Forty.

Stranger Come on. Don't pretend not to understand: how old were you when he died . . . for you . . . in your mind.

Freud (*not inclined to answer*) It's so long ago . . .

Stranger Let me guess . . . You must have been thirteen. After thirteen years on this earth it suddenly occurred to you that your father could be wrong. And that even when he was wrong he persisted in his error and that what you'd taken for a wise man's authority was in fact a foolish man's insecurity. And you saw that he had weaknesses. That he was frightened, that he would avoid difficult decisions, be afraid . . . of his neighbour, even his wife. And you realised that his principles were not timeless and eternal like the sun behind the clouds, but more like habits, familiar things like a battered pair of old slippers, things he used to repeat endlessly, hoping that they would find validity in their repetition. And that is when you realised that he was old . . . and not only old but getting older. His arms were getting flabby, his skin was getting dark, his back was rounding off and that his every thought was like his every step . . . cautious. In short, on that day you discovered that your father was merely a man.

Freud And that was the day I grew up.

Stranger You think so? That was the day you turned to God. You wanted to believe, but only on the rebound. That's what children do. They want to replace their natural father with a supernatural one. You took him up and plonked him in the skies.

Freud But . . .

Stranger Don't deny it, Sigmund, it's in all your books. It's called projection. According to you, that's where the idea of God came from. Man wants to believe in him so much that he exists. The need creates the object. (*Loudly.*) So I am only a figment of your imagination. A metaphysical fantasy. (*Shouting.*) Isn't that right?

Freud (*weakly*) Spot on.

Stranger Well then, if I'm your fantasy, you're dreaming.

In the building, a stampeding noise is heard and soldiers shouting.

You're old, you have a grown-up daughter who they've taken away, but they're also after you, so you're a little boy again who needs a father. For the first stranger who turns up at your house and is a little bit spiritual, a little bit obscure and, let's face it, a little bit incomprehensible, you throw out everything. Everything you've ever believed in, everything you've ever denounced.

The noises come nearer.

Freud No man under hypnosis would have said what you have said to me.

At that moment, there is a firm knocking at the door. Stupidly, **Freud** *looks at the* **Stranger** *in terror, as if to ask him what is going on.*

Stranger (*whispering*) Well, answer.

Freud Is that you, Martha?

There is no reply.

Freud (*murmuring to the* **Stranger**) Hide behind the curtain. I won't be long.

The **Stranger** *dashes behind the curtain. At the same moment, the* **Nazi Officer** *appears.*

Scene Five

The **Nazi Officer** *comes in, looking suspiciously around him.*

Officer No one's answering.

He waves to the other soldiers in the antechamber.

I'll go in alone.

Freud Where is my daughter?

Officer (*inspecting the room*) Gestapo headquarters.

Freud You're not bringing her back?

Officer We'll see. For the time being we're having a bit of fun with her. She is very accommodating. (*Suddenly.*) Were you alone?

Freud (*embarrassed*) Of course. As you can see.

Officer (*passing in front of the desk*) Ah, I see that you have our paper ready and waiting. (*He picks up the sheet and looks at it.*) You really should be a good boy and sign it.

Freud And my daughter?

Officer (*continuing absentmindedly to search the room, as if he were looking for someone*) Be patient, you're sure to get her back particularly if you leave . . . no one's going to pass up on a chance of getting rid of a few Jews.

Freud You will return her to me . . . intact?

Officer (*coarse laugh*) Why, are you still hoping to marry her off?

He plants himself in front of the bookcase and stops laughing.

I've got this thing about Jews, I've got a nose for them. Kind of sixth sense.

Freud Really? And you sniffed me out?

Officer (*laughing*) Absolutely!

Freud And what do I smell of?

Officer (*simply*) No, it's not you that smells, it's me, in your presence.

Freud And what do you smell of?

Officer Shit.

Freud (*very shocked*) Pardon?

Officer It's simple. Jews have always done that to me. Whenever I think I'm rotten and no good, whenever I say to myself that I haven't any money and I won't have any money tomorrow either, when I think that no woman in her right mind would want to touch me, all I have to do is look over my shoulder, it always does the trick because there's always a Jew looking at me. He makes me feel like shit. So at least I was right about that. Look at this lovely home, all this furniture, these pictures, these curtains, this desk, all these books, and I've never read one. I'm sweating and I've got a lump in my throat. Bet you anything I'm in the house of a Jew.

Freud That's odd: whenever I think I'm third rate, the only person I blame is myself.

Officer Of course: you're Jewish. As I said, with me, it's like a sixth sense.

Without any transition, the **Nazi Officer** *takes a paper out of his pocket. It is the reason for his visit.*

What is this?

Freud *does not reply. He is visibly embarrassed at the sight of the document.*

You should be delighted. You must have missed it. And a will is always a handy thing to have about the house, especially at your age and in these uncertain times.

Freud What are you getting at?

Officer Oh nothing. It's just that your will refers to bank accounts abroad. You might have told us. Naughty.

Freud (*weakly*) I don't remember you asking.

Officer It's not very patriotic, is it, old man, to put money aside for oneself . . . you are robbing the State . . . So, wouldn't you rather it reverted to us? Now.

Freud That money is for my children . . .

Officer And quite right too! It might be just what she needs right now. A few liquid assets may just soften the blows. Now. I'm the only person who knows about this paper. It just wouldn't do for me to go back to the Gestapo with this naughty paper, it would make a bad impression. And be ever so slightly unhelpful. For you. For her.

Freud (*beating a retreat*) What do you want me to do?

Officer Well, first you might stop and think . . . which I'm told is your speciality, Professor . . . (*Showing the will with one hand and the unsigned document with the other.*) Because, frankly, I'm afraid that this paper would cancel out the other one.

He turns towards the door and shouts to the soldiers who are in the corridor.

There is no one here, try the next floor.

Freud (*spontaneously*) What is going on? You're looking for someone?

Officer You haven't seen anyone? Then keep looking. (*He stops on the threshold.*) Stop and think and see what's to be done. If you ask me, it's a private matter, something best kept between you and me. Do you see what I'm saying? (*With a big smile.*) I'd love to call again . . . very soon.

Exit.

Scene Six

The **Stranger** *comes out from the curtains. His eyes are gazing into the distance, as if he had a vision.*

Stranger He's lying.

Freud (*still agitated*) Unfortunately, he isn't: I do have bank accounts abroad.

Stranger He is lying about Anna. She's not being interrogated.

Freud (*worried immediately*) What are they doing to her?

Stranger (*sharpening his vision*) She is at the Gestapo headquarters, she's in a corridor and she is waiting.

Freud That's good.

Stranger No, it's not good. She knows that if she stays in the corridor and is not interrogated, she is in danger of being rounded up this evening with all the other Jews and being sent to a camp . . . or shot.

Freud *calls out like an animal and rushes towards the* **Stranger**, *grabbing him by the collar.*

Freud Do something!

Stranger It's best if she's interrogated.

Freud Do something! Quickly!

The **Stranger** *pushes him away calmly, continuing to describe what he sees.*

Stranger She is feeling something in her pocket, I can't quite see . . . a glass phial.

Freud *suddenly falls on to a chair.*

Freud (*dully*) I know what it is. Veronal. She asked Schur, my doctor, for some. She wanted us to commit suicide.

Stranger (*distracted from his vision for a moment*) Her suggestion?

Freud Yes.

Stranger (*ditto*) What did you say?

Freud That we would be playing into the Nazis' hands and therefore shouldn't consider it.

Stranger (*returning to his vision*) For the moment she's happy to grip the bottle in her hand, it reassures her. Now she is lifting her arm to her mouth and . . .

He bursts out laughing.

Freud What is she doing?

Stranger (*still laughing*) She's biting it until it draws blood . . . that's brilliant . . . she's bleeding!

Freud (*mad with worry*) But what has come over her?!

The **Stranger** *suddenly detaches himself from his vision, as if he were extinguishing some piece of apparatus.*

Stranger No, no, everything is as it should be, things are taking their natural course.

Freud What's happening now?

Stranger (*very quickly*) The Nazis will kill thousands but they will always see to a single woman in distress. She has succeeded: she has drawn attention to herself, they are going to interrogate her. Don't worry: your daughter is no fool, Herr Freud.

Freud Yes, yes you're right.

The **Stranger** *nods. Smiling, he goes up to* **Freud**, *takes his hands, shakes them and calms him. He hands* **Freud** *the document and a pen, so he can sign it.*

Stranger There have been five hundred suicides in a

month in Vienna. Jews mainly.

Freud How do you know?

Stranger I read the newspapers. The Nazi authorities insisted on publishing a correction saying that the rumour had been exaggerated and that there had been only 487 voluntary deaths. They're such sticklers for detail.

Nazi footsteps in the hall are heard again and the **Nazi Officer** *busy shouting orders.*

Freud (*frightened*) He's here again! What am I going to say to him? If I accept, we shall have nothing left in the world.

Stranger Turn the situation round.

Freud How?

The **Stranger** *takes a photo off the desk and holds it out to* **Freud**.

Stranger Here, use this.

Freud How? What shall I say to him? Don't leave me!

Stranger Come on Freud, you're a big boy now.

Freud Stay with me! Speak to him!

Stranger Don't be silly. In any case, he can't see me. Only you can see me this evening.

Scene Seven

The **Nazi Officer** *has come in. The* **Stranger** *has jumped behind the curtains.* **Freud** *is still stupidly holding the photograph which the* **Stranger** *has given him.*

Officer Well, Professor Freud, have you given it some thought?

Freud, *opposite the* **Nazi Officer**, *at once regains his composure, although he still does not know what to do.*

Freud Indeed, I have.

He tries to gain time by walking up and down.

(*Pensive, staring at the* **Nazi Officer**.) Yes, I was thinking . . . (*He casts around as hard as he can.*) I came across this photograph of my Uncle Simon quite by chance (*He puts it under the* **Officer**'*s eyes.*) and I was thinking . . .

Officer (*without looking*) Stop playing for time. How will you get the money to me?

Freud (*finding his tactic*) I'm coming to it, I'm coming to it . . . so I came across this picture of my Uncle Simon and while I was looking at it I kept on thinking about what you were saying about having a nose for recognising Jews. A nose, that's what you said, isn't it? Well, it's funny that, because I was thinking . . . oh no! . . . I must be mistaken . . .

Officer What?

Freud No, I was just thinking this thing about the nose . . .

Officer (*worried*) Pardon?

Freud Well, it's your nose. It reminds me in every particular of my Uncle Simon's nose. My Uncle Simon the rabbi.

The **Nazi Officer** *instinctively puts his hand in front of his nose.*

No, really, it's almost uncanny, it's more than a family likeness. And I'll tell you what's odd – my nose is straighter than yours, but I'm the Jew. No one's ever seen me at the synagogue, but I'm the Jew. I don't think I've ever done anything mercenary merely for money, but I'm the Jew. Oh well. Surely someone must have mentioned your nose before now?

Officer (*backing away*) I must leave.

Freud No one in the family? No relatives?

Officer I must leave.

Freud Yes, you are right to persecute Jews and hunt them down and wipe them out. All of them! That's what makes the Jews so dangerous, you can never be sure of not being one! Anyway, you came to discuss my funds abroad?

Officer (*understanding the blackmail*) Perhaps we'll just forget it.

Freud No, go and see your superiors, I should be delighted to speak with them . . . about this money . . . about the fact that you didn't mention my will to them . . . about my amateurish little theories vis-à-vis physical attributes . . . no, it will be good to chat.

Officer I've never seen your will . . .

Freud And my daughter? Can I expect her back soon?

Officer (*understanding the blackmail*) Yes, soon.

Freud (*with an ironically humble smile*) Very soon?

Officer Perhaps. And you will leave soon?

Freud (*same smile*) Very soon.

Officer Good evening.

Freud Good evening. (*At the moment that the* **Nazi Officer** *turns around.*) Oh, by the way, Mr Gestapo-man, I've worked out what it is that makes me Jewish and you not. In a few days we'll be refugees, my wife, my children, with our suitcases, with our bundles, we'll be being moved on. And that's what it is to be a Jew.

Officer (*expressionless*) Good evening.

The **Nazi Officer** *leaves and* **Freud** *cannot prevent himself from rubbing his hands together for joy: it is a victory. And he walks towards the curtain where the* **Stranger** *is hidden in order to celebrate it with him. But the* **Nazi Officer** *reappears on the threshold, remembering, in spite of his agitation, why he has come to see* **Freud**.

Officer By the way, you haven't seen anyone?

Freud (*surprised but saying no as a reflex*) Nobody.

Officer (*satisfied*) Very well.

Freud What should I have seen?

Officer (*withdrawing*) There is no need since you haven't seen anything.

Freud (*rushing up to the* **Nazi Officer** *rather too quickly*) But what's going on? What should I have seen?

Officer Nothing, Doctor. Just a man who has escaped. He climbed into one of the buildings in the Berggasse. We have been looking for him for over an hour.

Freud (*quickly, anguished*) Well, there's no one here.

Officer I believe you. Good evening.

Again, he is about to leave.

Freud But where has he escaped from? Prison?

Officer No, the asylum. A madman. Someone saw him making for this block. So we're searching everywhere.

Freud What kind of madman is he? Hysterical? Depressed? Obsessive?

Officer (*with professional assurance*) A nutcase. (*Pause.*) But he is not dangerous; I believe he's a fantasist, the sort who thinks he's Goethe or Napoleon . . .

Freud (*anguished*) You mean a mythomaniac!

Officer Good night, Doctor. Shut your windows and lock your doors, just in case . . .

Exit.

Scene Eight

Freud, *devastated, too disappointed at having lost his new belief to move. The* **Stranger** *slowly comes out from behind the double curtains and goes and shuts the window. Then he turns round and looks at* **Freud**.

Stranger Walter Oberseit.

Freud (*expressionless*) Pardon?

Stranger Walter Oberseit. That's the name of the man they are looking for.

Freud You mean your name.

The **Stranger** *does not deny it. Pause.*

Stranger Walter Oberseit. A poor man who was brought up shut in a cellar for the first twelve years of his life. When he was set free, he had never heard a friendly voice or seen the light of day. He didn't make a sound for months. They thought he was a cretin. Then, when he learned to speak, he made up stories, marvellous stories with himself as hero, as if to make up for that lost life. No one had had any hopes or dreams for him, no one had ever leaned over his cradle and wished him love or success, or even wished him well. That's often the way with madmen . . . no one ever dreamed for them when they were young. (*Pause.*) And I feel very close to him.

Freud (*peacefully*) You tricked me, but it's odd, I don't seem to mind. On the contrary, it's like a great pain has been lifted from me – a boil lanced . . .

Stranger That was doubt.

Freud (*in front of the open window*) The whole world is in agony tonight. Ringing with songs of hate; my daughter has been taken away from me; and an unhappy man comes into my home and, for the first time, he's someone I do not wish to treat . . . I won't treat you. Not this evening, nor tomorrow. Never. I don't believe in psychoanalysis any more. Not in this world . . . (*To himself.*) Why save a sparrow when the whole city is burning? How can I believe in a cure? Why look after one man when the whole world is going mad? . . . (*Without turning towards the* **Stranger**.) Is it true that no one's loved you?

Stranger (*suddenly moved*) Really loved me? I don't know.

Freud (*without turning around*) The lack of love – loneliness. (*The* **Stranger**, *too moved, cannot even answer.*) If I did not love Anna, Martha, my sons, would I have been able to live?

Stranger But wrapped up in what you call your love,

there is their love, the love they give you in return . . .

Freud That's true.

Stranger . . . whereas when you are alone in loving, really alone . . .

Freud (*turns round and clumsily takes the* **Stranger**'*s hand*) I don't mind that you lied to me. But this evening, I can only wait for my little Anna, nothing else. Come and see me tomorrow. We . . . we shall talk. I . . . I shall perhaps not be able to . . . love you . . . but I shall treat you, which is perhaps another way of loving . . . (*Making his decision.*) I shall treat you.

The **Stranger** *keeps* **Freud**'*s hand in his and* **Freud**, *although very shy, does not feel strong enough to refuse that.*

You see here, there's only us here, two men and suffering . . . There is no God . . . The heavens are empty – merely a ceiling over man's pain . . .

Stranger You think so? Really?

Freud Reason has dispelled all the ghosts . . . Henceforth, there will be no more saints, only doctors. It is man who has charge of man. (*Pause.*) I shall treat you.

Stranger (*confidentially*) Tell me, just now, did you really think I was . . . (*Showing the sky.*) . . . Him?

Freud (*ashamed*) I lost my bearings – momentarily.

Stranger (*amused*) But you're all right now? (*Nod from* **Freud**.) Basically, you believe in Walter Oberseit more readily than in God?

Freud You know, Mr Oberseit, I am an old man. I have spent all my life championing the cause of intelligence against stupidity, treating my patients, fighting for men against men, unremittingly, without drawing breath, and what have I earned for it? Some days my throat stinks so much that even my dog daren't come anywhere near me – he stares at me, balefully, from the far end of the room . . . I would have preferred a crisp, neat death: I have earned only agony. So, any number of times I could have murmured God's name, any number of times I could have lapped the seductive honey of His mercy, any number of times I could have hoped that belief in a God might have given me the courage to suffer and walk gently into death. But I have always resisted. It was too simple. Just now, I very nearly gave in, but that was only because fear was thinking in my place.

Stranger It was necessary to give in.

Freud I take enough drugs, thank you very much, I don't need that one.

Stranger Why not that one?

Freud Because it anesthetizes the mind.

Stranger What if the mind needs it most?

Freud It is the animal in me which wishes to believe, nothing to do with the mind; it is the body which is tired of the hot, muck sweat of fear; it is a hunted beast, a cornered stag . . . God is a cry of fear – a scream from a corpse.

Stranger So you do not wish to believe because it might do you some good?

Freud (*violently*) I do not believe in God precisely because everything in me is disposed to believe! I do not believe in God because I long to believe in him! I do not believe in God because I would be only too happy to believe in him!

Stranger (*still somewhat jocularly*) But in the end, Dr Freud, if this wish is there, why suppress it? Why censor yourself? If I refer to your works . . .

Freud It is a dangerous desire!

Stranger Why dangerous? For whom?

Freud For truth . . . I cannot allow myself to be ensnared by an illusion, however tempting.

Stranger Truth is a very demanding mistress.

Freud And exacting . . .

Stranger And not very satisfying!

Freud Contentment is not an index of what is true. (*Explaining, with his eyes lost in what he is expounding.*) Man is locked in a subterranean vault, Mr Oberseit. What little light he has is from a torch that he has made himself with a few shreds of cloth and a drop of oil. He knows that the flame won't last for ever. Now the believer walks forward, believing that there is a door at the end of the tunnel which will open on to light . . . The atheist knows that there is no door, that there is no other light than the light that he made himself, such as it is . . . There is no end to the tunnel other than his own end . . . Therefore, inevitably, it hurts him all the more when he bashes himself on the walls . . . It is more awful for him when he loses a child . . . It is harder for him to behave decently . . . But he does it! He finds the nighttime terrible, merciless . . . But he goes on. And pain becomes more painful, the fear makes him more fearful, death is more final . . . And life seems no more to him than a terminal disease.

Stranger Your atheist is just a man in despair.

Freud There is another name for despair: courage. The atheist has no illusions, he has cashed them all in for courage.

Stranger And what does he gain?

Freud Dignity.

Pause. The **Stranger** *walks up to* **Freud**. *He seems gentle, sincere.*

Stranger Sigmund, you are too fond of your 'courage'.

Freud Dr Freud to you.

Pause.

Stranger Do you hate me?

Freud I'm too raw to hate.

The **Stranger** *again takes his hands.*

Stranger Thank you. (*Pause.*) You hate me for not

coming until now. But if I'd shown myself sooner to you, that wouldn't have changed anything. You would have lived the same life, Freud, dignified, generous, good . . .

Freud (*tired*) Walter Oberseit, stop playing God. The healthy part of you must know that it's a mean trick.

He detaches his hands.

Stranger (*recapitulating with a smile*) So, to recap, you don't believe in God, but you do believe in Walter Oberseit. (*With a bow.*) I'm very flattered for him. (*Amused.*) But who proves to you that Walter Oberseit exists?

Freud (*without smiling*) I am exhausted.

Stranger No, you are not, you are thinking about Anna. It would be touching if it wasn't somewhat insulting . . .

Freud (*with an angry gesture*) At any rate, for you, it is better that you should be whoever you are . . . an impostor . . . because if you had been God . . .

Stranger (*very interested*) Yes?

Freud (*standing up*) If you had been God, you would have picked a really bad evening . . . yes, if God existed . . . and was here in front of me! . . .

Stranger If God existed?

Freud I'm not angry with you . . . But with God, if he came out of that dark void where I stowed him away . . .

Stranger If you had God in front of you?

Freud If God manifested himself here, I would ask him for some explanations. I would ask him . . .

Becoming angrier, he stands up suddenly.

Stranger (*encouraging him*) Yes?

Freud I would say to him . . . (*Vehemence overcomes him.*) Let God put his nose out the window! Does God not know that evil is oozing about the streets in jackboots – here and in Berlin, soon all over Europe? Does God not know that hatred now has its own party, a democratic one in which all shades of hatred have a vote: hatred of the Jew, hatred of the gypsy, hatred of the unmanly, hatred of the minority?

Stranger (*to himself*) How can he ignore it?

Freud It wasn't necessary for evil to become so very spectacular, it doesn't have to take up arms or be dyed with blood, I've always seen evil everywhere. Ever since that day on the kitchen tiles – when I called and no one answered. That is the ultimate evil – and that is what I would reproach God with if he were here – a broken promise!

Stranger What do you mean?

Freud Evil is a broken promise. What is death but the promise of life stated unequivocally in the rushing blood, the pulsing heart . . . and then broken? Death is nowhere implicit in life – when I allow myself to revel in the sheer reckless intoxication of being alive – I feel immortal – death is nowhere to be felt, not in my stomach, nor in my head – and if I know about it, it's only by hearsay. If I hadn't heard tell of Death, would I ever have guessed? I mean, from my lived experience? Death is an assailant who strikes from behind. The evil doesn't lie in the dark, endless void – it's in the broken promise of life eternal. And that's God's fault.

And what of pain? The body is a machine with the capacity for work and enjoyment – yet there's a manufacturer's trick, a built-in obsolescence. It is vulnerable, broken, ravaged. And those wounds also wound the soul, not just the flesh. Pain is another broken promise and it's God's fault.

What of moral evil? War. There is an implicit promise in a rounded head between a mother's breasts, in the soft, sweet sounds which gurgle up from every tiny throat, perplexing and delighting us, and in the simple concord between us and the world when that world consists merely of pairs of loving hands giving us succour, or sleep, or comfort; all that love and trust is God's promise to mankind. So why all this war? Broken again. And it's God's fault.

And perhaps the ultimate evil, the hardest to forgive or forget, is that he has given us intelligence, but not enough. We believe we are capable of the most astounding leaps of thought, prodigious calculations and connections – but the walls of the mind are transparent. We may think we see forever but we will never transcend our limitations. We are shown flashes of the whole picture but the mind goes blind along the way. We will not know everything nor will we understand very much. For what it's worth, I know that if we were to live 300,000 years longer than our allotted span, the stars in the firmament would still be unfathomable things for all that we could name and even visit every single one of them. I'd still be trying to work out what on earth I was doing on earth. The built-in limits of a mind made to seem limitless to its owner. That is God's last and greatest trick. The last broken promise.

Life would be beautiful if it wasn't a fraud. Life would be easy if we'd not been led to believe it would be long or happy or fair.

Stranger You were expecting too much.

Freud I would have to have been created much more stupid than I am for me to hope for less. There you are, Mr Oberseit. If God existed, he would be a lying God. A God who gave his word and never kept it. He would be a God of evil. For what is evil but a broken promise?

Stranger Let me explain.

Freud No. To explain is to absolve: I do not want any explanations. If God was content with what he has done with this world, he would be a peculiar God, a cruel God, a cunning God, a criminal, a liar, the author of men's ill! It would be better for him not to exist. Basically, if there were a God, he could only be the Devil . . .

The **Stranger** *gives a sudden start.*

Stranger Dr Freud!

Freud Walter Oberseit, you are an impostor, a brilliant

impostor, but you should recognise the greatest impostor of all. God. If he existed.

Stranger You're delirious.

Freud So if God were here this evening, an evening when the world is in tears and pain, and my daughter is in the clutches of the Gestapo, I would say to him: 'You cannot exist! If you are all-powerful, then you are evil; but if you are not evil, you are not that powerful. You are either a complete bastard or a complete incompetent. And either way you are a God who's not quite up to being God. Don't bother existing . . . it's not worth the effort. Chance, atoms, random collisions. Any number of things could quite satisfactorily explain the random workings of an unjust universe. When all is said and done, you are no more than an unnecessary hypothesis.

Stranger (*quietly*) And if God were here, he would probably say something like . . . well . . . this . . . If you could see, as I can, the future, the unfolding panoply of the years, you would be twice as angry as you are. But I think you'd direct your anger in the right quarter. At the responsible party. If you could see as far as I can see . . . This century, for instance. People will doubtless dub it the century of man. Wrong . . . It's the century of plague. There'll be the Red Plague from the East and the one that's incubating nicely here and now in the west . . . the Brown Plague. The first blisters can be seen here in Vienna, on the walls and in the streets, but you wait, it'll spread and grow and infect the whole world, for there will be no resistance, none. You're being sent away out of your homeland, Herr Doctor. Count yourself lucky. All the others, all your friends and family and followers, all the innocents, are bound for the slaughter in their thousands, in their tens and hundreds of thousands. In their millions. Led to showers with gas instead of water. And the dead men's brothers will shovel the dead away. And, guess what, the Nazis will make soap from them to wash their asses clean with the thing they hate the most.

And there will be other plagues, oh yes. But the source of all the plagues will be the very cause of your not believing in me. Human pride. It's always been around but it's having its heyday. There was a time when pride was happy merely to defy God, and fair enough, I suppose. But now it wishes to supplant him. Nothing less will do. You've cleared the decks, wiped the slate. The world is now no more than a concatenation of random molecules. A rudderless ship . . . And in the absence of the captain, man has assumed command. This need to rule, to be the master, never before has this madness held such sway. To be master, say, of nature . . . and you soil the earth and blacken the clouds. To be master of matter . . . so you can make the whole globe quake. To be master of politics . . . so you can create totalitarianism. To be master of life itself, so you can pick your offspring out of a catalogue, to be master of one's own body and to be so afraid of illness or of death that one would accept any life at any cost. Happy not to thrive but merely to survive, anaesthetised like forced rhubarb in a greenhouse. And to be the master of morality . . . only to believe that it is men who invent laws, so everything is as right or as wrong as everything else, and nothing is intrinsically worthwhile. And so the only lasting God will be Mammon. And his temples will cover the earth. Every thought, every deed will be hollow, without form and void in the absence of God.

And at first you'll all pat yourselves on the back for having killed off God. For if nothing is due to Him it all devolves to you. At first vanity will preclude misery. You will attribute all intelligence to yourselves. Never will the world have seen more pessimistic yet happier philosophers. But you cannot yet see that man will have denied himself Light. When a young man, in a dark night of turmoil and of doubt, the like of which all men have when young, asks his elders, 'What is this meaning of it all?', there will be an embarrassed silence and a shrug. He will have no answer. And it'll be your job, henceforth, you and others, to elucidate, to explain man in terms of man, life in terms of life. And what will man be, in your universe? A madman in a padded cell playing an endless game of chess between his conscious and his subconscious. After you, and after those who will come after you, man will be in solitary confinement with no hope of release. You still have the heady delirium, don't you, of the conqueror, of the pioneer. But think of the rest, those who are yet to be born. What kind of world will you have bequeathed them? Atheism revealed! And that would be a superstition twice as stupid as any it replaced!

Freud But that's not what I intended, honestly not.

Freud *then realises that he has just spoken to the* **Stranger** *as if he were God . . . He takes his head between his hands, groans and tries to control himself.*

Walter Oberseit, you are a remarkably intelligent creature and doubtless you are also a very unhappy one. Unfortunately, prophecy has never been my field, I have little taste for it and less skill, and I think that it would be better for you, for us both, if you went home now.

Stranger What, to the asylum?

Freud We shall see each other tomorrow, I promise.

Stranger So hand me over to your friend the officer: he will be delighted with the catch and your stock will soar!

Freud No, you will go back to your bedroom . . .

Stranger (*correcting*) . . . to my cell! (*Slight pause.*) . . . For my own safety. Certainly it's safer being mad nowadays, than being out on the streets.

Pause. **Freud**, *extremely nervous, lights a cigar in spite of his burning throat. The* **Stranger** *watches him do so tenderly and comes and sits down again opposite him.*

But why not just give in?

Freud (*spontaneously*) Never! What to, anyway?

Stranger To me . . . Just let yourself believe . . . you know you want to!

Freud (*almost obsessive*) What would I have achieved if I had 'given in'? I would be a little old Jewish doctor on a pension; all my life I would only have treated colds and sprains! I do not need faith, I have to have certainties.

Positive results. And it is not enough that a madman, however brilliant he may be, makes a speech which . . . (*Suddenly having an idea.*) Are you Walter Oberseit, yes or no?

Stranger What do you think?

Freud I am asking you a question. Are you Walter Oberseit?

Stranger I ought to say 'no', but Walter Oberseit would say the same.

Freud (*getting his energy back*) Very well: you claim that you are God? Prove it!

Stranger I'm sorry?

Freud If you are God, prove it! Seeing is believing.

Stranger You can see me.

Freud I see a man.

Stranger Well, obviously I had to incarnate myself. If I had turned up as a spider or as a chamber pot, you wouldn't have given me the time of day.

Freud Do a miracle.

Stranger Are you joking?

Freud Do one.

Stranger (*bursting out laughing*) Freud, Dr Freud, one of the greatest minds of the century, indeed of all time, is asking me for a miracle . . . What had you in mind? A nifty metamorphosis? A swan, a bull, the sun? Or Christ oozing blood, or a Virgin at the back of a grotto? I generally reserve my miracles for idiots.

Freud (*furious*) No. Idiots see miracles at every turn. A scientist is not so easily bamboozled! It's a shame that God has never performed a miracle at the Sorbonne or in a laboratory.

Stranger (*sarcastic*) If you believed me, that would be miracle enough.

Freud Come on. A miracle!

Stranger Ridiculous! (*Suddenly giving in.*) Oh well, if you insist (*He seems to reflect.*) Ready? Oh, could you hold my stick for me?

He holds out his stick to **Freud** *who, as a reflex, seizes it: at that moment the stick turns round, turning into a big bunch of flowers. The* **Stranger** *bursts out laughing at* **Freud***'s comical expression.* **Freud** *understands the trickery and the ridiculousness of his request; he throws the bunch of flowers on the ground.*

Freud Get out! You're not only a fantasist but you're also a neurotic and a sadist.

The **Stranger** *continues to laugh,* **Freud** *is increasingly irritated.*

A sadist who takes advantage of my night of hell! A sadist who revels in my weakness.

The **Stranger** *suddenly stops laughing. He seems almost severe.*

Stranger If it were not for your weakness, how could I get in?

Freud That is enough. No more! Go back through that window again and home.

Polite knocks are heard at the door.

(*Testily.*) Yes!

Scene Nine

The **Nazi Officer** *enters, almost respectfully. As soon as he sees him, the* **Stranger** *nimbly hides in a dark corner of the room.* **Freud***'s expression is sarcastic at his behaviour.*

Officer (*obsequiously*) Professor, I thought I would just pop back and return this document . . . your will . . . a document which plainly I have never had in my possession.

He looks at **Freud** *questioningly, to know whether* **Freud** *is ready to corroborate his version.*

Freud Where is my daughter?

Officer They are in the process of interrogating her, but that will not last for long. It is strictly routine, I am sure. In any case, I have taken it upon myself to insist that that should be the case.

In reply, **Freud** *holds out his hand to receive his will.*

Freud Very well. I will not detain you.

The **Nazi Officer** *clumsily gives a vague salute and is about to leave.*

Officer Oh yes, I also wanted to tell you . . . about the madman who had escaped . . . he's been found.

Freud Sorry!

Officer You know, the nutcase from the asylum . . . He'd been hiding round behind the dustbins in your yard. He has been given back to the orderlies.

Freud Why are you telling me this?

Officer Forgive me, you seemed interested earlier on.

He again makes to leave.

Freud You are quite sure about that?

Officer About what?

Freud The madman? It was definitely him?

Officer Yes.

Freud Walter Oberseit?

Officer Something like that . . . You knew him? In any case, the staff were particularly pleased to get him back so soon. It appears that when he is in top form, he will make anyone believe anything, whatever he wishes! Anyway, there we are, he's safely under lock and key: after all, we are very good at what we do. Good evening.

Freud (*devastated*) Good evening.

The **Nazi Officer** *exits.*

Scene Ten

The **Stranger** *goes up to* **Freud**, *not triumphant but, on the contrary, with compassion. He slowly takes the cigar from him and puts it out in an ashtray.*

Stranger Death is already burning you up. There is no need to stoke the fire.

Freud *allows him to do it, as if calmed. Pause.* **Freud** *looks at him very intensely.*

Freud Why have you come?

Stranger (*slightly embarrassed*) Are you saying that because you believe in me, in my coming or just to get rid of me again?

Freud Why?

Stranger I do not feel you are sincere.

Freud (*full of the great practitioner's gentle authority*) It is you who is not sincere. Why have you come? You cannot hide the truth from me.

Stranger So be it. I'm going to show you . . . (*The* **Stranger** *suddenly seems to be prey to an attack. Worried.*) Freud! My neck is swelling.

Freud (*calmly*) I can see, and you are also very red . . .

Stranger My skull is throbbing. What is happening?

Freud It's called embarrassment.

Stranger Does it always happen when you tell the truth? Now I understand why men tell so many lies. (*Amused.*) I've done a very thorough job on the old incarnation, don't you think?

Freud (*looking at him intently*) Stick to the point. Why have you come?

Stranger Well, obviously not to convert you.

Freud Why, then?

Stranger Out of boredom.

Freud Are you serious?

Stranger Beware of flippant answers, they are often true. (*Pause. Then slightly provocatively.*) No, all right, it wasn't out of boredom, it was out of hate. I resent you.

Freud What for?

Stranger For being human, for being stupid, for being limited. Who'd want to be God? (*He sits down, crossing his legs elegantly.*) I have everything. I know everything. I am everything. What could I want? I've been stuffed to the gills, totally sated, since the dawn of time. What do I lack that I don't already have? Nothing. Nothing except an end. An expiry date. Since there's nothing beyond me, no death, no boundary, what is there that I can believe in, that lies beyond myself? Have you any idea what it's like being God? It's the only prison from which there is no possible escape.

Freud What about us?

Stranger Who do you mean, us?

Freud Man? (*Hesitating.*) Aren't we . . . a distraction?

Stranger Do you ever re-read your own books?

Shake of the head from **Freud**. *The* **Stranger** *sums up the world.*

There is nothing above, everything is below. And all of it was made by me. Wherever I go, I only meet myself or my creations. Men are so presumptuous, it would never occur to them what unexciting company God is forced to keep. To be everything is so boring . . . and so lonely . . .

Freud (*gently*) The loneliness of royalty . . .

Stranger (*dreamily*) Quite . . .

In the street, the noise of a chase is heard. A couple is being chased by the Nazis. Anguished cries of the fugitives. Baying of the Nazis. **Freud** *and the* **Stranger** *shiver nervously.*

(*Suddenly.*) Do you believe me?

Freud Not at all.

Stranger Fair enough.

In the street, the woman and the man have been arrested. They can be heard crying out under the blows. It is unbearable. **Freud** *stands up very suddenly to go to the window. The* **Stranger** *stands between him and the window and bars his way.*

No, please.

Freud You let them get on with it!

Stranger I made man free.

Freud Free to commit evil!

Stranger (*preventing him from passing, in spite of the cries which are getting louder*) Free to do good as well as evil, otherwise freedom is nothing.

Freud So you are not responsible?

The **Stranger***'s sole response is suddenly to stop holding* **Freud** *back.* **Freud** *rushes towards the window. The cries die down. Only the sound of boots going off into the distance is to be heard. The* **Stranger** *has collapsed on to a chair.*

They have arrested a couple. They are taking them away . . . (*Turning to the* **Stranger**.) Where to?

Stranger (*weakly*) To the camps . . .

Freud The camps?

He is aghast at this news. He walks up to the **Stranger**, *who is much more ravaged than even he is . . .*

Stop them! Stop it all! How can you expect to be believed in after all that! Stop!

He grabs hold of his collar.

Stranger I cannot.

Freud (*vehemently*) Go on! Intervene! Stop this nightmare!

Stranger I can't. Not any more!

The **Stranger** *detaches himself, collects all his strength in order to* *go and shut the window. At last, the noise of boots fades away . . . He leans up against the window, exhausted.*

Freud You are almighty.

Stranger Well, actually, no, I'm not. The moment I made man free, I lost omnipotence, lost omniscience. I would have been able to control everything and know everything in advance if I had constructed automata – mere machines.

Freud Why did you do it, then?

Stranger For the reason which underlies all the stupidest decisions, the only reason for anything really . . . for love. You look embarrassed, Freud. You don't want any part of any of that, do you, a God who loves? You'd prefer a God who scolds, an angry old man, with a knotted brow, a red face and a thunderbolt. A cross old dad, rather than a loving, caring father.

He goes up to **Freud**, *who is sitting down, and kneels down in front of him.*

And why would I have made you if it was not out of love? But you don't want any part of it, you want no part of a God who weeps . . . who suffers . . . (*Tenderly.*) Oh, yes, you'd like a God to prostrate yourself to but not a God who'd kneel to you . . .

He is on his knees before **Freud**. *He holds out his hand to him.* **Freud**, *too shy, looks away. The* **Stranger** *stands up shyly and goes to the window through which music is coming in. He opens it. The Nazi songs can then be heard.*

It's beautiful, isn't it?

Freud Unfortunately, yes. If only it were ugly.

Stranger Beauty . . . You prize that particularly, don't you, you men?

Freud (*surprised*) You don't?

Stranger Not really . . . (*Remembering.*) Oh well, yes, once, I was rather caught off my guard. Once there was . . .

Then he looks up, seeming to breathe in the air with all his nostrils, and a song which becomes clear is heard. **Freud** *listens.*

. . . something. I know many sounds. The murmuring of merging clouds, the wild songs of the wild geese as they cleave the air, strung round the sky like a bow bent taut and bound for Africa. I know the mumblings of moles. I know the love cry of the earthworm. The headlong scream of shower of meteors. But . . . that, I did not know.

The music rises. It is the Countess's aria, 'Dove sono', The Marriage of Figaro.

At first, I thought one of the Earth's shimmering winds had got trapped in the Milky Way . . . I thought that I had a mother, I who have no mother, who was opening her arms to me from the furthest end of infinity . . . I thought . . .

Freud What was it?

Stranger Mozart. Enough to make God believe in man . . .

The music continues. **Freud** *is at his desk with his head leaning on his hands, listening to the music with his eyes shut. The* **Stranger** *steps behind the curtain without him noticing.*

Scene Eleven

Anna *comes quickly into the room. She stops when she sees her father at his desk.* **Freud** *has not yet either seen or heard her. She stands in front of the desk and says emotionally:*

Anna Papa!

The music fades away. **Freud** *comes out of his dreamy torpor and with a rattling noise in his throat in which are mixed extreme pain and joy, he murmurs:*

Freud Anna!

They throw themselves in each other's arms.

(*With tears in his eyes, caressing her like a little girl.*) My Anna, my joy, my pride, my baby.

Anna *responds to his embrace.*

Did they hurt you?

Anna They did not touch me.

Freud *holds her even more tightly.*

They interrogated me about the society ... They actually wanted to know if the International Association of Psychoanalysis was a front for a seditious political movement ... I managed to convince them otherwise ... Papa, you're hurting me ... (**Freud** *holds her a little less tightly.*) I described us as a group of harmless amateurs. I'm really ashamed. (*Collecting herself.*) We can't wait a minute longer. I have heard terrible things down there, I spoke to other Jews, I listened behind doors: they take Jews to camps and, once there, nothing more is heard of them ...

Freud (*sombrely*) I know.

Anna *looks surprised.*

Anna (*going on even still*) But there is something even more serious: the Jews are keeping quiet, Father. They are letting themselves be shut up by the Gestapo, they wait for hours and hours without a murmur of protest, they are insulted, they are spat upon, they are deported and still they say nothing. (*She is walking about, furious.*) They are behaving like guilty people! But what have they done? Been Jewish? Where's the crime in being Jewish? Little Macha, your new grand-daughter, what is she guilty of? Of being born? Of existing?

Freud We are going to leave.

Anna We shall leave and we shall speak. We shall speak to the whole world.

Freud We shall leave and we shall be silent. Because my sisters will remain in Vienna and because they would be made to pay. Because Jews will remain behind us and they will suffer for our stupidity.

Anna You too! You are going to stay silent too?

Freud What are the odds? The death in my throat will ensure my silence one way or the other.

Anna *throws herself in his arms.*

We are going to leave, little girl.

Freud *then begins to cough violently.*

Anna You have been smoking!

Freud I was waiting for you.

Anna That's no excuse – you know you mustn't smoke!

Freud *grabs his throat where he is now very sore.*

Freud The noose is tightening, Anna. (*Gathering his strength.*) We are going to leave. I was irresponsible, I was making you take too many risks staying here, I was only thinking of my own skin which, in the greater scheme of things, isn't that important . . .

Suddenly, he realises that the **Stranger** *is no longer there.*

But where is he? I must introduce you. He was here a moment ago . . .

Anna What are you talking about?

Freud (*going and lifting up the curtains*) I had a visit during your absence, a remarkable visit.

Anna Who was it?

Freud (*triumphantly*) A stranger! A visitor, well worth knowing. That's all I can tell you. Now where's he got to? He didn't go out through the window, nor the door . . . no, we were just talking when you came back.

Anna You were alone.

Freud Well, yes, but that's because he went and hid as soon as he saw you. We were in the middle of a discussion.

Anna (*tenderly*) Papa, when I came in, you were in your 'I might just have a little nap' position.

Freud (*outraged*) I was not sleeping. Completely impossible.

Anna Then where's your mysterious visitor?

Freud *bangs violently in the curtains.*

Freud I wasn't sleeping, I wasn't! Didn't you hear the music?

Anna I'll make us a hot drink and you can tell me all about your dream.

Exit.

Scene Twelve

The **Stranger** *comes through the door, a few seconds after* **Anna** *goes out. He looks at* **Freud**, *who is still looking for him, tenderly and but not without some mockery.*

Stranger I would have felt out of place, I wouldn't want to spoil that reunion.

Freud (*turning round*) Where were you?

Stranger (*elliptically*) The necessities of physical incarnation.

Freud *does not understand. The* **Stranger** *indicates to him that he has been to urinate . . .*

Stranger A fascinating phenomenon: like a hose pipe . . . it didn't stop.

Freud Stay here. Anna has to see you.

Stranger No.

Freud Yes.

Stranger You will tell her . . .

Freud She needs you, particularly this evening.

Stranger If she's as pigheaded as you are, it might be a long night.

Freud Please.

Stranger (*giving in*) At your own risk . . .

Scene Thirteen

Anna *comes in, bearing a tray with a rich tisane set. She does not immediately see the* **Stranger**. *There then takes place a silent action in which* **Freud** *is trying to place the* **Stranger** *in her field of vision but from which she always finally turns away. Finally, in desperation,* **Freud** *speaks.*

Freud Can't you see my visitor?

Anna *turns around, sees him and says calmly in an almost gloomy voice:*

Anna Oh it's you. (*She picks up the empty teapot. With commanding politeness.*) Well, sit down. You'll have a tisane, I'm sure. I'll just fetch another cup.

She goes out again, leaving them stunned.

Scene Fourteen

Freud, *bewildered by* **Anna**'*s everyday calmness, turns to the* **Stranger** *and asks:*

Freud 'Oh, it's you'! What does she mean: 'Oh, it's you'? You know each other?

Stranger I'm as surprised as you are . . .

Anna *has already returned.*

Scene Fifteen

She brings the hot water and extra cup.

Freud You know this gentleman?

Anna Yes, of course. Well, by sight . . .

Freud Who do you think he is?

Anna Sorry?

Freud Who do you think he is?

Anna Well, I know exactly who he is . . . All too well.

Freud (*irritated*) Who, for God's sake?

Anna A man who has been following me every afternoon in the street for a fortnight, every time I go to the kindergarten. He always smiles at me, and I always ignore him. He always winks at me, and I always pretend not to notice. In short, Monsieur is a rude man.

Stranger I assure you that I never . . .

Anna Do not insist, sir. Your forward behaviour is one thing but laying siege to my father in order to get to me . . . really! You are exhausting him and you are not changing my attitude to you one jot . . . On the contrary.

Stranger I assure you that it isn't me.

Anna Oh, really! Then you must have a double! Or an identical twin! It is a miracle. I'm leaving you, Father, I'll come back when your guest has left.

Exit **Anna**.

Scene Sixteen

Freud *stands rigid. The* **Stranger** *helps himself to a cup of tisane.*

Freud I demand an explanation. You could have foreseen all that. You should have done if you know everything.

Stranger Well, almost everything.

Freud I can't bear it.

Stranger There it is again, Freud. The old fawn. You're starting to doubt again. I hope you're not going to continue.

He offers **Freud** *a cup of tea, much as the lady of the house would.*

Or perhaps you are standing back for a bit, taking a longer view.

He laughs. A pause.

Nobody can see me, everyone projects the image that suits him on to me or the one that is obsessing him: I have already been white, black, yellow, bearded, clean-shaven, ten-armed and even a woman! I think that deep down your Anna doesn't find her stranger as repugnant as all that . . .

They drink. The **Stranger** *is unable to restrain a little laugh.*

Freud Why are you laughing?

Stranger I'm wondering if, what with all this tea, I'll be able to do the hose-pipe trick again. It really was quite spectacular. (*He laughs again and looks at* **Freud**.) Dr Freud finds me childish. But surely to marvel is to become a child again . . .

He suddenly stops bantering and puts his hand on **Freud***'s shoulder.*

I'm leaving, Freud. I have no father, no mother, no gender, no unconscious. Plainly you could have done nothing for me but listened. But you have listened and for that, much thanks.

Freud You're leaving me?

Stranger I have never left you.

Freud I shall never see you again?

Stranger You will. As much as you wish but not with your eyes.

Freud How then?

Stranger (*puts his finger on* **Freud***'s heart*) I was there, Freud, I have always been there, hidden. And you have never found me; so you have never lost me. And when I heard you saying that you did not believe in God, it was like hearing a nightingale say that it didn't believe in music. (*He hands* **Freud** *the document and a pen.*) Dr Freud, you can go now. Take as many people with you as you can, save their lives.

Freud *signs the document at last. The* **Stranger** *seems relieved.*

He turns, picks up his elegant evening coat and moves towards the window.

Goodnight.

Freud But . . . I still don't know . . . (*Suddenly aggressive.*) You have to stay.

Stranger (*peacefully*) I said goodnight, Freud.

Freud *stands across the window to prevent him from getting past.*

Freud Out of the question. I will not allow you to leave by the window like a human being, like a burglar. You will disappear in front of my eyes!

Stranger (*smiling*) The thorn. Still the thorn.

He goes to the window and, staring at **Freud**, *causes him to withdraw, as if moved by an invisible power.*

Good night.

Freud *recovers his wits and suddenly picks up the revolver that he had left on the table. Holding it at arm's length, he takes aim at the* **Stranger**.

Freud I'm going to shoot.

Stranger (*smiling*) Ah yes?

Freud I'm going to shoot.

Stranger Of course you are. (*Pause.*) But if I were the madman who escaped this evening, Walter Oberseit, or even that man who pays undue attention to Anna every afternoon, you would have a corpse on your hands. One bullet: one dead man. Think, Dr Freud, losing your faith and freedom in one fell swoop and ending up on trial for murder – is it worth the risk?

Freud (*trembling*) I am confident. You will not fall.

Stranger Well, then, why not leave it at that? Faith must feed itself on faith, not on proof.

Freud (*with shaking hands*) Why are you mocking me? That's what the devil would do.

Stranger A God who manifests himself quite simply as God would not be God – merely the king of the world. I wrap myself in obscurity, I move in mysterious ways, otherwise what would remain for you to decide? (*Putting the barrel of the weapon on his heart.*) I am a mystery, Freud, not an enigma.

Freud I am not converted.

Stranger But Sigmund, only you can convert yourself: you are free! It is always man who makes voices speak . . .

Freud I have gained nothing.

Stranger Until this evening, you thought that life was an absurdity. Henceforth, you will know that it is in fact a mystery.

Freud Help me.

Stranger Au revoir, Freud, or rather 'adieu'.

He disappears.

Scene Seventeen

Freud *makes as if to catch the* **Stranger**, *but he escapes.*

Freud He's disappeared! (*He leans out of the window.*) Now you're making fun of me! You can't make off like that . . . not shinning down the drainpipe like a common thief. (*Enraged.*) Not like that!

He runs to the desk, from which he picks up his weapon again and goes up close to the window. He shuts his eyes and fires a shot in the direction of the **Stranger**. *Coughing through the smoke, he leans out in order to see. Then he turns around, with the revolver smoking.*

Missed!

Curtain.

Enigma Variations

translated by Jeremy Sams

Variations énigmatiques was first performed at the Théâtre Marigny, Paris, on 24 September 1996. The cast was as follows:

Abel Znorko	Alain Delon
Eric Larsen	Francis Huster

Directed by Bernard Murat
Designed by Nicolas Sire
Lighting by Jacques Wenger and Laurent Castainet
Sound by Michel Maurer

Characters

Abel Znorko, *a writer*
Erik Larsen, *a journalist*

Setting

Abel Znorko's study at his house on Rösvannöy, an island in the Norwegian Sea, the present day.

Same set throughout.

The study of **Abel Znorko**, *winner of the Nobel Prize for literature. He lives in retirement on his own at Rösvannöy, an island in the Norwegian Sea. His office is baroque, fantastic, all books and wood, and opens out on to a terrace beyond which can be seen the distant waves.*

The passage of time can be read in the sky, which shows passing clouds and wild birds flying by from time to time. This afternoon is the very one when, after a northern day lasting six months, the winter night lasting six more months will begin. In the centre of the scene, twilight is beginning to colour the horizon with a violet glow.

The action takes place in a single scene.

As the curtain rises, the room is empty. Elgar's Enigma Variations *can be heard coming from a record player. Then, outside, two clear shots ring out. Noise of rapid steps. The sound of running footsteps.* **Erik Larsen** *enters through the bay window at a run, breathless and very frightened. He is a man between thirty and forty who still has a quality of youth, something lively, gentle, about him . . . He looks around, anxious to find help.*

Abel Znorko *enters from the side. Tall, proud-looking, with piercing eyes, he looks at the intruder with the expression of a hunter. As soon as he comes into the room, everything becomes focused on and reorganised around him. He receives his visitor like a demigod at the heart of his creation. Having enjoyed* **Erik Larsen***'s discomfiture for a moment, he turns off the music abruptly.*

Erik Larsen *turns round, sees the writer and rushes towards him.*

Erik Larsen Quick, quick, do something, will you! Just now . . . Someone just shot at me. There's a bloody madman on the island . . . coming up the path, two bullets went right past my head . . . they hit the gatepost.

Abel Znorko Yes, I know.

Erik Larsen We've got to take cover.

Abel Znorko You're safe here.

Erik Larsen But what's going on?

Abel Znorko Nothing that dramatic. I just missed, that's all.

Larsen *can't believe his ears.*

Erik Larsen You what?

Abel Znorko I missed. I don't mind admitting my mistakes; obviously I didn't shoot as well as I used to. That's age, I suppose. Do you honestly think I'd wreck my own front gate on purpose? Only a madman would do that! It was a nice new wooden one too . . .

Larsen *turns towards the bay window to find a way out.* **Znorko** *prevents him by blocking his path.*

Abel Znorko Don't be scared. I only shoot at people when they're on the way up to the house: once they're inside, they're my guests. Firing at intruders is fair enough . . . natural distrust, but shooting at a guest would smack of homicide, not to mention inhospitality . . . (*Charming, now, he starts to take his coat. He adds with a strange smile:*) So, guest or corpse, your choice . . .

Erik Larsen (*frozen*) I don't know . . .

Znorko *laughs, as though they were exchanging polite nothings.* **Larsen** *tries to steer the conversation into ordinary channels.*

Erik Larsen Mr Znorko, I think you might have forgotten our appointment.

Abel Znorko Our what?

Erik Larsen We'd made an arrangement to meet . . . here . . . at Rösvannöy, around four o'clock. And I've travelled three hundred kilometres plus an hour's boat ride to get to the island.

Abel Znorko And who are you?

Erik Larsen I'm Erik Larsen.

Znorko *looks at him, still waiting for a reply. After an instant,* **Larsen**, *thinking he hasn't heard, repeats more loudly:*

I'm Erik Larsen.

Abel Znorko And that's it?

Erik Larsen Well . . .

Abel Znorko (*with joyful irony*) When you wonder about yourself . . . at night, say, under a silent sky, peppered with countless stars, when you ask yourself 'Who am I, who is this fat-arsed, shivering skeleton marooned in a hostile or at best indifferent universe?' you reply: 'I'm Erik Larden'? I mean, that's answer enough for you, is it, that rattle of unconnected syllables, 'I'm Erik Larden' . . . ?

Erik Larsen (*automatically*) It's Larsen . . .

Abel Znorko (*facetiously*) Oh, oh, excuse me, Larsen . . . see . . . of course that makes all the difference, the whole essence of your being resides in that 's' . . . Larsssen . . . (*Mockingly.*) Of course, Larsen . . . Erik Larsen . . . the secret of the universe . . . something that fills the aching void of all creation . . . yes, yes, of course, the whole of Kant and of Plato seems nothing, a mere puff of metaphysical hot air when set beside the sibilant solidity of that 's' . . . Larsen . . . of course. Now why didn't I see that sooner?

Erik Larsen I am a journalist with the *Nobrovsnik Gazette* and you agreed to give me an interview.

Abel Znorko Pure fiction! I hate journalists and I only converse with myself. (*Pause.*) I can't think of any earthly reason why I should allow my privacy to be invaded.

Erik Larsen Indeed. That's what puzzled me. Nevertheless . . .

Pause. They look at, or rather stare at, each other. **Larsen** *says slowly:*

But you confirmed it in writing.

Larsen *holds out a letter to him. Somewhat pressurised by his insistence,* **Znorko** *takes the letter and glances at it. He enjoys disconcerting his visitor.*

Abel Znorko Did I now? Fancy that. (*Pause.*) Any idea what made me agree to an interview?

Erik Larsen I have a few theories.

Abel Znorko Aha?

They look at each other. Pause.

Erik Larsen OK. One theory.

Abel Znorko Aha! (**Znorko** *finally smiles and is suddenly charming again.*) I do believe we're going to get on. (*He claps his hands.*) Good, let's get to work. I presume you have one of those machines that makes me sound like a eunuch who mis-stresses every other word, now what're they called, oh yes, tape recorder? (**Larsen** *takes it out of his bag.*) It's always the people who tape me who always misquote me. Paradoxical, that, isn't it? Like getting crutches in order to walk worse. (*He sits down in an armchair.*) So. Do you like my books?

Erik Larsen Who's asking the questions?

Abel Znorko We haven't started yet. Do you like my books?

Erik Larsen (*setting up his tape recorder*) I don't really know.

Abel Znorko What?

Erik Larsen Well, it's a bit like God, I don't really know.

Abel Znorko (*annoyed*) You aren't being very clear.

Erik Larsen Well . . . with God, you hear so much about him in advance it's hard to decide, honestly, what you really think about him. You're already influenced . . . prejudiced if you like, certainly intimidated from the outset . . . you say to yourself, men wouldn't have gone on about him for so many thousands of years if he really didn't exist. Well, your reputation has the same effect on me: it has always stopped me having an objective view. Nobel Prize-winner, translated into thirty languages, dissected in minute detail in all the major universities, you are too dazzling for me; you blind me.

Abel Znorko (*simply*) Nobel Prize . . . don't let yourself be dazzled by a silly medal.

Erik Larsen Well, yes, but you have to have one not to be impressed. You can afford to be modest.

Znorko *bursts out laughing.*

Abel Znorko Me, modest? I'm not sure modesty exists. Look at somebody modest, so-called . . . his blushes and embarrassed contortions are such an effort, and merely an index of his immodest desire to try to chalk up extra brownie points. (*Abruptly, he fixes the journalist with a stare.*) So, you're trying to say, politely, that you don't like my books.

Erik Larsen No, but it is so frequently proposed as a given that you are admirable that my admiration is hamstrung. No, I'll have a better notion of what I think when you've been dead a couple years . . .

Abel Znorko Charming . . . But, you've read me, at least?

Erik Larsen (*seriously*) Like no one else has . . . (*Pause. Slight unease on both sides.*) OK, can we start?

Znorko *clears his throat and nods.* **Larsen** *starts the tape.*

Erik Larsen You have just published *Unconfessed Love*, your twenty-first book. It takes the form of a romantic correspondence between a man and a woman. Their passion is physical at first, and they have a few months of the most intense happiness, then the man decides to end it all. He enforces a separation, a physical separation; he demands that their passion shall henceforth only be expressed in writing. The woman, unwillingly, agrees. They write to each other for years, fifteen years, I believe . . . and the book consists of their correspondence, their sublime correspondence, which ends abruptly a few months ago, last winter, for no apparent reason . . .

Abel Znorko I got bored writing them.

Erik Larsen You caused quite a stir with this book: the first time you have ever spoken about love. Your normal predilection being for the philosophical; your stories have as their arena the lofty regions inhabited by the solitary soul, divorced from any kind of reality, in a world which is yours and yours alone. But now, suddenly, you're describing an affair, something everyday, almost commonplace. The affection of a man, a writer admittedly, for a woman, a story of flesh and blood, throbbing with the pulse of life. Real life. In everyone's view, it's your best book, your most sensitive, your most intimate. The critics, who have sometimes given you a rough ride, have praised it to the skies. You've had unanimous raves.

Abel Znorko (*sincerely astonished*) Really?

Erik Larsen Don't you read the newspapers?

Abel Znorko No.

Erik Larsen You don't have a radio, or television?

Abel Znorko I don't like being invaded, least of all by everyday trivia. (*Perturbed.*) So . . . they liked it, did they? Well, really, I'll never understand those guys . . . nor will they, for that matter. Whether they're hailing something or trashing it, they're just chattering away and understanding nothing. (*Facetiously.*) Twenty-five years at cross-purposes with the critics, hardly a great career, is it?

Erik Larsen But how does it affect you that your twenty-first book has been unanimously acclaimed as your masterpiece?

Abel Znorko (*simply*) Well, it makes me sad for the others.

Larsen *looks at him, astonished.* **Znorko** *is touching, suddenly.*

Erik Larsen You really do love your books, don't you, as if they were your children.

Abel Znorko (*evasively*) I've lived off them; I'm a kept father, but not an ungrateful one.

Erik Larsen (*persistently*) Now you sound bitter. You have it all, success, talent, prizes . . . and you don't seem that happy.

Abel Znorko (*clamming up*) Let's stick to the point. Where were we?

Erik Larsen (*returning to the interview*) Could we talk about this woman . . . Eva Larmor?

Abel Znorko I'm sorry?

Erik Larsen This correspondence is signed Abel Znorko–Eva Larmor. I have some knowledge of your life, but I don't know anything about her. So. Let's talk about Eva . . .

Abel Znorko But there's no such person.

Erik Larsen So the whole story's a fiction?

Abel Znorko Look. I'm a writer, not a photocopying machine.

Erik Larsen But you depict yourself in the book!

Abel Znorko Do I?

Erik Larsen You are the man, one half of the correspondence! Otherwise why are the letters signed Abel Znorko?

Abel Znorko Because I wrote them.

Erik Larsen What about the others, the ones signed Eva Larmor?

Abel Znorko I wrote them too, and the woman I was when I wrote them happened to be called Eva Larmor.

Erik Larsen You mean she doesn't exist?

Abel Znorko That's right.

Erik Larsen And she wasn't inspired by anyone in particular?

Abel Znorko Not as far as I know.

Erik Larsen (*suspiciously*) Not by a woman, or women, that you've been in love with?

Abel Znorko What's it to you? What makes a mystery

beautiful is not the truth it conceals, but the secret it enshrines. (*Abruptly dry.*) When you go to a restaurant, do you enter by the kitchens? Or do you rummage about in the dustbins on your way out?

Larsen *looks at him. He senses that* **Znorko** *may bite, but he is brave enough to press him further.*

Erik Larsen I thought perhaps, stupidly perhaps, that there were certain details which couldn't have been invented.

Abel Znorko 'Stupidly' is right. What sort of detail would it be that can't be invented? Isn't that what a novelist does, invents details that can't be invented, but which seem real? If a work rings true, it doesn't owe its authenticity to real life, but to its author's skill. Literature doesn't regurgitate life, Mr Larden, it invents it, provokes it, surpasses it.

Erik Larsen (*standing up to him*) Larsen. You back off every time I ask you a personal question.

Abel Znorko I prefer intelligent questions.

Erik Larsen I'm just doing my job.

Abel Znorko All you pea-brained lobotomised dimbos ask the same dim dead question: Mr Znorko, is your work autobiographical? The more you churn out your sad little columns, the more you dribble out your etiolated syntax, the more you copy, and recopy, report and rehash the world . . . the more you have become the cripples of creativity. And you think everyone who writes is like you. Well, I'm not. I don't report, I create. Would you have said to Homer, 'What was Mount Olympus really like? Oh, and is your work autobiographical?'

Erik Larsen So you think you're Homer, do you?

Abel Znorko No, but I think you're a journalist, meaning a hack, meaning everything I hate most!

Larsen, *furious, gathers up his things.*

Erik Larsen Very well. I won't waste any more of your

time. There is nothing for me here! I . . . I'm sorry to have disturbed you.

Abel Znorko (*rather astonished*) But my dear chap, what is the matter? We're only having a quiet chat. (*Smiling.*) Actually, you seem a deal less dim than most of your colleagues. What's the problem? I'm answering your questions, aren't I?

Larsen, *annoyed, doesn't know how to take this.*

Erik Larsen Yes, by insulting me.

Abel Znorko That's the only answer to certain questions.

Erik Larsen So you think you're superior to your interviewer?

Abel Znorko So you're saying you're more important than I am?

Erik Larsen No, Mr Znorko, I'm not saying that. I am no great writer, I am not really much of a writer at all. I've never written a single sentence worthy of being remembered by anyone, but I have always had respect for people and try to give a straight answer to a straight question.

Abel Znorko What a deplorable attitude!

Erik Larsen Yes. Well, goodbye, sir.

Znorko *tries to detain him.*

Abel Znorko But I don't get what you're playing at. I give you the rare privilege of an interview and you up sticks and leave. What is it that I'm not giving you?

Erik Larsen The truth.

Abel Znorko Don't be vulgar. Do you tell the truth, Mr Larsen? I mean always . . .

Erik Larsen (*embarrassed*) I try.

Abel Znorko I don't.

Erik Larsen I know your works, I know your fiction. I

know what everyone knows. I wanted to meet *you*, to find out more about you.

Abel Znorko How can you be sure that 'the truth' tells you more than a lie?

Erik Larsen Cos it's the truth!

Abel Znorko (*impassively*) Oh, for God's sake. Look, I'm a forger, nothing more than that. If you want truth, you've come to the wrong shop: I only deal in artifice. But interesting how you contradict yourself: you come to see a famous man who famously tells lies and you ask him for the truth . . . You might as well pop into the baker's and say, 'Oh, just half a pound of sausages, please!'

Erik Larsen You're right, my mistake. Bye-bye.

He goes to the door. Suddenly, very nimbly, **Znorko** *blocks his way. He is smiling again; he is charming.*

Abel Znorko (*amused*) Well, well, I underestimated you, you're less of a coward than I thought: I thought you were unrileable, like the rest of your colleagues. No, I like you. (*He pats him amicably on the back.*) Come on, old man, don't be cross now, let's have a nice quiet chat. I want you to stay. Really I'm listening. All ears . . .

Larsen *hesitates, then sits down again on the sofa.*

Abel Znorko Will you have something to drink? A little drinky-poo. A teeny-weeny dinky-donk? (*Humming.*) There's nothing like a little drink to clear the throat and help you think.

Larsen *accepts a glass and drinks, exhausted by the conversation.*

Erik Larsen When they said you were hostile, I thought they were overstating the case.

Abel Znorko A word of advice: never believe anyone who speaks well of me, only listens to those who do me down . . . they're the ones who take me at face value.

Erik Larsen Anyone'd think you enjoyed being nasty . . .

Abel Znorko God, sooner that than being 'nice'. There's

this ghastly fashion nowadays for it, for 'niceness'. Everyone being sweetness and light to each other, like puppy dogs licking each other and holding out their silly fat paws. . . . 'Nice', is that the best we can do?

Erik Larsen Your reputation as a misanthrope plainly isn't exaggerated. How long have you lived on this island?

Abel Znorko A dozen years. Or so . . .

Erik Larsen Don't you ever get bored?

Abel Znorko (*simply*) With my own company? Never.

Erik Larsen (*slightly ironic*) Isn't it exhausting, living with a genius?

Abel Znorko Not as exhausting as living with an idiot. (*He looks towards the bay.*) I'm happy at Rösvannöy. Dawn lasts for six months, twilight takes six more. So I am spared the tedium of nature, the seasons, the climates, the stupid to-and-froing of night and day every day and night! Here, near the Pole, Nature doesn't get overexcited, she takes it easy, and floats. (*Pause.*) And then there's the sea, the sky, the grass, vast great blank pages that write themselves without any help from me.

Erik Larsen How can one go for years without seeing other people?

Abel Znorko How can one go for years seeing them every day?

Erik Larsen Even so, your novels are so full of precise observations about human nature that it has to be said that even if you have no dealings with people, you certainly know all about them.

Abel Znorko Thank you. But that's not much to boast about. The two most boring species in the animal kingdom are men and dogs. They both kind of do what they do and that's it . . .

Erik Larsen So what do you admire?

Abel Znorko Clouds . . . Cats . . .

Erik Larsen I don't much care for cats.

Abel Znorko I spotted that the moment you came in.

They look at each other. They fall silent.

Znorko *sits down opposite* **Larsen** *and stares at him fixedly. He murmurs in a soft voice, as if he were reading* **Larsen***'s brow.*

Abel Znorko You have that look . . . the open, candid look of the sentimentalist . . . you expect too much of others; you'd even sacrifice yourself for them. Which makes you brave . . . a brave man. And therefore dangerous . . . to yourself. So beware.

Larsen *bows his head, touched, embarrassed. He tries to break the spell.*

Erik Larsen Let's get back to your book. Can we touch on your feelings about love?

Abel Znorko What do you mean 'we'?

Erik Larsen I'm speaking for my readers.

Abel Znorko Bollocks! Spare me that, that's pure megalomania. You can't claim to speak for the people just because there's a regular supply of morons who buy your rag probably to wrap their vegetables in.

Erik Larsen (*correcting himself*) Tell me about your feelings about love.

Abel Znorko I hate love. It's a feeling I've always wanted to avoid. And guess what, it avoids me, too.

Erik Larsen (*astonished*) You mean you've never been in love?

Abel Znorko No, I have, when I was eighteen, when I was trying out the other stuff . . . booze, smoking, cars, girls, you know, all the other rituals they invent to make you feel a bit more like a grown-up. But not long after that I expunged love . . . I eschewed it.

Erik Larsen But . . . you have been loved?

Abel Znorko Oh, desired, yes, enormously. Female

readers invest a writer with any number of qualities. When I went to a book fair, or a signing, there'd be women swooning at me like I was a rock star. I've lost count of the number of pretty things who've offered me their bodies, their lives.

Erik Larsen Aha! And . . . ?

Abel Znorko And nothing. I took their bodies and spared them their lives. (*Laughing.*) No, when I was younger, my speciality was married women; all a matter of peace of mind: adultery obviates emotion.

Erik Larsen You weren't afraid of the husbands?

Abel Znorko Husbands don't kill out of jealousy. They get tired long before that. Then they drop off to sleep. So . . . (*Pause.*) Is your machine not working?

Erik Larsen No, it is.

Abel Znorko (*with an ambiguous look*) Perhaps you'd better check it.

Erik Larsen (*leaning over*) No, no, the tape's going.

Abel Znorko (*continuing with a little smile*) It isn't always easy to avoid the beaten path. People fall into the norm, in spite of themselves, and believe me, you have to run long and hard to escape the clutches of mediocrity.

Erik Larsen How can you think of love as something mediocre?

Abel Znorko Listen, my dear Larsen, Larden, whatever . . . I'll tell you an old story from these parts. One that the fishermen tell, you might hear them mumbling it to themselves, to others, as they're mending their nets. And it goes like this.

There was once a time when the earth afforded great happiness to all mankind. Life tasted of oranges, of clear fresh water, of sleeping in the sun. There was no such thing as work. There was only eating, drinking, sleeping, and men and women just slotted their bodies into one another, totally naturally, every time they felt that tingling in the groin; and there were no repercussions, there were no couples, only coupling, there were no particular laws concerning the region above the thighs and below the navel. The only rule was pleasure. In a word, paradise.

But paradise, like happiness, is boring. Men began to realise that perfect sexual satisfaction was even more monotonous, more predictable, than the sleep that inevitably followed. The gymnastics of orgasm began to weary them. So men created forbidden fruit. They decreed that certain relationships were illicit. They found, like showjumpers, that the course became more exciting when there were obstacles in the way. Something to surmount which gave them the whiff, the tang, the sometimes bitter taste of sin.

But that wasn't enough. One gets tired of scaling the same fences, climbing the same mountains. So men invented something even more complex than vice; they invented the impossible; they invented love.

Erik Larsen That's absurd!

Abel Znorko Love is nothing more than a perversion of sex. A detour, a mistake. A sideshow for those who are bored with copulation.

Erik Larsen That's nonsense!

Abel Znorko Well, you say so, but think of the pluses: pleasure is the work of the moment, fleeting, pointless, something that is always about to vanish; love's essence is durability. At last there's something solid, something that can be tussled with, something with substance! Love introduces a new dimension. Time. It creates fascinating new episodes, approaches, refusals, pain, sighs, ecstasies, setbacks: in short, love offers all the attractions of a labyrinth. (*Simply.*) There, my dear Larsen, love is nothing more than that: a story made up by people who don't know how to make up stories the way I do, in words.

Erik Larsen Is that really a folk story, or just off the top of your head?

Abel Znorko What do you think?

Erik Larsen So who wrote it?

Abel Znorko Who writes folk stories? Folk.

Larsen *sighs and takes up his notebook.*

Erik Larsen Are you saying that in your life you've avoided love and contented yourself with sex?

Abel Znorko That's exactly what I'm saying.

Erik Larsen (*mockingly*) That must be tricky, living all alone on an island.

Abel Znorko (*amused*) Oh yes? How do you think I eat? I don't live on bark and berries. No, I have everything delivered, bread, vegetables, meat, women.

Erik Larsen Yes, I know . . . I know . . . When I was coming over, on the boat, the ferryman mentioned these women . . . he even told me what they called you, your nickname.

Abel Znorko Oh yes?

Erik Larsen Do you know it?

Abel Znorko No.

Erik Larsen The wicked ogre of Rösvannöy.

Abel Znorko *bursts out laughing.*

Erik Larsen (*mysteriously*) The wicked ogre. It's wonderful, like a fairy story . . . Who writes folk stories, I wonder? (*Pause.*) And what truth do they protect?

They eye each other scornfully, silent for a moment. They avoid a direct confrontation once again.

Znorko *returns to the professional interview.*

Abel Znorko To go back to your original question, no, I am not the man in my book. I hate complications. They appal me. I've steered clear of love, which is my great strength.

Erik Larsen It's odd . . . because you describe the condition of being in love like no one else.

Abel Znorko Why, thank you.

Erik Larsen And even more convincingly, the condition of being frustrated in love. (**Znorko**, *annoyed, gives him a hard look.*) So there's no such woman?

Abel Znorko No.

Erik Larsen Very well. The first page has a dedication to H.M. Who's that?

Abel Znorko If I'd wanted people to know, I'd have written out the name in full.

Erik Larsen So they're the initials of the real woman whom you really corresponded with?

Abel Znorko That's pure fantasy.

Erik Larsen I don't believe you.

Abel Znorko And I don't give a toss.

Erik Larsen If you don't care about anything, what do you want from me? Why did you let me come here? Why me?

Znorko *looks at him without speaking. He suddenly seems beaten. He drops down into a chair.* **Larsen** *looks at him with compassion.*

I get the feeling you're in pain . . .

Abel Znorko Really?

Erik Larsen . . . that you're not happy.

Abel Znorko (*simply, reflectively*) Happy, what's the point of that? (*He is silent and stays absorbed.*)

Erik Larsen Your silence speaks volumes.

Abel Znorko (*tiredly*) Spare me your sophistry, I'm fine.

Larsen *goes over to him and puts his hand on his shoulder.*

Erik Larsen Let me help.

Znorko *jumps, but* **Larsen***'s hand eventually pacifies him. He lets himself enjoy this strange contact for a moment.*

Erik Larsen (*softly*) I'll tell you who I am. I'm one of those total strangers you tell your life story to, just like that, just one evening, just by chance, not really knowing why. I am of no importance. I can listen to anything ... I'm safe. No repercussions ...

Znorko *sighs.*

Erik Larsen (*softly*) So. Tell me about her.

With sudden irritation, **Znorko** *gets up and throws his glass against the wall, smashing it.*

Abel Znorko Leave me alone. Sod your compassion. It smells like an old wet dog. Piss off! Give me some air!

Larsen *looks at him affectionately, without moving, not taking him seriously.* **Znorko** *becomes angry, ill at ease.*

Go on, piss off! Your curiosity, your solicitude, it's unbearable. It's suffocating being in the same room as you. I need some air! Go away. Thank you. Goodbye!

And he moves hurriedly to the terrace, to get his breath back, as if he is unable to bear **Larsen***'s physical proximity.* **Larsen** *gathers his belonging together, tape recorder and notebook. But before leaving, he goes up to the record player and starts the* Enigma Variations *playing again.*

Znorko *is taken aback, and gives him a black look.*

Abel Znorko Who said you could do that?

Erik Larsen *Enigma Variations*, my favourite. (*Pause.*) And yours too.

Abel Znorko But ...

He stops speaking, then shrugs scornfully and studiedly contemplates the countryside. **Larsen** *takes up his raincoat.*

Erik Larsen You pretend not to love anyone, but it's a façade. I know what you do with your money.

Abel Znorko I hoard it. The wicked ogre.

Erik Larsen No you don't. You give it all to medical research.

Abel Znorko (*jumping*) What? How did . . . ? (*Then, fearing to say too much, he stops.*) Anyway it's not true. (*He goes back to being silent, looking into the distance.*) It's not true.

Erik Larsen Goodbye, Mr Znorko.

Abel Znorko Goodbye.

Larsen *goes out.*

Znorko *comes back into the room thoughtfuly. He looks around him, hesitating. He thinks carefully. Then he goes out by the inner door. The music continues.*

A few seconds later, two shots are heard again, followed again by the sound of running footsteps. **Larsen** *re-enters, breathless, this time more furious than frightened.*

Calmly, regally, **Znorko** *reappears.*

Erik Larsen You're mad, totally mad! You missed me by a couple of inches.

Abel Znorko And what do you conclude from that? That I'm a good shot or a bad shot?

Larsen *throws his belongings angrily on the floor.*

Erik Larsen What do you want from me?

Abel Znorko (*enjoying himself*) A reaction. What's it like being shot at? How does a rabbit feel?

Erik Larsen What do you want? Tell me, and let's get on with it!

Abel Znorko Won't you have something to drink? A little drinky-poo. A teeny-weeny dinky-donk? (*Humming.*) There's nothing like a little drink to clear the throat and help you think.

Erik Larsen Oh, don't play mine genial host, that's a joke. When you shoot at someone, you don't offer them a drink thirty seconds later!

Znorko *pours a glass for himself. When he puts it to his lips,* **Larsen**, *furious, snatches it from him and drinks it down in one.*

Znorko *calmly pours himself another.*

Erik Larsen It would have been so easy just to have refused an interview, like you do with all my colleagues. But you've not only invited me here, now you prevent me from leaving. Now what do you expect me to do?

They look at each other.

Abel Znorko What are you after? How do you know what I do with my money? I keep it a total secret.

Erik Larsen I made enquiries. You give huge sums to medical research. Anyone else would have blazoned it from the rooftops if they'd given a tenth of the amount. So why keep shtumm?

Abel Znorko (*grumpily*) I don't give out of the goodness of my heart, I give out of fear. (*Rapidly changing the subject,* **Znorko** *shrugs. He takes the tape recorder from* **Larsen**'*s bag and shows it to him.*) What are you playing at? You're the first journalist ever to make a tape recorder work without a plug or batteries.

Erik Larsen I . . .

Abel Znorko You hadn't noticed, perhaps? When I asked you, you assured me it was going.

Erik Larsen Yes . . . but . . . it got broken on the way here . . . in any case, those machines are pointless . . . OK, I was pretending . . . but my memory is good enough . . .

Abel Znorko (*sceptically*) Oh yes?

Larsen *sits down. He stares at* **Znorko**, *defying him.*

Erik Larsen No, I'll stay. There's something delicious about liars: it's that sooner or later they can't resist telling the truth. That's what I'm waiting for.

Abel Znorko Then you'll be waiting for a while. Did you bring a packed lunch?

Erik Larsen I'll be fine.

Abel Znorko What?

Erik Larsen You?

They eye each other scornfully. **Znorko** *ends it lightly.*

Abel Znorko What do we want from each other? Men. People. We carry on seeing each other precisely because no one can answer that question.

Erik Larsen So. What do you want?

Abel Znorko How about you? (*Pause.*) What an impasse: two people, and neither wants to go first.

He pours them another drink. Pause.

Well, while we're waiting, why not tell me about yourself.

Erik Larsen I don't think there's anything I care to tell.

Abel Znorko Are you married? (**Larsen** *doesn't reply.*) Yes, of course you are. Married, and in love with your wife. At least, you think you are.

Erik Larsen What makes you say that?

Abel Znorko I get a strong whiff of bourgeois platitude off you: it smells of slippers by the fire, of 'stopping in', the car on Saturday, the garden on Sunday, oh, and lavender sachets in the linen cupboard . . . I don't see you taking the risk of any happiness other than other people's happiness. Everything is totally banal, totally normal and totally dismal. (*He starts to laugh.*)

Erik Larsen Do I seem ridiculous?

Abel Znorko Worse than that, ordinary.

Erik Larsen You judge humanity as if you lived on some sort of higher plane.

Abel Znorko I am overbearing, pretentious, insupportable, anything you like to call me, but ordinary? Not ordinary.

Erik Larsen It's an odd habit you have. Forcing people

to stay so that you can pitch into them . . . what's it hiding?

Abel Znorko (*smiling*) Aha. Good question.

Erik Larsen You seem to hate me. Why? Where does this hatred come from? Hatred never has hatred as its prime cause; it's always about something else . . . a symptom of, I don't know . . . suffering, frustration, jealousy, pain . . .

Abel Znorko Spare me the cracker-barrel philosophy.

Erik Larsen Love speaks in the name of love, for itself, but hate always speaks for something else. So what's making you suffer?

Abel Znorko You, at the moment. These pearls of compassion . . . do you have to look at the world like an agony aunt? I mean, can't you do better than that?

Erik Larsen (*simply*) When I look at a man, I merely see someone who's going to die.

Abel Znorko Bit morbid.

Erik Larsen That's why I don't get angry, that's why I don't insult people, why I can't strike anyone. I see the skeleton beneath the skin.

Abel Znorko (*furious*) Well, there's nothing wrong with me!

Erik Larsen Oh really? You are so broken down by loneliness and by boredom that you mount a complete three-ring circus to stop the first person who comes here from leaving.

Abel Znorko But you're not exactly the first person.

Erik Larsen Is that so? How's that? (*Pause.*) It's time you explained yourself.

Znorko *hesitates, then finally sits down.*

Abel Znorko Very well. we've spent enough time sniffing around each other. (*He decides to speak frankly.*) I . . . I made you come here because I saw that you lived in . . . Nobrovsnik. You do live in . . . ?

Erik Larsen (*glad to see the turn the conversation is taking*) Yes, I do.

Abel Znorko Well, I'd like to hear what's going on there.

Larsen *relaxes and gives a big smile. He doesn't seem very suprised by* **Znorko***'s question.*

Abel Znorko Tell me about Nobrovsnik!

Erik Larsen You know it?

Abel Znorko Yes . . . no . . . let's say I've never been there but I've heard about it . . . Why do you ask?

Erik Larsen Well, in your book . . . in *Unconfessed Love*, your description of the town where the woman lives, the woman you, he, whoever loves, well . . . I got the feeling that the town was my home town!

Abel Znorko (*put out*) You did?

Erik Larsen Well, of course you give it a different name, but when Eva Larmor describes the spiral layout of the streets, when she mentions the iron church with the blue beams, she's describing Nobrovsnik.

Abel Znorko What a coincidence . . .

Erik Larsen What about when she lingers by the seventeenth-century fountain which commemorates King Gustav's defeat of the Poles? There's only one seventeenth-century representational fountain. And it's in Nobrovsnik . . . Incredible, isn't it, for someone who's never heard of the place.

Abel Znorko Yes . . . yes . . . well, we writers sometimes have these visions . . . but you can hardly be the only inhabitant to have spotted the resemblance.

Erik Larsen Maybe not . . . but it's only a small town and it may be that your readership isn't that extensive.

Abel Znorko (*disappointed*) Oh, right. So you haven't talked to anyone about my book, I mean, there?

Erik Larsen No, not that I can think of . . . (*His face lights up.*) No, I tell a lie, there is someone who reads your stuff, who really loves you as a writer, who worships you . . . how come I didn't think of them sooner!

Abel Znorko (*almost feverishly*) Tell me, tell me . . .

Erik Larsen The vicar. He's bonkers about you. And he's no pushover, by any manner of means. He's sophisticated, cultured.

Znorko *seems to be deeply disappointed and* **Larsen** *is highly amused by his disappointment.*

Abel Znorko But hang on, I seem to remember . . . yes, that's right . . . that I had a couple of letters from Nobrovsnik . . . part of my considerable postbag, you understand . . . letters from a woman, a teacher of literature in your town . . . wait, perhaps I can remember the name . . .

Erik Larsen A woman . . . a teacher . . . a beautiful woman?

Abel Znorko Yes, very beautiful! (*Catching himself.*) Well, I don't know, one assumes, after all it was only a letter . . . But she wrote with the calm, beautiful confidence of a woman men will do anything for . . . now what was her name . . . Helen something?

Erik Larsen Helen Metternach.

Abel Znorko That's it! Helen Metternach! Do you know her?

Erik Larsen Of course! It's not that big a town.

Abel Znorko Well, how's she doing? I mean, I haven't heard from her for the longest time.

Larsen *gets up, with manifest astonishment.*

Erik Larsen So you're saying that you agreed to see me just to hear the latest news about Helen Metternach?

Abel Znorko No . . . no, obviously not . . . that would be ridiculous . . . but since she cropped up . . . have you ever mentioned me to her? I mean, my name?

Erik Larsen Not that I can think of. No. Um . . . no. We've never discussed you or your work or anything.

Znorko *gives a pleased smile.*

Abel Znorko Obviously not. Why would you?

Erik Larsen Why indeed? (*Pause.*) Oddly enough, you dedicated your book to someone called H.M. . . . that's not her, is it, Helen Metternach?

Znorko *bursts out laughing.*

Abel Znorko What a ridiculous idea . . .

Erik Larsen You're laughing a bit too heartily.

Abel Znorko Do you think I'd dedicate a book to a fan, to a teacher living in the arse end of nowhere, just because she wrote to me once or twice to say she liked my work? If I did that, I'd be dedicating twenty novels a day: that's the number of letters I get.

Erik Larsen That's a long answer to a short question. So, H.M. is in fact Helen Metternach?

Abel Znorko Look, if it'll make you any happier, I'll tell you who H.M. is. It's Henry Metzger, my first publisher. I owe him my entire career. But as he's now dead and I've since changed publishers, I just put his initials so as not to offend.

Erik Larsen I see . . .

Abel Znorko I warned you: the truth is always disappointing.

Larsen *rises, takes his coat and bag.*

Erik Larsen Well, Mr Znorko, I won't take up any more of your valuable time. Thank you very much indeed for this exclusive. I'll get it back and type it up and send it in.

Abel Znorko What do you mean? We haven't finished.

Erik Larsen I've talked to you about Nobrovsnik. You've given me a few profound statements. I've got more than enough to use. So thank you and bye-bye.

Abel Znorko What do you mean? I haven't said a thing!

Erik Larsen Well, you know, to be honest, the arts section in a newspaper this size isn't ever going to be that extensive, even for someone of your . . . I'm unlikely to get more than half a page on Wednesday. So really I've got plenty to be going on with.

Abel Znorko Wait . . . wait . . . A Nobel Prize-winner gives an exclusive interview to some local rag . . . I mean, doesn't your editor realise . . .

Erik Larsen No, he doesn't, he's completely illiterate. (*He puts away his tape recorder.*) No, to be frank, the only way to get an arts piece in would be to have some kind of angle, some news value, some local interest.

Abel Znorko What sort?

Erik Larsen Well, say, for the sake of argument, that you'd lived in Nobrovsnik for some years . . . That you'd met the love of your life in Nobrovsnik . . . That you'd spent time together as lovers in Nobrovsnik . . . obviously that would be of interest to the good burghers of Nobrovsnik . . . otherwise you would just have the space normally set aside for contemporary literature, which to be frank isn't that enormous.

Znorko *blocks the way to the door.*

Abel Znorko All right, if you want a news story, I'll give you a news story. I'll give you a scoop, an exclusive. I'd hate to think you came all this way for nothing.

He makes a strenuous effort to keep **Larsen** *from leaving.*

You want a revelation? OK, I'll give you one.

Erik Larsen Now, why would you do me a favour like that?

Abel Znorko It's not a favour, it's a swap. I give you information, you do something in return.

Erik Larsen (*still stern*) What?

Abel Znorko Take a letter and deliver it in person.

Larsen *sits down again. Pause.*

Erik Larsen You're going to tell me more lies.

Abel Znorko I'd much rather, given the choice.

Erik Larsen But how shall I recognise the truth?

Abel Znorko By its indelicacy. A lie is delicate, it's artistic, it describes the world as it ought to be, whereas the truth is merely what actually is. Compare an academic with a conman – it's the conman who is the artist.

Erik Larsen Very well. I'm listening.

Abel Znorko (*slowly*) All right. In my book, Eva Larmor is inspired by a real person, a woman I did love. And yes, your fellow townswoman, Helen Metternach.

Larsen *shows marked surprise.*

Erik Larsen Really?

Abel Znorko Yes really. We met fifteen years ago. (*He laughs, glad to be reliving his memories.*) I first met Helen Metternach at a conference on 'Early Nordic Literature'. She was there as a student, third row, legs were sticking out into the aisle. From what I could see, I felt there was something familiar about her. Had I seen her somewhere before? I hadn't. But as I looked at her, I worked out what it was that was familiar: it was her ugliness.

Erik Larsen Sorry?

Abel Znorko The faces of handsome people have a certain architecture, even when they aren't expressing anything very much; those who aren't beautiful are forced to smile, forced to make their eyes sparkle, compelled to make their lips move in order to animate a face that has in itself no real form. Looking at her face, one was looking at emotions, not features. Helen was condemned to express herself all the time.

And that wasn't all. She had this skin, this particular skin, which disturbed me. When I looked at her, I sort of shivered with embarrassment, as if her skin were offering itself, tangibly . . . I hardly dared look in her direction, I felt that someone might catch me in the act of touching her, of feeling her. 'That poor girl's skin', I thought to myself, 'is positively indecent.'

Her figure didn't improve matters either. Objectively speaking, Helen had a beautiful body, but there was something about it that turned my stomach . . . I was nauseated by something like . . . compassion . . . yes, I felt a kind of distasteful affection, tenderness almost, for those too-firm, too-high, too-pointed breasts, those too-well-rounded buttocks, those too-well-sculpted calves; her body seemed to jut out, obscenely; she was stark naked beneath her clothes; I felt like a voyeur. I looked at my colleagues surreptitiously; I was certain that we had all spotted her blatant display of her flesh.

This sense of unease didn't go away.

That evening, over drinks, we chatted a bit. She had a charm. A voice. A smile. A way with words. She seemed completely unaware of the incongruity of her body.

That night, I went to bed thinking about her: 'That poor girl', I thought, over and over again, 'has every imaginable quality apart from the ability to make a man fall for her.' I thought of her naked and I began to laugh. I thought, God, Nature is so thoughtless, so unfair. Which was cruel of me, I thought, but there we go.

So I studied her every day, and every evening I thought of her as I fell asleep. One day at lunch I heard that one of my colleagues at the seminar had his eye on her. Which gave me pause. Was he going to make fun of her?

My immediate reaction was to protect her. I left the table, found her in her office and asked her out to dinner that very evening. I was not unpleased with myself: at least I'd saved the poor girl from his weaselly maraudings. His sarcasm. That evening, I had fun dolling myself up as if it were for a real date. So it was the tux, the taxi and the best restaurant in town. And almost absent-mindedly I set about seducing her. It was fun. Basically I was doing her a good turn, offering her something that no other man would. I was smug to bursting with my own good nature, I was high as a kite on my kindness of heart.

At midnight I took her home. She suggested one for the road. I accepted, rather amused I said yes. If she'd been playing along, you see, the game would have been even more fun. We drank, we chatted, I looked at her sitting on her little studenty bed, I wanted to make love. 'What a pity she's so ugly,' I thought.

Who made the first move?

And an hour later we were in each other's arms. It was dazzling, a night like a beautiful morning . . . What did I say about her body? Her body was perfect, her skin was silk, I swam in her, I flowed in her, I was drunk on her. (*Pause.*) So, beware of ugly women, they're completely irresistible . . .

Erik Larsen I'm simpler than you: I thought her magnificent from the moment I saw her.

Abel Znorko That's my doing. The chemistry of our love; since me, all men see her with my eyes.

Erik Larsen (*doubtfully*) It still doesn't explain how you seduced her.

Abel Znorko I didn't, she seduced me. When a man falls, what woman can resist? (*He pauses, looking back into the past, sincere.*) I was defenceless, I was five, I was ten, I was twenty, I was myself at every age I've ever been. It was only with her that I finally experienced my childhood, my young manhood and all that at the age of forty. (*Continuing, too happy to be able to tell his story.*) We lived together for some months, never leaving each other's side; I'd rented a little flat, not far from the university. My pretentiousness she found humorous; and guess what, I made her laugh. I honestly think I became almost charming, because that's how she saw me. I showered her with gifts, the first time in my life I knew what to do with my money. And she loved me so much that she even made me love myself.

Erik Larsen Why didn't you marry her?

Abel Znorko (*laughing*) Marriage for a writer? Having someone trying to hoover your desk! Come off it! (*Pause.*) No, I prefer short-term madness to long-term stupidity.

Erik Larsen Don't be glib. Why did you split up? Are you allergic to happiness?

Abel Znorko I really cared for Helen. When we swore to love each other 'for ever', I wanted that 'for ever' to really last for ever. Lovers swear to be true for eternity, but generally that eternity passes very quickly.

Erik Larsen You were afraid that your passion would fizzle out?

Abel Znorko Obviously. One might as well promise to have a high temperature for ever. I imposed a separation so that our love would be stronger.

Erik Larsen I still don't understand.

Abel Znorko You don't understand? Life as a couple became unbearable! Living side by side in the same room, in the same bed, we were constantly reminded of our essential separateness. I have never felt so alone as when I was brushing against her all the time. We threw ourselves on each other in order to slake a thirst greater than ourselves, an unassuageable thirst that bordered on madness, we made love night and day . . . we made love for hours, furiously . . . we wanted to melt into the same flesh . . . each separation was an amputation . . . if we couldn't touch each other, I'd scream with rage, I'd beat the walls . . . if she went away for a single day, I'd go into a decline . . . before long, we'd never go out at all; we spent, we must have spent, five months in each other's arms.

With her I discovered everything that is painful in love.

Have you ever felt the potential cruelty in every caress? The hidden claw ... Do you think that touching makes us closer? It separates us. The caress irritates, itches almost; distance burrows its way in between the hand and the skin, and there is pain beneath each caress, the pain of never really being really close to each other; caress is a living paradox, a misunderstanding, a misreading ... a loneliness that's longing to come closer yet longing for the other loneliness, for her loneliness, to come to you ... it's at cross purposes ... the more excited you get, the more you recoil ... you think you're caressing a body, but in fact you're opening up a wound. And so we crushed our lips, our teeth together, mingling tongues and saliva; like two lifesavers or two drowning people, we breathed breath to breath, heart to heart, I tried to push myself into her, she tried to be engulfed in me, we tried to chip away the granite, to erode everything between us, to be annihilated in each other, to forge one being in a final fusion. And so we screamed and writhed, but all in vain: I remained the visitor, she the host. I stayed me, she stayed her.

We couldn't fuse, we couldn't conjoin, but we still had hope, the hope of orgasm: we felt it mount, irresistibly, that split second when we would flow into each other, and perhaps, at last, at long last ...

A spasm. Another spasm. And then the loneliness again ... Orgasm. That sad little thing, which merely serves to show us we're apart, which disunites. The opposite of love. Un-love. We'd each roll to our own side of the bed, back to the cold, to the wilderness, to silence, to death. That's what we were. Two separate beings. For ever and ever. Yet the memory remained of that moment when I had believed I'd lost myself, a melancholy heady memory as bitter as magnolia on a summer's evening ... Pleasure is merely a way of redefining one's own solitude.

Erik Larsen I see things differently.

Abel Znorko (*now well-launched into his story*) You don't see anything at all. It was no longer love, it was slavery. I wasn't writing any more, I thought of nothing but her, I needed her.

Erik Larsen So you sacrificed her.

Abel Znorko Sorry?

Erik Larsen You sacrificed Helen to your work. That's murder.

Abel Znorko Not at all. We made our love purer, more essential, ultimately stronger.

Erik Larsen Oh really? So your ideal lover is one who isn't there.

Abel Znorko (*amused by* **Larsen**'s *aggressiveness*) Now, now, calm down. From the minute we stopped jumping on each other, our relationship was able to develop into another dimension. When we wrote, we talked of literature, of philosophy, of art; she gave me notes on everything I wrote and didn't spare my feelings either; I honestly think Helen was the most sincere critic I've ever had. The only one. And in my darkest moments, when I felt emptier than the eye of the hurricane, she gave me new faith in myself.

Erik Larsen How handy.

Abel Znorko (*increasingly amused*) Look, journalist, I honestly think you're overreacting. You wanted an exclusive and I'm giving it to you. You ought to be thrilled, not getting worked up about it. (*Peremptorily.*) Sex only goes rotten when it gets all mixed up with love. Helen and I owed it to ourselves to rise above such pathetic little spasms. (*He reflects, hesitates a moment, then takes a letter out of his pocket.*) Anyway, I want you to do me a favour. Take this letter, give it to Helen Metternach and make her read it out loud.

Erik Larsen Why? Doesn't she open your letters any more?

Abel Znorko Look, just do it for me and don't ask questions.

Larsen *takes the letter. But he takes up the previous conversation again.*

Erik Larsen I just don't understand it . . . to enforce that separation, to deliberately deprive yourselves.

Abel Znorko (*calmly*) Tristan's sword.

Erik Larsen Sorry?

Abel Znorko Tristan's sword. You know the legend of Tristan and Isolde. It's another big favourite around here . . . The greatest lovers of all time end their mortal lives lying side by side on the same bed for all eternity, with his sword between them . . . Isolde could only be happy with his sword there.

Erik Larsen You only love love if it's a disease.

Abel Znorko Don't be stupid.

Erik Larsen You need Helen Metternach in order to burn, to be consumed, to lament your fate . . . to die, not to live.

Abel Znorko (*sarcastically*) I need to die, oh yes, of course, that's my lifetime's ambition.

Erik Larsen Anyway, you don't even know who she is.

Abel Znorko (*laughing at* **Larsen***'s belligerence*) Why should you care one way or another?

Erik Larsen You don't love Helen, you love your own agony, and your unnatural relationship, and the pain of a separation entirely of your own making . . . It's not Helen's presence you need, but her absence. Not the Helen that is, but the Helen that you don't have. It's just as well you didn't tell the public that your book was drawn from life: they would have seen that Abel Znorko, the great Abel Znorko, was nothing but a spotty adolescent who'd been mooning about for the last fifteen years, waiting for the mail to arrive!

Znorko *is very put out by* **Larsen***, as much by what he says as by the way he says it; but he decides to laugh it off.*

Abel Znorko Keep your hair on, please. Look, really, this is completely inappropriate.

Erik Larsen You should never have left her. You killed her.

Abel Znorko You won't let it lie, will you! Look. Everything we had was strong, our caresses, our separation, everything. There was no question of sacrifice, we agreed. Otherwise, why do you think she would have accepted?

Erik Larsen My guess is that, like all those who love passionately, she was predisposed, in some profound way, to misery. (*Pause.*) And then of course . . . she loved you. She agreed for your sake, simply that.

Abel Znorko Well, well!

Erik Larsen So there were two of you to pander to the needs of the great Abel Znorko, her and you.

Znorko *bursts out laughing.*

Abel Znorko Well, you're very defensive. Unbelievably touchy. It must be a really tight-knit community, Nobrovsnik. (*Amused.*) Such concern for a fellow citizen . . . Do you know Helen Metternach well?

Erik Larsen Yes, very well. (*Pause.*) She's my wife.

Znorko *is dumbfounded.*

Abel Znorko What?

Erik Larsen Helen Metternach became Helen Larsen . . . Larsen, you know, with the magic 's', which fills the aching void of all creation.

Reeling, **Znorko** *sits down.* **Larsen** *looks at him, very amused and not at all surprised.*

Erik Larsen Will you have something to drink? A little drinky-poo. A teeny-weeny dinky-donk? (*Humming.*) There's nothing like a little drink to clear the throat and help you think. (*He thrusts a glass into his hands.*)

Znorko *jumps and takes a hold on himself.*

Abel Znorko And of course you're lying! You've just made that up to drive me mad! Prove it, prove you're her husband . . .

Calmly, **Larsen** *takes a photograph out of his wallet.*

Erik Larsen Perhaps you'd like to see the wedding photos?

Looking at it, **Znorko** *nearly retches. He is, firstly, very moved.*

Abel Znorko I haven't seen her since we parted . . . (*Unable to stop himself.*) God, she's so beautiful . . . (*Then, deliberately, he changes tack, his state of emotion changing to mocking scorn.*) God, it's grotesque . . . is that you dressed up as the groom? . . . Look at your tie, was it stapled on? . . . Do you pay to hire that stuff or do they pay you? . . . And look, a flying saucer's landed on Helen's head. Oh no, it's a hat . . . No, it's a joke! It has to be. This has got to be a fancy dress ball you both went to, or a let's-dress-up-like-a-cunt-for-a-laugh party. (*Reassuring himself.*) Nice try but no cigar! I'm sure you've met Helen Metternach, I'm sure you know her, but actually she's lived on her own for the last fifteen years. And she's written to me every day for the last fifteen years. Helen is not married. Not to you, not to anyone. Good trick, though. (*He returns the photograph.*) Very good. Very humorous.

Larsen *then takes out another paper from his wallet.*

Erik Larsen Well, continuing that vein of humour, here's the marriage certificate. April the seventh, twelve years ago.

Abel Znorko Twelve years . . .

He looks, then pushes the paper away. He is completely nonplussed. He eventually asks, very reluctantly:

And do you have any . . . children?

He is afraid of the answer. **Larsen** *looks at him and tells him, frankly and with pain.*

Erik Larsen No.

Znorko *sighs, relieved that he has been spared this cruelty. Then he abruptly seizes his book and leafs through it furiously.*

Erik Larsen What are you doing?

Abel Znorko I want to see what she wrote me on the seventh of April twelve years ago, what she had to tell me about her wedding day! (*He finds the page.*) No letter that day.

Larsen *smiles.* **Znorko** *doesn't give up.*

Abel Znorko And the next day? (*Reading.*) 'April the eighth. My love, I stared at the sunrise and I thought of you. I said to myself that maybe we were both looking at the same sun, on the same earth, at the same instance, but even then, I couldn't feel happy.' (*With disillusioned humour.*) There we have it. The love song of the new bride. It's not that hot for either of us, is it?

Larsen *shrugs.* **Znorko,** *exhausted, puts down the book.*

Abel Znorko And how about me, what was I doing that day? How could I have not known? Perhaps I wasn't well ... (*He thinks.*) You knew, didn't you, you knew all along.

Erik Larsen Of course. Why else would I have asked to come and meet you?

Abel Znorko (*distraught*) Why did she never write to me about it?

Larsen *fixes his gaze on* **Znorko** *and says the questions and replies for them both, as if he is reading the writer's thoughts and sharing his inner turmoil.*

Erik Larsen What do you know of her, when all's said and done? You were content to rub up against her for, what, five months, and then you sent her away. You never began to be a proper couple, you ran away before all that could even begin to start!

Abel Znorko (*nastily*) I don't see why you're complaining. You wouldn't have had my cast-offs otherwise.

Erik Larsen Falling in love, anyone can do that, but to really love someone ...

Abel Znorko (*finding his energy again*) Oh, please ... don't compare your half-hearted cohabitation to a relationship of fifteen years; Helen and I thought continually about each other . . . we wrote every day . . . we told each other everything.

Erik Larsen (*ironically*) Everything? (**Znorko** *is silent, touched.*) What do you know about Helen? In her letters, she became what you wanted her to be. Faithful, considerate, self-effacing, attendant on your every wish, subservient to your genius. Funny that, the Crown Prince of Lies can only tolerate his own?

Abel Znorko She should have told me . . . about your marriage.

Erik Larsen Perhaps she wanted to spare your feelings? To spare you the fact that life could go on without you. That you were actually replaceable. To spare your pride, in other words nine-tenths, not ten-tenths, of your being. Let's face it: there is life after Abel Znorko. (*For a moment he drives it home with a certain cruelty.*) Didn't you think it odd that she should be a widow after your separation? You always assumed that she'd stay single?

Abel Znorko Yes. Our passion was a thunderbolt which can only leave ashes . . .

Erik Larsen Well, your ashes still seem pretty active.

Abel Znorko What do you mean?

Erik Larsen Your special deliveries. Your girls-to-go.

Abel Znorko That's a different matter altogether. Don't confuse the two. Not one of those soft pink sluts could begin to replace Helen. I love them for what they are and I leave them for what they're not. It's a matter of hygiene . . . I'm a man. I need a receptacle for certain bodily urges.

Erik Larsen And a woman doesn't have urges?

Znorko *turns viciously on him.*

Abel Znorko Oh, so that's why she chose you, is it? As her stud, her hot lover? You? You look about as sexy as an overcooked leek!

Erik Larsen Oh, so you're an expert on men, are you?

Abel Znorko I can spot a man who likes women; I can tell him by his nostrils: he has the nose that likes the sniff, a nose that likes to get right up close, a roving nose, a nose that pokes into folds, into nooks, and elbows and armpits and the rest . . . You have a thoroughly respectable nose.

Erik Larsen Do I, now!

Abel Znorko (*making his point*) Put it this way. Helen is the most sensual woman I've ever known. How have you managed to satisfy her?

Erik Larsen (*frankly*) Helen doesn't set much store by that sort of thing. We rarely make love.

Abel Znorko Well, quite!

Erik Larsen It was her decision. She assures me she doesn't need it.

Abel Znorko That's her sweet way of telling you that what you do best in bed is sleep.

Larsen *quietly bursts out laughing.* **Znorko***'s vituperations don't affect him at all. It's clear he is totally prepared for this confrontation.*

Erik Larsen I'm beginning to get what it is that rings false with you.

Abel Znorko Oh yes?

Erik Larsen Your rudeness.

Znorko *falls back into his seat. Deep down, he knows that* **Larsen** *is right, and changes his tone wearily.*

Abel Znorko Go now. This situation is awful for both of us. That's the reason I chose to live on this island . . . to get away from this sort of banality.

Erik Larsen I'd really rather stay.

Abel Znorko The husband, the wife, the deceived lover, all so hackneyed, all so vulgar. I bet you've even got a revolver in your pocket.

Erik Larsen I haven't.

Abel Znorko (*with a sigh*) Pity.

Erik Larsen 'Helen is the most sensual woman I've ever . . .' But what makes you think we know the same woman? There are two Helens: yours and mine. Why should Helen be the same all the way through, like seaside rock? If she chose us, two such different people, it's because she wanted to be different people with both of us. With you it was passion; with me it was love.

Abel Znorko (*sarcastically*) Love! Poor little boy. How long have you been married now?

Erik Larsen Twelve years.

Abel Znorko Twelve years? That's not love, that's inertia. (*Reassuring himself.*) You kid yourself your strength is in some sort of animal proximity, like two cows in a barn, but everyday life doesn't break down the barriers, or bridge the distance. On the contrary, it builds invisible walls, walls of glass, which get thicker and thicker as year turns into year, making a prison where you can always see the other person but never reach them. Everyday life! Clear and simple, you think. Far from clear. Far from simple. Love, you say, lovely love. That sleeps in a sump of habit, that's silted up with compromise and disillusionment, that's dull and damp, and made of smelly socks, and picking your nose and crafty farts under the sheets.

Erik Larsen That's real. It's only when you don't love life that you invoke the sublime.

Abel Znorko And it's only when you don't love the sublime that you get bogged down in real life.

Erik Larsen Our relationship is real, we're close, we talk to each other, we touch each other every day. I see the nape of her neck when I wake up. We've taken a gamble: either we're satisfied with each other, or we're disappointed. You never had the courage to be part of a couple.

Abel Znorko You mean the cowardice!

Erik Larsen No, the courage! The courage to commit, to trust. The courage to stop being the sort of man women dream of and to be a real man. Do you know what true intimacy is? It's knowing your own limitations. You have to say goodbye to your power and your glory, and you have to reveal the little inglorious being that you really are without flinching an inch. You've avoided intimacy in order to avoid ever facing up to your own limitations.

Abel Znorko Spare me your bourgeois philosophy; it reeks of mothballs and boiled beef.

Erik Larsen You're one of those people who love without discovering anything.

Abel Znorko There's nothing to discover, not about love.

Erik Larsen Oh yes, there is. The other person . . .

Znorko *comes up to* **Larsen**. *His eyes dart flames. He has just understood something fundamental.*

Abel Znorko It's your fault she stopped writing! You read my book, you found out about our relationship, you made a big scene, you put your stupid fat foot down.

Erik Larsen (*ambiguously*) You can think what you like.

Abel Znorko Yes, that's it, you threatened her, you were mad with jealousy, you made her cry. I know her, she hates violence. She was afraid to hurt you, and so gave me up! But even if she'd decided, she could have warned me, or explained . . . Those letters, the last letters, you intercepted them, didn't you? You wanted to let me bleed myself dry these last few months. That's it, isn't it?

Erik Larsen That's precisely it: you no longer receive her letters because I've had enough of the whole thing.

Abel Znorko And what about my letters, the letters I've been sending her for the last four months? Where are they? Did she get them?

Larsen *takes out a bundle.*

Erik Larsen Here they are.

Znorko *falls on it.*

Abel Znorko You bastard! They haven't even been opened.

Erik Larsen Would you rather I'd read them?

Znorko *is beside himself with rage. He walks furiously round the room, ranting.*

Abel Znorko But what on earth has it go to do with you, you little meddler! You pathetic moron. We could have gone on living together by letter if you hadn't put your oar in!

Erik Larsen You shouldn't have published! On a whim you reveal fifteen years of intimacy to the world. Changing her name changes nothing: you've made it all public, commonplace. It's obscene. And what for? For a book? To make money?

This hits **Znorko** *hard and he slumps into a chair, his head in his hands.*

Abel Znorko I . . . I had my reasons.

Erik Larsen Oh yeah?

Abel Znorko Yes. And they are my business . . . and Helen's obviously . . . It's all in the last letter . . . the one you're going to give to her.

Erik Larsen (*holding out his hand*) So hand it over.

Znorko *hesitates, then takes it out of his pocket.* **Larsen** *takes it. He looks at it; he would clearly like to open it.* **Znorko** *stops him.*

Abel Znorko It's not for you.

Larsen *puts the envelope in his pocket.* **Znorko** *returns obsessedly to the past.*

Abel Znorko She told me her day every day of her life and you didn't even rate a mention.

Erik Larsen She told you the truth: she told you about

the day she spent with you, not with me. And she didn't tell me about the day she spent with you. She had two truths, that's all: the truth with you and the truth with me.

Abel Znorko Two lies, you mean.

Erik Larsen What makes you think Helen is one entity? Is any of us? Helen is a passionate lover with you – that's true – and she's my wife from day to day – and that's true too. There are two Helens. Maybe more. Neither of us knows both of them. Neither of us can satisfy both of them.

Abel Znorko (*maliciously*) Well, hubby seems to be taking it all on the chin.

Erik Larsen I never thought I could be all men to Helen.

Znorko *shrugs. He is still angry.* **Larsen** *goes to the record player.*

Erik Larsen You were listening to the *Enigma Variations* when I arrived?

Abel Znorko Do you want to know what I had for breakfast as well?

Erik Larsen Did she give it to you?

Abel Znorko Look, just piss off, will you! You smug little cuckold. You already look a complete cunt; I'd quit while you're ahead if I were you.

Erik Larsen (*persistently*) Was it her who introduced you to the Elgar? I'm sure it was.

Abel Znorko Yes. (*Remembering.*) The first day we said we loved each other, she gave me the record, she smiled at me sweetly and said, 'We say words of love to each other, but who are we? When you say I love you whom are you saying it to?'

Erik Larsen (*smiling*) '... And whom am I saying it to? We don't know who it is we love. And we'll never know. So I'm giving you this piece of music so you can think about it.'

Znorko *looks at him in astonishment.*

Abel Znorko How do you know that? I cut it out of the book.

Erik Larsen She said the same thing to me the first time we said we loved each other.

Abel Znorko (*disappointed*) Ah!

Erik Larsen Maybe it's the only thing you and I have in common.

Abel Znorko (*bitterly*) I'm sorry, but I haven't had time, like you have, to get used to all this . . . Sharing things isn't really my style.

Larsen *goes to the piano and begins to play the opening of the* Enigma Variations.

Erik Larsen Variations on a theme that one never hears . . . Elgar claimed that it was a well-known theme, but no one has ever really identified it. A hidden melody, which one senses, the shadow of a song which comes and goes, a melody one has to imagine, as enigmatic, as elusive and as distant as Helen's smile. (*Pause.*) Women are melodies that one imagines and which one never hears. Whom do you love when you love? We never really know.

Abel Znorko (*inscrutably*) We don't. (*When* **Larsen** *has finished playing, he asks suddenly:*) How many variations are there?

Erik Larsen Fourteen. Fourteen ways of hearing an absent melody.

Abel Znorko So you think there are . . . fourteen of us?

Larsen, *taken aback, looks at him. Seeing his face,* **Znorko** *bursts out laughing.*

Abel Znorko Only joking. (*He's at the end of his tether.*) Look, I think we've said all that needs to be said. You've told me Helen's married and that she's kept it from me for twelve years, well, fine! And now I even know her husband, a very presentable, very upright man, a positive orgy of propriety. And that's fine. And I now know why she doesn't write to me any more. And that's fine too. I think we can usefully bring down the curtain. I think . . . that I don't find all this all that amusing any more, if it's all the same to you. (*He takes up his last book and looks at it with irritation.*) Actually, push comes to shove I was being more truthful than I thought when I told you that my book was pure fiction. Actually, I was pretty near the mark. That woman has come entirely out of my own head, she never existed. (*He throws the book into the fireplace.*) It's the most imaginative novel I've ever written, and I didn't even know it.

Erik Larsen Don't apologise.

Abel Znorko (*painfully*) Twelve years of lies upon lies! And she was the writer, I mean the real one! What an imagination! She told me all her thoughts were dedicated to me, when in fact she was having lunch with you, having dinner with you and sleeping in the same bed as you!

Erik Larsen (*shocked*) You're being cruel.

Abel Znorko (*his anger rising*) And she played her part to the hilt. Honest, caring, attentive, critical-but-supportive and I believed every bloody word. Like a kid with its mother. What a fool.

Erik Larsen Stop it, you'll regret it.

Abel Znorko (*beside himself*) What could make me regret it? I fled the world to escape from the all-pervasive vulgarity of everything, I restricted myself to this one woman, I hung upon her tiniest word or whim with religious zeal, and I find that she's just calmly lied to me. What's going on in her black heart? What vile mush does she have in lieu of a conscience? Go home, tell her I never want to hear of her again, that I take it all back. All the time, all the care, all the consideration I gave her, that I take back all the secrets I shared, all the thoughts and feelings I coined just for her, that I hereby renounce everything and that there's just one thing I stand by, and that's the act of publishing our letters. Because, bottom-line, like all the great bitches of the world, she's also a fairly decent writer. Tell her.

Erik Larsen I shan't.

Abel Znorko You will! And as for the book, I disown it! She can keep all the royalties! It's no longer mine! It's all hers! Reassure her that her delicious little hoax, apart from being one big barrel of laughs for her, will be a nice little earner. Tell her that I'll never share anything with her again, and that she can fuck off and die.

Erik Larsen I won't tell her.

Abel Znorko Oh yes, you will! Like the good little hubby you are, the little puppy dog who laps it all up! And when you're home, she'll be all twitchy and impatient; dying to know how our meeting turned out, chuckling inside. Do send her my very worst wishes, and tell her she's not worth fly shit, and that I won't have a second's peace until the day (and dear God, let it come soon) when she'll have been completely erased from my mind, when as far as I'm concerned she'll be wiped out, vaporised, extinguished, blown back into the limbo of mediocrity she somehow crawled out of, and exposed as the impostor, the sad, crabby, shitty little cheat she was and is and always will be.

Erik Larsen (*beside himself*) I won't tell her!

Abel Znorko Why the hell not?

Erik Larsen Because she's dead!

Larsen'*s words echo in the silence. It's as if* **Znorko** *has been stabbed with a knife. He reels.*

Larsen, *without looking at him, goes on quietly.*

Erik Larsen Helen is dead. It took three months. Three months, a long time to die, a short time to live.

Abel Znorko *listens with pain as* **Larsen**, *seating himself behind him, takes up the tale.*

Erik Larsen When the doctors first made their diagnosis, she rebelled. She became very angry and she decided to fight. But that anger wasn't her; it was whipped up, the froth. The next day she gave in to reality. She didn't get up, she stayed in bed, she looked at me like a naughty little girl. 'I don't want to go to the hospital. I want to be cared for here.' When she said 'cared for', she was thinking of another word, a word which was too hard for her. A word she couldn't say. So with the doctors' consent, I became hospital and medical staff all rolled into one. I lived for her needs; I gave her her medicine, fed her, made sure she slept, told her stories, tried to get her to laugh; I knew that it was all pointless, that it was fighting the inevitable, but it was the only way I could go on showing her I loved her. She accepted my attention, my anxiety, quite naturally; she hardly seemed to be aware of it.

I'll tell you the worst thing about a slow death, Mr Znorko: it's that you lose the one you love long before they die. You see them fading away between the sheets, getting heavy and dull, under dull, heavy pain, folding in on themselves and moving into a secret, inaccessible place, their eyes wandering, as if seeing a place they no longer want to talk about. Helen was still there and yet somewhere else. The painful part for me, Mr Znorko, was that, occasionally, all my care, all that desperate manifestation of my love for her seemed merely to produce profound indifference.

The last few days, she didn't even speak. She had become so slight that she didn't seem to be lying down, more that she'd been carefully placed on the bed, weightless, like a bird, a poor little flightless bird. It took two hours to feed her an apple. I began to want her dead and I was ashamed to think it. She was suspended between life and death, as I was between love and hate. You'll find death warps everything and everyone, Mr Znorko.

She died on the first day of spring. The snow had melted two weeks before, the roads were caked with mud; the river had burst its banks, the traffic was logjammed. And when dawn broke that morning, it gave the first glimpse of green and of yellow, and of new blades of grass seeking the sun.

And she fell asleep for the last time.

That morning, there were larks in the sky.

Znorko *takes* **Larsen** *warmly in his arms.*

Abel Znorko Thank you. Thank you for being there for her.

Larsen *shrugs. For him, it was the obvious thing to do.*

Abel Znorko (*with pain*) I'm ashamed . . . I . . . I . . . never did anything for her.

Erik Larsen Oh yes, you did.

Abel Znorko All that time, I was only thinking of myself. Maybe I was raging against her – I was thinking about my book . . . and for what . . .

Erik Larsen (*gently*) You're wrong. Your absence, your silence, were good for her. As she was dying, for those three long months, she was, at least for you, still Helen, still attentive, intelligent, beautiful, still round and firm. For you she was still just as you wanted her to be, just as she would have wanted to be for you. Thanks to the distance between you, she remained for you alive, intact, curled up in your dreams, both of your dreams, a perfect vision of herself that allowed her to refute the degradation which became more visible, more appalling day by day. By knowing nothing, you made her happy . . . And now I know that in her dreams and in her silence she came here, to you . . .

Abel Znorko You should have called me.

Erik Larsen The day after we buried her, I burned the mattress which still bore the imprint of the weight of her body . . . I threw away the clothes she would never wear . . . I gave away the armchair she liked sitting in; it had begun to look like an old dog, asking me with plaintive eyes where his mistress was . . . Then, towards evening, I unlocked her desk and I found the letters – your letters – and the rough drafts of hers.

Abel Znorko I'm sorry – that must have made it even worse.

Erik Larsen (*hesitating, then going on*) No – I was happy to know that she had known more happiness than I had thought, more joy than I had been able to give her. No, it was a sort of relief that life hadn't been too mean to her.

Znorko *is very moved by what* **Larsen** *is telling him.*

Erik Larsen The letters she never sent you, they're the ones that hurt. The ones in which she said what couldn't be said, how much she misses you, when she screams with a love quite unrestrained, when she tells you that she'll never love again, not like that, and when I saw that you were the most important man in her life . . . They were letters for herself, not for you, still less for me . . . no one was meant to hear that silent scream. (*At the memory, he puts his head in his hands, in a gesture of isolation.*)

Abel Znorko *is disconcerted, like a child. He suddenly becomes very close to* **Erik Larsen**.

Abel Znorko I . . . I should like to come home with you . . . to give her flowers.

Erik Larsen (*simply*) All right.

Abel Znorko I'll go with you.

Larsen *looks between them, at the sofa. He puts his finger mysteriously to his lips, as if they should both keep very quiet.*

Erik Larsen (*gently*) Can you hear? (*Pause.*) I've the feeling she's here. Here with us. For the first time.

Abel Znorko (*as gently, indicating the empty space*) Here?

Erik Larsen There.

And for a moment, the two men commune together as they remember Helen.

Then **Znorko**, *too upset, rubs his eyes, looks around rather helplessly and begins to shiver.*

Abel Znorko I just have to pack a bag, that's all . . .

Erik Larsen You won't need much.

Abel Znorko (*suddenly afraid*) It's just that . . . I haven't left the island for years . . . and . . . I don't know what to take . . . what will I need?

Erik Larsen (*understanding*) Would you like me to help?

Abel Znorko Yes, if you would, I'm afraid I'm rather hopeless at this sort of thing . . . (*And suddenly the tears start to flow, like a child.*) Helen . . . (*He is shaken with sobs. Grief has taken hold of him, without warning.*)

Erik Larsen (*disconcerted*) I never thought you'd cry.

Abel Znorko (*drunk with despair*) I never have. Helen, Helen! No!

Larsen *goes up to him, full of respect for his grief. He tries to comfort him by putting his arms round his shoulders.*

After a few seconds, **Znorko** *gently frees himself.*

Abel Znorko I'm sorry, I can't be held . . . not by a man.

Larsen *respectfully drops his arms. He is about to get up when* **Znorko** *holds him back.*

Abel Znorko One day, Helen said to me, 'I would like to see myself die, I'd like to be there at my own death; I wouldn't miss it for the world.' . . . And in the end, that's sort of what happened . . .

Larsen *is moved.*

Abel Znorko Ten years ago, she had a scare. All the women in her family had died of cancer, so of course I was afraid. And I thought I would have to leave my island and we'd have to live together again, and that I'd have to break our ridiculous contract. For weeks and weeks she couldn't even write. And then the tests showed that the tumour had been reabsorbed and all was well. Helen had won.

Erik Larsen And since then, you've given your money to research. Is that the reason?

Abel Znorko You don't need much to live here. (*Owning up.*) All right, yes, that's the reason, she's the reason. (*Pause.*) That crisis brought us even closer, made us more intimate, as if fear had made us both grow a little. But still we never spoke of death.

Erik Larsen That's exactly what did her so much good: you loved her as if both of you were immortal. It was sort of childlike. With me, it was the opposite, I loved her like an old man. (**Abel Znorko** *smiles gently.* **Larsen** *carries on.*) Mine is an anxious kind of love – always has been. I thought when Helen stumbled, she'd snap. When Helen bled, she'd bleed to death; when Helen coughed, she'd die of it. Of course she'd tease me about it. I loved her desperately . . . despairingly . . . as if she were something ephemeral, destined to be taken from me. (*Pause.*) And I was right.

Abel Znorko (*sincerely and simply*) Being you is beyond my gifts. So I'm glad you exist. (*Tonelessly.*) Really I'm nothing but a pompous old windbag of the worst sort, the sort that is listened to and, God help us, respected. I fear I invented my own literary cult simply to escape the pain, the pain of living which terrified me. So to the world, my self-denial was heroic whereas in reality I doubt if I'd have the nerve to free a rabbit from a trap. I never wanted to live life, I wanted to write it, to compose it, to control it, from my armchair in the middle of my room, in the middle of my island, in the middle of the wide wide world. I didn't want to live in time, not the time allotted to me, too proud for that, and I didn't want to live in other people's time either, so I invented time, my own version of time, regulated by the hourglass of my writing. Pure vanity! The world goes round, the grass grows and withers, children grow old and die, and I get the Nobel Prize! You are your own man, quite unobserved, you make total sense in your own obscurity . . . I am one of those creatures who are so worthless they can only be venerated. (**Znorko** *rises and says, somewhat lost:*) Sorry – what shall I take?

Erik Larsen I'll get some things.

Abel Znorko Right . . . I feel a bit, you know, but . . . yes, thank you. (*He indicates the bedroom to the side.*) It's in there. Pack whatever.

Larsen *smiles and goes into the bedroom.*

Erik Larsen (*off*) I didn't know you were so out of touch with practicalities.

Abel Znorko (*trying to make light of it*) I can't even make a bed or boil an egg.

Erik Larsen (*off*) What about the washing up – how do you get that done?

Abel Znorko (*smiling weakly*) By mouth – I give orders. I have a woman who comes and does. She's an angel, well, not in looks, obviously.

Larsen *enters with some shirts which he puts on the sofa.*

Erik Larsen Which shirt? Blue or white? (**Znorko** *doesn't know what to say. So* **Larsen** *shows him the blue one.*) Yes, that's fine – goes with your eyes.

Abel Znorko (*embarrassed by what he's just heard*) Ah . . .

Erik Larsen (*going out again; off, very natural*) Helen was the same as you: hopeless around the house. I had to do everything.

Abel Znorko In the five months we lived together, the dirty washing had acquired a life of its own, you needed a map and a torch to find anything – we became potholers. (*He stands in front of the mirror to see how the shirt looks. He says to himself:*) Yes, I think it does rather suit me.

Erik Larsen Pants or boxer shorts?

Abel Znorko (*shocked by the triviality of the question*) You can't be serious.

Erik Larsen Come on, I need to know: pants or boxer shorts?

Abel Znorko I never use those words. They're kind of . . . obscene.

Erik Larsen (*surprised*) Which ones? Pants? Boxer shorts?

Abel Znorko The whole thing – I don't even want to think about it: 'pants' sounds like knickers being slipped off;

'boxer shorts' sounds like knickers being pulled up again.

Erik Larsen (*laughing*) I still don't know which to pack.

Abel Znorko (*crossly*) The ones that go up.

Larsen *comes back with a pile of underclothes and puts them on the stool.*

Erik Larsen There, that's the lot. Eight pairs of socks, two pairs of trousers, eight pairs of – if you'll pardon the expression – boxer shorts, two cardies . . .

Abel Znorko (*embarrassed*) Yes, thanks, that's fine. (*He is rather irritated by the simple way in which* **Larsen** *puts his belongings into a bag.*) But anyway, I'm only coming for a couple of days, not for a week . . .

Erik Larsen Oh, it'd be a shame to come all that way for such a short time. And then, you'll see, you'll like it at the house . . .

Abel Znorko (*repeating mechanically*) . . . at the house . . .

Erik Larsen It'd be my pleasure to put you up. Ever since . . .

Abel Znorko . . . ever since . . .

Larsen*'s joy troubles* **Znorko**. *He comes closer, ill at ease, clearing his throat.*

Abel Znorko Look . . . I don't want there to be any misunderstanding . . . I appreciate everything you've done for Helen, and your whole attitude and everything, enormously . . . and I'm grateful . . . but I want to make it clear that I'm coming for her . . . not for you.

Erik Larsen (*a little tensely*) But of course.

Abel Znorko You understand that, basically, obviously, we can never be . . . friends, you see what I'm saying.

Erik Larsen Indeed. (*With a practical, unembarrassed air:*) Where's your bathroom stuff?

Abel Znorko (*humiliated and irritated*) Look, leave all that, I'll do it.

He goes out. **Larsen,** *left on his own, goes up to the record player, and starts the* Enigma Variations *playing again.*

When he re-enters, **Znorko** *turns the music off.*

Abel Znorko I'm sorry, but . . . I'm not used to sharing this piece. Sharing anything, actually.

Erik Larsen Understandable. I wanted to ask you something else: when you make love with a woman, do you keep the light on or turn it off?

Abel Znorko That's a completely uninteresting question.

Erik Larsen Please . . .

Abel Znorko Off.

Erik Larsen (*smiling*) I thought so. One more question, just the one. (**Znorko** *acquiesces, feeling constrained.*) Have you ever been to bed with your best friend?

Abel Znorko You're mad.

Erik Larsen I'm serious. Have you ever been to bed with your best friend?

Abel Znorko I don't have any friends.

Erik Larsen Please answer me.

Abel Znorko Where's this leading to?

Erik Larsen What's the answer?

Abel Znorko It'd be no.

Erik Larsen Helen was my best friend. That's what she came as when she came into my life: shared smiles, discussions, secrets, all of which soon became a habit. I told her about my emotional ups and downs, and she was amused, and concerned, and gave me advice . . . We practically lived together in each other's homes. And then one day we discovered that we were also man and woman. So I made love with my best friend. It's a different thing; it happens in the light, so pleasure can have a face at last.

Abel Znorko (*annoyed*) You're a fool. Sex is far better with your eyes closed.

Erik Larsen You're the fool. It's far far better with your eyes open. I've got my own little theory about it. Helen and I . . .

Abel Znorko (*impassively*) Look, I'm not interested. (*Suddenly he remembers something.*) Of course – Erik . . . You're Erik as in Erik 'my friend Erik' – she mentioned you, God, it must have been years ago.

Erik Larsen And then she stopped mentioning me twelve years ago when we got married . . .

Abel Znorko I don't remember your being a journalist.

Erik Larsen No, music teacher. Still am, actually. The *Nobrovsnik Gazette* doesn't exist. It was my invention to get myself invited here. You were rather gullible as far as that was concerned. Or maybe impatient.

The two men look at each other. **Znorko**, *arranging his bag, breaks the silence.*

Abel Znorko (*sorting out his luggage*) Let's go. The boat should be due soon. (*He looks out at the blue and violet twilight over the bay.*) What a shame to be leaving today! Just when day is turning into night. The first twilight for six months. And the last for a year. You had to come now . . . (*He asks, in a harmless sort of way.*) When did she die, exactly?

Larsen, *who seems to have heard, doesn't reply, however.*

Abel Znorko I asked you when Helen died.

Erik Larsen It was a Tuesday. Tuesday the twenty-first of March.

Abel Znorko (*remembering*) That's right, you said it was spring.

Erik Larsen Yes, the first day of spring . . . ten years ago.

Znorko *doesn't take it in straight away, then stops, struck dumb, and looks at* **Larsen**.

Erik Larsen I only lived with Helen for two years. The day after she was buried, when I was sorting everything out, I found the letters, your letters . . . I found the ones she had wanted to write during the first days of her illness and which she never sent you. I discovered your love for each other, what it had been, what it had become . . . I missed her terribly . . . So, that evening, I . . . I took up my pen and I wrote you. I've always been able to do other people's handwriting, especially hers – my party trick; it drove her crazy, sometimes . . .

Abel Znorko (*in a colourless tone*) So it was you?

Erik Larsen For ten years. Several times a week. Almost every day.

Znorko *jumps on to the sofa, distraught.*

Erik Larsen I'm sure you find that quite inexcusable.

Znorko *doesn't reply.* **Larsen** *looks at him sadly.*

Erik Larsen I didn't want her to die. And when I wrote to you she was still alive. And when I received your replies, she was still alive. She was so happy to read them, so very happy. And you too were happy that she replied. And I was happy in between . . . You were right, just now; we do need lies. It's the dead who keep us alive.

Long silence between them.

Znorko *seizes the book abruptly. He opens it and reads.*

Abel Znorko 'I kiss your lips, your lower lip, which is so sensitive, I love the way it swells when we make love . . .' You wrote that?

Erik Larsen Stop, you're embarrassing me!

Abel Znorko You wrote it!

Erik Larsen I . . . I looked back over the earlier letters . . . I did my research . . .

Abel Znorko 'I caress the top of your thigh, on the inside, the soft warm part where the shivers come from that convulse your whole body . . .'

Erik Larsen (*ill at ease, falsely naive*) That's what mine does – doesn't yours?

Znorko *stands up, threateningly. There is something pitiful about* **Larsen**, *as if he has been broken.* **Znorko** *brandishes his rifle and comes up to* **Larsen**.

Abel Znorko Go on, get out. . . . And run, run fast . . . This time I won't be aiming at the gatepost.

Larsen *looks at him without flinching.*

Erik Larsen Whatever. Why did you publish our letters?

He looks fixedly at **Znorko**. *Neither of them moves. And suddenly,* **Larsen** *snatches the rifle from* **Znorko**. *He keeps it by his side.*

Erik Larsen I only came here to ask one question: why did you publish your letters? Why?

Abel Znorko None of your business.

Erik Larsen It is my business. For ten years, I have known everything about you and I've kept Helen alive. By publishing, you've killed her. Murdered her! If the book hadn't come out, I could've gone on writing till the day I died.

Larsen *holds out the rifle abruptly and thrusts it into his hands.* **Znorko** *is once more in the dominant position but doesn't comprehend the situation.*

Erik Larsen My death doesn't matter. But before you kill me, you have to tell me why.

Znorko *doesn't reply.*

Larsen *says to him, with the air of casting a spell on him:*

Erik Larsen Abel Znorko, I am Helen. For ten years we have loved each other through her, we have told each other everything through her person. You killed Helen by publishing that book. What on earth can have possessed you?

Abel Znorko (*suddenly feeble*) The answer's in there. (*He lowers the gun and indicates the letter in* **Larsen***'s pocket.*) In the last letter. The one you were to take to her.

Larsen *takes out the letter.*

Abel Znorko (*automatically*) No, it's not for you . . .

Larsen *smiles sadly.* **Znorko,** *also sadly, lays down the gun.* **Larsen** *opens the letter and reads it. At the same time* **Znorko,** *with the air of a sleepwalker, explains.*

Abel Znorko I was very afraid. Very afraid. I wanted to see Helen. She refused.

Erik Larsen That was the deal.

Abel Znorko That was the deal.

Larsen *finishes reading the letter and folds it up again. He looks at* **Znorko** *with a certain tenderness.*

Erik Larsen (*gently*) You should have just told me the truth. I would have come. Instead of forcing the issue by publishing.

Abel Znorko (*exasperated*) But I have nothing to say to you! I didn't force anything and I don't want to see you! (*Exhausted, he drops on to the sofa.*) When my doctor told me about the cancer I decided I wouldn't have any treatment. My one wish was to see Helen, but without letting her know that it would be for the last time. She refused to come; she reminded me of our deal. So I had to force the issue. And so, when my publisher came to visit, I took the plunge. I gave him the packet of letters and said: here's my new novel. He published at once. And I waited for Helen's reaction. I waited for her to be angry, to turn up . . . nothing happened.

Erik Larsen Where's the cancer?

Abel Znorko Lungs . . . same as her . . .

Larsen *makes a despairing gesture.*

Erik Larsen I envy your being so close to her . . . and even dying like her, perhaps.

Abel Znorko I don't think I will die. I thought I would.

But they've done some more tests. Everything is being reabsorbed.

Erik Larsen (*doubtfully*) Is that true?

Abel Znorko It is true. (*With a bitter laugh.*) I'm one of those corpses who have to be buried several times.

Erik Larsen Really?

Znorko *doesn't reply.* **Larsen** *comes up to him and tenderly puts his hand on his shoulder. The gesture appeases* **Znorko**.

Abel Znorko (*gently, without thinking*) Either way, it doesn't bother me much, dying . . . as long as I can still write. (*Pause.*) When all's said and done, I've always thought that life is a bit of a con-trick. We're dumped here without being consulted and flushed out again whether we want it or not. And as soon as we think we've touched something – it vanishes. The people we love turn out to be phantoms and all the others are simply enigmas who resolutely remain unsolved. (*With a painful laugh.*) I used to think that when I died, the veils would be lifted just for an instant – the beautiful, thick veils, like underskirts – and for that instant I should see unadorned truth with its naked thighs. I must be dead already.

Erik Larsen I'll stay with you.

Znorko *rises and considers* **Larsen** *severely.*

Abel Znorko No, it's better you go. Obviously I shan't be coming with you. I shall mourn Helen here.

Larsen *sees that he can't argue with the wounded man. He gathers his belongings, ready to leave. As he goes out, he searches for a look from* **Znorko**, *in vain.*

Znorko, *at sea, alone at last, staggers a little, then sits as if by instinct at the piano. He begins to play the* Enigma Variations.

After a few seconds, **Larsen** *reappears, moving softly in rhythm to the music. He goes up to* **Znorko** *and says gently.*

Erik Larsen You know, when she was buried, ten years ago, I thought that love had been buried with her. But then there was you, and her through you, and I realised that the world wasn't so empty after all.

Abel Znorko Well, it is for me.

Erik Larsen But what is shared love? Two dreams that coincide by chance, a happy misunderstanding, a misunderstanding perfectly understood by both parties . . . Can't we talk to each other through our dreams?

Abel Znorko (*no longer playing the game*) Sorry. My dreams aren't the same gender as you.

Erik Larsen What I've learned over these ten years is that love has no gender.

Abel Znorko Get out!

Erik Larsen (*docilely echoing*) Out. (*He goes to the door and stops.*) It may be the dead who keep us alive. But the living do too.

Abel Znorko Out!

Erik Larsen (*echoing docilely*) Out.

He looks at the falling night. He shivers. Suddenly, it is clear how terribly lonely he has been these past months.

(*As if to himself.*) I didn't love you at first, Abel Znorko; you are nothing but arrogance. Your work has flashes of genius, it's true, but God – the stuff in between. I only wrote to bring Helen back to life. But then, behind all your shortcomings, I discovered a tiny flicker of something, the little candle flame that fuelled you – your fear. (*Coming closer.*) And that's what you are – nothing but fear. Fear of the life you run away from, fear of the love you run away from, fear of the women you merely fuck. So you took refuge here in your books. That's how you became a Great Man, and that's why every reader finds himself in you: you are even more afraid than they are. Everything is exaggerated with you, anger and love, selfishness and tenderness, stupidity and intelligence; everything sticks out, is jagged, lacerating; one walks in the labyrinth, one wanders about, one gets lost, but at least it's alive. (*Pause, then timidly:*) I need you.

Abel Znorko Out.

In the distance can be heard the foghorn signal from the boat.

Erik Larsen (*defeated*) Out. (*He cannot steel himself to leave.*) What are you going to do?

Abel Znorko Grow old. Since I met you, I feel ready.

Erik Larsen Not you.

Abel Znorko I'll grow old in peace, without worries, without heirs. Lots of money and nothing to do. I shall become an utter idiot, Erik Larsen, but a happy one. I don't believe in anything any more. I have no higher hopes from this existence than good digestion and deep sleep. The void, Erik Larsen, the void, at last. Thanks to you. Thank you and goodbye.

Larsen *looks at the evening, which has now fallen. He shivers.*

Erik Larsen It's night . . . it's cold . . . (*Pause.*) Goodbye, Abel Znorko. (*He trembles, he seems all small.*)

The boat sounds its signal again in the fog. **Larsen** *goes out.*

Once alone, **Abel Znorko** *thinks, then abruptly goes out through the door at the back.*

Two shots ring out.

Silence.

Then the sound of running footsteps.

Larsen *reappears. This time, he is smiling broadly, as if this summons satisfies him.* **Abel Znorko** *re-enters, darkly, the gun in his hand. He looks at* **Larsen** *without saying anything.*

Erik Larsen (*good-humouredly*) You'll have to replace your gatepost. It's shot to bits.

Abel Znorko (*tentatively*) I just wanted to say . . .

Erik Larsen Yes?

Abel Znorko I'll . . . I'll write . . .

Between Worlds

translated by John Clifford

Hôtel des Deux Mondes was first performed at the Théâtre Marigny (Salle Popesco), Paris, on 23 September 1999. The cast was as follows:

Julien Portal	Jean-Ives Berteloot
Le Mage Radjapour	Rufus
Doctor S . . .	Victor Lazo
President Delbec	Bernard Dhéran
Laura	Laurence Côte
Marie	Catherine Arditi
Young Man	Fabrice Archirel
Young Woman	Benoîte Gazeres

Directed by Daniel Roussel
Designed by Philippe Miesch
Costumes by Sophie Perez
Lighting by Franck Thévenon
Sound by Didier Beaudet

Characters

Colin Gates
Magus
Doctor S . . .
Chairman
Laura
Jessie Smith
Young Man in White/Assistant/Angel
Young Woman in White/Assistant/Angel

Setting

A hotel lobby, present day.

Translator's note: I would like to thank the staff of the Collège International des Traducteurs Littéraires at the Espace Van Gogh in Arles for their invaluable help in preparing this translation.

I am certain of only one thing: uncertainty.
François Villon

The first thing: a strange noise, like the sound of a huge wind . . .

We have the sense that this wind has infinite power, that it is strong enough to blow away everything that stands in its way: ships, trees, houses. To carry everything away on the wings of its breath.

It roars louder and louder, it moans and it moans. The sound becomes unbearable and then suddenly disappears. As it dies away, we can hear the sound of a lift.

The lights come up.

We are in a hotel reception.

It has a kind of unostentatious comfort. No daylight enters. The lighting is subdued and artificial. There are the usual armchairs grouped around the usual low tables. For the moment there is no one at the reception desk. Its residents, when they arrive, are sent off in one of two directions: either down a corridor marked 'D', or down another marked 'A'.

The luminous sign above the lift door tells us that someone is about to arrive. The bell rings. The doors open.

Colin *enters. He looks dazed, as if in shock. He is still young, and he wears a light raincoat. He rests one arm against the wall; he rubs his eyes with the other hand; he recovers himself slowly and he walks on to the stage. He walks a bit uncertainly, as if he's just had an accident, which has left him a bit off balance.*

He looks around him for a moment, then goes up to the reception desk. A slim and elegant **Young Man**, *dressed in white, appears immediately and smiles sympathetically.*

Colin *leans on the counter.*

Colin Where am I?

The **Young Man** *says nothing: he simply hands him a room key.* **Colin** *grabs it.*

Colin Yes. Yes, you're right. I should have a rest.

The **Young Man** *makes a sign and a* **Young Woman** *appears. She, too, is dressed in white, and is as slim and as elegant as the man. She goes up to* **Colin** *and it is as if she has spoken to him.*

Colin Yes, yes, I do have some luggage and it's all in the car but . . . (*And he starts to look in his pockets for his car keys but does not seem able to find them. At that he seems to lose heart and says:*) Well, it doesn't matter . . . I'll sort it out later . . .

The **Young Woman** *takes his arm and starts to take him down the corridor marked 'D'.* **Colin** *suddenly stops and goes back to the desk.*

Colin But shouldn't you take a note of my name? Maybe . . . maybe someone will want to phone me . . .

So the **Young Man** *shows him his name in the hotel register.*

Colin Oh, I see . . . You've already got it down . . . fine . . . (*This seems to disconcert him.*) Yes, yes, of course . . . you're right. I should go and lie down.

The **Young Woman** *needs to keep hold of his arm. Together, they disappear into the corridor 'D'.*

Two people appear from the corridor 'A'.

The **Magus**, *wearing an opulent robe, looks around the reception area.*

Magus I'm telling you: there's someone new.

He is followed by the **Chairman** *of the Board, a cold man, a conventional man. A man in a business suit.*

Chairman Never heard a thing.

Magus As usual. That's because you're as deaf as a bucket.

Chairman (*annoyed*) What?

Magus Exactly. Deaf as a post. Deaf as a kitchen implement. Deaf as a whole set of aluminium saucepans! (*He turns to the* **Young Man** *at the reception desk.*) Raphael, someone's just come, haven't they?

The **Young man** *smiles.*

Magus (*understanding that to be assent*) I thought so.

Chairman (*surprised*) You call him Raphael? I call him Gabriel.

Magus And he replies?

Chairman Of course.

Magus So we must both be right.

Chairman We can't be. (*And he turns to the* **Young Man** *at the reception desk.*) That's your name, Gabriel, isn't it? Not Raphael. Gabriel.

. . . *But the* **Young Man** *has already disappeared.*

Magus (*sitting down*) How come you've always got to be right? Why can't you accept we might both be?

Chairman Because we can't be. It's obvious.

Magus Not to me it isn't.

Chairman You say one thing, I say another. One of us has to be right and one of us has to be wrong. But we can't both be right. Either I'm right and you're wrong. Or you're wrong and I'm right.

Magus So whatever's true for you cannot be true for me.

Chairman Absolutely not.

Magus So truth cannot be shared. Just as a man can't share his wife.

Chairman I'm not sharing my wife with anybody.

Magus I know you're not. I saw her photo yesterday.

Chairman (*annoyed*) What?

Magus I said I saw her photo yesterday!

The **Magus** *unfolds his newspaper and starts to read. This doesn't stop the* **Chairman** *talking to him.*

Chairman Have you seen Doctor S . . . today? (*The* **Magus** *is about to reply. The* **Chairman** *ignores him.*) I haven't. I filed a request for an appointment this morning and I still haven't had a reply. It's disgraceful. How is one supposed to do business with such people? I'm asking you.

(*The* **Magus** *is about to reply.*) No, I'm telling you. It's impossible. And unacceptable. Absolutely unacceptable. It should surely have been possible to build up all the necessary information to do with our case, and Doctor S . . . should have set it all in train. Do you think that doctor really knows what he is doing? (*The* **Magus** *is about to reply.*) Now I know perfectly well that common sense has nothing to do with the way they train doctors nowadays, that they're just stuffed with facts like Christmas turkeys and they're not taught the one thing that really matters: how to run a business. With courtesy and efficiency. Doctors nowadays don't know how to behave like human beings. They treat you like a statistic. Like a statistic that doesn't have the right to the most basic information. Don't you agree? (*The* **Magus** *is about to speak.*) You're right, it's the welfare state. It's a whole generation brought up on benefit, that knows nothing about enterprise. That can't be bothered to move its arse, that just relies on the nanny state to look after it. That's what the trouble is.

Magus I am so glad you appreciate my replies.

Chairman What?

Magus I said I am so glad you appreciate my replies!

Chairman I'm glad. It's always a pleasure to talk to you but please don't interrupt.

The **Magus** *sighs and goes back to his newspaper.*

Magus I hope I don't disturb you when I read. The thing is I sometimes have to turn the page.

Chairman What?

Jessie *enters.*

Jessie I've made my bed four times. I've cleaned the washbasin five times and I've lost count of all the times I've straightened up my curtains, and now I don't know what to do with myself. You haven't got any buttons that need sewing, have you? Any little jobs I can do? Do your hems need doing?

Chairman (*taking no notice*) Has the doctor spoken to you?

Jessie No. Even though I've asked.

Chairman It's unacceptable. They treat us like dirt. As if we were cleaners.

Magus (*outraged at his rudeness*) Oh, for heaven's sake!

Jessie (*delighted*) But he's right. After all, I'm a cleaner. I should know.

Chairman Do we have to share the same reception area?

Magus Shocking, isn't it. No business class.

Chairman Yes. Status matters. And I suppose you believe in equality. You amaze me. I'm surprised there's any of you left.

Magus Status is an utter irrelevance. What matters is that a person be themselves.

Chairman What pathetic drivel. Pathetic dangerous drivel!

Jessie (*to the* **Magus**) No, I think the man's right. You can't compare the Chairman of the Board to a cleaning lady. There is a difference.

Chairman You see. You see. She knows. My dear lady, please tell us, in your own words, exactly where you think the difference lies?

Jessie Well . . .

Chairman No, no, please go on. I insist. You can instruct our friend and (*Speaking loudly.*) tell Doctor S . . ., if he happens to be listening, what you think the difference is between a charlady and the chairman of the board.

Jessie You really want me to tell you? Well, it's mainly got to do with the office . . .

Chairman (*encouraging her*) Yes.

Jessie The chairman makes the office dirty and the

cleaning lady cleans it.

Magus (*amused*) Go on.

Jessie And then the way I see it is that a chairman treats everybody like dirt and a cleaning lady knows that as far as he's concerned that's really all she is. So she treats everyone different.

Magus What else?

Jessie Well, a chairman might have a whole lot of letters after his name, and a whole load of titles that tell everybody who he is, like 'Chairman of the Board of So and So and somebody else', and he'll maybe even be Lord Somebody or other. He's bound to have lots of names, while a cleaning lady usually just has one, like Jessie, only usually because people like him have very little memory for unimportant people's names she loses that too and just ends up being 'you'. If she's lucky.

Magus How right you are. And isn't it extraordinary that in spite of all the really important differences between you, Doctor S . . . still hasn't found the time to see you either.

This is when **Colin** *enters. He's looking a little better.*

Colin Morning.

The others get up to greet him.

I'm Colin. Colin Gates.

Magus This is the Chairman of the Board, and this is Mrs Smith.

Jessie Only people usually call me Jessie.

Magus And I am the Magus.

Colin I'm sorry, I don't want to seem stupid, but I'm a bit confused. I'm not sure what exactly I'm doing here. I don't remember booking a room in this hotel, but when I got here there was my name in the register. I mean, who's in charge here? And where are we, exactly?

Magus What exactly do you mean by 'exactly'?

Colin I mean what place is this? What road is it on?

Magus I have absolutely no idea.

Colin What do you mean? Have you just come here too?

Magus Not at all. I am the hotel's oldest inhabitant. I've been here exactly six months.

Colin And you don't know where it is? I'm sorry, I must be off my head this morning, or something, because I really don't understand what's going on.

Pause. **Colin** *looks at each guest in turn. They say nothing.*

He scratches his head.

Jessie *puts her hand on his shoulder.*

Jessie You must have had a car accident.

Colin No. Maybe . . . (*He tries hard to remember.*) I don't know. It's true I was on the motorway and it was dark. I'd had a drink or two, I think, but I was in total control, in total control of my car. It's a Ferrari, the C6, latest model. Know the one?

Magus I only know two kinds of car: the ones that say 'Taxi' on the front and the ones that don't.

Colin I was driving fast, but I knew what I was doing. I was on my way home.

Jessie Was someone waiting for you?

Colin No.

Jessie What a shame. It's important to have someone at home. Someone waiting for you. That way you don't have accidents.

Colin (*indignant*) But I haven't had an accident.

They look at him in kindness and in disbelief.

Colin (*protesting*) I haven't had an accident. I haven't. I haven't had an accident.

They say nothing. **Colin** *sits down again.*

I must have started to drop off and that's why I checked into this motel.

Magus A motel! That's really very droll. A motel!

Jessie *and the* **Magus** *can't stop themselves laughing. The* **Chairman**, *too, utters a forced laugh.*

At this moment, the **Young Man** *in white walks across the stage. He looks at them briefly with an affectionate smile.*

They stop laughing at once.

Jessie (*a little bit ashamed*) You're right, Emmanuel, it isn't nice to laugh.

Chairman (*surprised*) You call him Emmanuel?

The **Young Man** *has gone.*

Colin Could you help me?

Magus Believe me, the fact is the only way to find out where you are is to ask each one of us what they were doing just before they came here.

Jessie *nods. A little later, the* **Chairman** *nods too.*

Chairman It's possible it really might help you.

Colin It makes no sense.

Magus There really is no other way.

Jessie He's right. Ask me. (*No response.*) For heaven's sake, ask me! (**Colin** *makes a dumbfounded kind of gesture which she interprets positively.*) See, he's asked me. (*She sighs happily and starts to tell her story.*) Right, then. Now, it all begins with my mum and dad who called me Jessie. And it was more than just giving me a name, it was like they branded me with some kind of sign that told everybody I was just going to be a cleaner because that's what people always expected of me and that's what I've always done. They say some people get born with a silver spoon in the mouth, it's like I was born with a hoover in mine. And that's not what I wanted, that struck me as a lousy idea, personally, but there's nothing I could do about it, was there? Anyway. My dad worked on a farm. Good-looking man he was, hairy. Very hairy. The kind of man who shaves in the morning and by midday looks as if he hasn't shaved for a week, and all that hair can only mean one thing, I mean all those hairs growing and growing, that means there's a lot of sperm in there and all it wants to do is find an outlet. If you know what I mean. So my mum was always coming out with these babies, every spring there'd be a new baby, sometimes a boy and sometimes a girl, and sometimes a boy and sometimes a girl. And I was the first and then there were twelve came out after me. And the thing was that the thirteenth, and his name was Jimmy, he had a face like a squashed cabbage and he wasn't right in the head, and my dad said it had to be something to do with the stuff they were giving him to spray on the cauliflowers, and after that he discovered condoms. Course, the other way of looking at it would be to say that my mum's cunt was worn out after repeated use.

Chairman Do we really need to know all this?

Jessie I don't know. You're getting it anyway. See, I don't normally get the chance to talk and when I get started there's just no stopping me. Anyway, where was I? Cleaning, cleaning from first thing in the morning till last thing at night, eighteen years old and this guy touched me up in a nice kind of way at a dance, and before I knew what had happened he was fucking me in the bus shelter. And then we got a council flat for him, me and the kid. I chose him because he was hairy. He was hairy everywhere, even all his hands, and the thing was it wasn't a very good system, for choosing someone, I mean. I mean, OK, my dad was hairy too but my dad worked, whereas this little shit just did nothing at all. I mean, someone who does that little is normally dead. Anyway, that was how it was: I did the work and he did nothing at all. And I fed him and his daughters, and he just sat there and ate, and watched the telly and took no notice. Acted like I didn't exist. And that makes you feel bad, that does. Fucking's important, I think, even if like him you're not very good at it. It makes you feel human somehow.

Chairman Do we really need to –

Jessie Like I said, you're getting it.

Chairman But all he needs to know is the last few minutes.

Jessie Well, he'll get them in the end, but in the meantime he's getting this. I mean, there's not much happened in my life and nobody usually wants to know but when they do they get the lot. I can't pick and choose. Anyway, one day he got out of his chair to get some fags and he never came back, and that was something of a relief. Though it didn't do much for my self-esteem. Anyway, there I was, me and my three daughters, and the thing about them was all they wanted to do with their lives was fuck boys. I mean, they changed boys more often than they changed their knickers and I don't know where they got that from, their grandad, maybe, they were sort of hairy inside, if you see what I mean, and I had no end of trouble getting them to settle down and stop chasing after pricks, and eventually it got to be time for my retirement. Now I'd always promised myself that my very last day at work I'd tell my boss to fuck off and you know what, there I was just about to put my hoover away when I kind of felt heavy all over and started shivering, and before I knew what had happened there I was, flat out on the carpet. And it wasn't even my carpet. At least it was clean, I'd seen to that, and they were very nice to me in hospital and they said the trouble was I'd been working too hard all my life and my heart was exhausted, and what I needed to do was rest. And it was brilliant in hospital, it was really clean, it was one of those private places that was being used by the NHS and it was gleaming. It was the first place I'd ever been to in my own life that someone else kept clean and I really liked it. There was even a garden and every morning someone put a carnation by my bedside. I felt like I was in heaven and one day they said to me I could go for a walk in the garden and I was just thinking that I had the time, at last, to look about me and think about the world, and that there was some kind of new life just about to begin and it was like I could hear things breathing, and

I was just thinking 'Maybe this is what people mean when they talk about happiness' and then all of a sudden, wham!

Colin Wham?

Jessie Another heart attack.

Colin And then?

Jessie Here I am.

Colin So this isn't a hotel at all? It's a hospital?

Magus Don't jump to conclusions. The Chairman will set the record straight.

Chairman I will be brief. The last thing I remember before coming here happened the morning of the day before yesterday. I left my house at eight o'clock sharp, as I always do, and I had just stepped on to the pavement when I noticed a cyclist coming towards me. He shouted something at me about getting out of the way but I had every right to be on the pavement and he had no right to be there at all. 'So he's bound to stop,' I thought, but the next thing I knew I'd been knocked over and had hit my head against the corner of the wall. And here I am.

Magus Was he wearing lycra shorts?

Chairman Of course. Yellow ones.

Magus Another fashion victim.

Chairman He was a typical cyclist. Young. Without respect for the law. I was completely in the right.

Colin (*to the* **Magus**) What about you?

Magus Diabetic coma.

Colin So where are the doctors? Where are the nurses? Why aren't we in hospital beds?

Magus Because we are not in hospital.

Colin You mean we are not in intensive care?

Chairman No.

Magus Think about it.

Jessie What corridor are you in? Corridor 'D' or corridor 'A'?

Colin This one.

Magus Corridor 'D'? Then you haven't had an accident!

Colin Of course I haven't had an accident, that's what I've been telling you all along. (*Thoughtfully.*) What does it mean, 'D'? Why's there a corridor 'D' and a corridor 'A'?

Magus I'm sure Doctor S . . . will explain it all.

Colin One minute you tell me this place isn't a hospital and the next you tell me it's run by a doctor.

Jessie It's run by Doctor S . . .

Colin Then I want to see him now.

Chairman But listen, my friend, it's not so easy to see Doctor S . . .

Magus Sometimes the fact that you want to means that you can't.

Jessie Are you sure you didn't do it on purpose?

Colin Do what on purpose?

Jessie Crash into your tree.

Colin What are you talking about? What tree?

Magus Do you really mean to say that you still don't understand? After everything we've told you? Think about it. Coma . . . heart attack . . . road accident . . . Don't you see any connection?

Colin (*getting up and looking about*) Are you trying to tell me that . . .

They all nod.

Magus You see, the thing is that our last memories are all . . . last memories. It's all terribly terribly sad.

Colin (*hardly daring to put his thought into words*) So . . . this place . . . are you telling me we're . . . dead?

The others all burst out laughing.

Colin (*shouting*) Dead! I'm dead!

This makes them all laugh the more.

Colin (*shaking the* **Magus**) For Christ's sake, talk to me! I'm fucking dead and you just laugh at me!

Magus But you see, if you're dead, we must be too. And being dead is so funny.

And that makes them laugh all the more.

Colin I'm getting out of here. The place is full of loonies.

The **Chairman** *has a little laugh on his own.* **Colin** *makes a furious dash for the lift.*

Jessie Oh, I know he's going to break something.

Colin *frantically looks for the lift call button.*

Colin I want out of here!

Magus You can't call that lift.

Colin Then I'll try the fire escape.

Magus There isn't one.

Colin You're crazy. They should lock you up.

Magus (*cheerfully*) They already have.

The guests all start laughing again. **Colin** *starts to run down the corridor.*

Jessie It's like laughing at a funeral. And I always do. Can't help myself.

Colin, *beside himself with fury, dashes across the stage.*

Colin I'm getting out of here!

He runs down the other corridor.

Magus (*shrugging his shoulders*) Poor thing. He's got to try.

Jessie Of course he doesn't believe. It's normal. He

never saw himself go . . .

Magus The first night here I even tried to dig myself out.

Colin *returns, out of breath and covered in sweat. He goes to the reception desk.*

Colin I don't believe it. There's no exits and no way of opening the windows. Unless someone shows me the way out right now, I'm going to have to break the glass and throw myself out the window.

Magus (*without even looking at him*) On you go, then.

Jessie I told you he was going to break something.

Colin *disappears down the corridor 'D', goes into his room; and we hear him throwing furniture at the windows.*

Jessie I hate breaking things. It breaks my heart. Poor things, when they've done nothing to deserve it.

Magus But why does it matter?

Jessie 'Cause I'm a cleaner. Must be an occupational hazard. See, when you're a cleaner, you get so used to being alone in the house and having to take care of things that you end up talking to them. So when you clean the silver, it's like you're giving it a bath. And when you put wax polish on a table, it's like you were feeding it. So when I break something, I feel so bad about it, it's like hurting somebody, I have to say sorry, and when I throw the bits into the dustbin I feel ever so guilty.

Colin *comes back, exhausted and defeated.*

Colin I couldn't break the windows. I couldn't even break the furniture. It doesn't make any sense. Is this a prison or what? Tell me it isn't real!

Magus You never chose to come here and you can't choose to leave either.

Colin *looks as if he's about to faint. The* **Magus** *quickly goes up to him to support him.*

Magus Come and have a seat.

Colin (*pale*) It's not true . . . I'm not dead . . . I'm not dead . . .

Jessie I think he's beginning to understand.

They sit him down among them.

Colin (*feverishly*) But I'm alive, aren't I? Aren't I alive?

Magus Don't take it all so much to heart. You've already been in stranger places. Think of your dreams. You're alive then, you're in your body, you're swimming in the deep blue sea . . . But you're also in bed in your pyjamas.

Colin (*touching himself*) I'm alive . . .

Magus To really prove that you're alive, you'd have to kill yourself. Now supposing you succeeded: that would prove that you were once alive. But on the other hand, if you failed, that could mean one of two things: either that you're dead already, or that you're really immortal.

Colin I'm going mad.

Magus That too.

Chairman That's a third possibility.

They **Young Man** *and the* **Young Woman** *suddenly come on stage, as if preparing the way for someone important.*

Magus Doctor S . . . is coming.

Chairman (*standing up*) I've an appointment with him.

The **Young Man** *and* **Young Woman** *look intently at the* **Magus**, *at* **Jessie** *and the* **Chairman** *of the Board. They all seem to understand something.*

Jessie (*disappointed*) Oh well.

Magus (*ditto*) If you say so.

Chairman (*angry*) But I was here before him. (*Angrily turning to* **Colin**.) And who, may I ask, are you?

Colin (*in a toneless voice*) I edit a motoring magazine.

Chairman And hasn't it occurred to you that the chairman of three international companies is more important than some wretched little editor?

The **Young Man** *and* **Young Woman** *insist.*

The three guests get up. The **Magus**, *in a kind way, leans over to* **Colin** *and explains.*

Magus You're the one the doctor wants to see.

Colin But who told you?

Magus Raphael!

Chairman It was Gabriel!

Jessie Emmanuel!

They leave the stage.

The **Young Man** *and the* **Young Woman** *follow them off.*

Colin *waits.*

A woman enters. She is simply but elegantly dressed, and she carries files under her arm, like a doctor doing her rounds.

Doctor S . . . Colin Gates?

Colin Yes?

Doctor S . . . Good day. I am Doctor S . . .

Colin *looks surprised.* **Doctor S . . .** *smiles at him in a way that puts him at ease. With a gesture, she invites him to sit down.*

Doctor S . . . (*gently*) Are you afraid?

Colin A little.

Doctor S . . . Do you understand where you are?

Colin Tell me it isn't true!

Doctor S . . . You were driving at a hundred miles an hour. Your car left the road and hit a tree.

Colin (*incredulous*) I don't remember a thing.

Doctor S . . . Of course you don't. You were fast asleep.

(*Looking through her papers.*) Excuse me while I consult your file.

Colin (*to himself*) So that's what it was. A tree. I ended up smashed against a tree. Lucky I was on my own.

Doctor S . . . (*mechanically*) That's one point in your favour.

Colin, *as if waking up from a dream, begins to pay attention to* **Doctor S . . .**. *It is as if he starts to fancy her.*

Colin I never thought you'd be like this.

Doctor S . . . By which you mean?

Colin Attractive.

She smiles, and then looks down again at her file.

Doctor S . . . Aged forty. Born into a rich family. Good school record. No major surgical interventions. No serious illnesses.

Colin (*cynically*) At least I died in good condition.

Doctor S . . . Several attempts at a professional career. An innate instability of character drove you to change jobs every two years. Single.

Colin Are you going to turn me down?

Doctor S . . . I'm not here to judge. It's just a question of going through your record.

She crosses her legs.

Colin (*caught between amazement and desire*) I never imagined death would have good legs . . .

Doctor S . . . Are you trying to seduce me?

Colin What have I got to lose?

Doctor S . . . It's not a course of action I would recommend. Your file mentions an insatiable pursuit of women . . .

Colin The thing about women is they always try to run.

So I had to chase them.

Doctor S . . . And you would go after them. And then once you'd had them you ran away from them. You deserted them all.

Colin It's just you know it's not to going to work out. Usually it doesn't take long. And then I'd walk out of it. Is that really such a crime?

Doctor S . . . (*ironically*) You'd walk away fast enough.

Colin I never came across a woman capable of keeping me faithful.

Doctor S . . . As if that had nothing to do with you.

Colin (*irritated*) I gave a lot of pleasure and I caused a lot of pain. I worked hard and I played hard, and it all comes down to the same. Anyway, most of the women I met didn't want love. All they wanted was a love story. And they couldn't bear to be told the truth. (*Suddenly getting up in fury.*) And what are you on about anyway? Aren't you going to write all this down? Or are you really going to try to make me believe that it's true, all that old shit about paradise? About heaven and hell and the sheep and the goats and the Day of Judgement? I won't let you judge me. I'm dead! What else do you want?

Doctor S . . . You are completely and utterly mistaken. (*Calmly.*) For one thing, I am not God. I am simply Doctor S . . . The next thing you need to understand is that you are not dead.

Colin (*shaken*) What?

Doctor S . . . Of course not. You are not dead.

Colin (*exultant*) I knew it! I knew it! Thank Christ for that! (*He boxes the air.*) I'm alive! I'm alive!

All of a sudden, he looks like a young man of twenty.

Doctor S . . . (*watching him with a certain amusement*) That's not quite what I said.

Colin What?

Doctor S . . . I never said you were alive.

Colin Now look, I don't give a shit about what you're trying to tell me. I'm not even going to try to understand it. Since I'm on my feet, I take it I can go?

Doctor S . . . That's not for you to decide.

Colin Are you going to try to stop me?

Doctor S . . . (*gently*) That's not my decision either.

Colin Look, Doctor Arsehole, I don't think I quite understand how I've ended up in your so-called clinic, maybe I did fall asleep at the wheel, and maybe I did bang my head against a tree, and maybe that is why I don't remember being brought here. But right now I feel fine, absolutely fine, and I don't need to be seeing you. So if you don't mind, I'll just kiss your arse and be on my way. Goodbye. (*He frantically pushes the lift button.*) And tell this fucking lift to come when I tell it to.

Doctor S . . . Are you going to start this again? Doing the rounds? Which will it be first? Trying to find the stairs? Or maybe trying to break the windows?

Doctor S . . . *makes a sign and her two* **Assistants** *appear. She posts them at the entrance to each corridor. She gestures to* **Colin** *to calm down.*

Colin You're crazy. Is this supposed to be some kind of jail? Where am I?

Doctor S . . . You are in danger. In very grave danger. We should talk about it. Then perhaps you'll understand.

She makes another sign and the two **Assistants** *go to the back of the room. They slide back a panel in the wall. A screen appears, rather like some kind of strange control panel the audience cannot yet see.*

Doctor S . . . Less than an hour ago, your car was driven at approximately one hundred miles an hour into this tree. I'd rather not describe the state your car is in, because I know you were proud of it. Still less do I wish to describe to you the state your body is in.

Colin What are you trying to tell me?

Doctor S . . . *takes him by the hand and guides him towards the screen.*

Doctor S . . . The ambulance has just taken you to casualty. You're unconscious and you've lost a lot of blood. You have multiple fractures: to both knees, your ribs, your pelvis and your skull. They are assembling a medical team. They are taking you into theatre. They've hooked you up to a life-support machine. No one rates your chances. They just do what they can.

She shows him the control panel. There are lights that blink, and luminous indicators that go up and go down.

Everyone who stays here is living through a crucial time. On earth their bodies are full of tubes. They are fed by saline drips. They are monitored by electrodes. Their progress is assessed by a medical team. They are watched over by their families. You call it being in a coma. In other words, the state between life and death. In other words, here.

She leads him back to the armchairs. In a state of shock, he moves like a sleepwalker.

And this is where you wait. Here, in the space between worlds. Think of it as a kind of hotel. A place which sets you free of the agony endured down there by your poor body.

Colin (*on the point of believing her*) I don't believe you. Do you really want me to believe that my body's somewhere else?

Doctor S . . . Let's take your ankle. Remember, two days ago you sprained it. It was swollen and painful, and hard to walk on it. Does it hurt you now?

Colin *moves his foot without any difficulty.*

Doctor S . . . You see. Your body of flesh and blood and nerves, your wounded and vulnerable body, is in intensive care. You are here to wait.

Colin Wait for what?

Doctor S . . . Wait for your case to be decided. If your life is saved, then the lift will take you down to earth. If not, then the lift will take you up.

Colin *receives this information like a blow. Struck by it, he slowly looks around.*

Colin Up?

Doctor S . . . That's quite enough information for the time being.

Colin You mean death?

Doctor S . . . What you call death, yes.

Colin What else can you call it?

Doctor S . . . Perhaps the suppression of this form of life. (*Pause.*) My work consists in giving you the necessary information to help you through the transition.

Colin Then who employs you?

Doctor S . . . *sees a light flashing on and off above the entrance to corridor 'A'. She prepares to leave.*

Doctor S . . . I must be going.

Colin What does that mean, corridor 'A' and corridor 'D'?

Doctor S . . . You mean you haven't guessed? 'A' stands for accidental; 'D' for deliberate. Which is another way of saying for suicides.

Colin Then there must be some mistake! I shouldn't be in corridor 'D'. I didn't try to kill myself, I just had an accident!

Doctor S . . . Oh yes?

Colin I didn't deliberately crash into a tree!

Doctor S . . . Really? (*Fiercely.*) Mr Gates, at the time of your accident there was alcohol in your blood. Well over the acceptable limit. And not only that, Mr Gates, but your drinking habit dated back over two decades. Of course, you've tried other drugs: some gentler, some more violent, some more exotic. But alcohol has always been your drug of choice. It's the one that helps you best, helps you run away, Mr Gates, run away from yourself. Your life was falling apart, Mr Gates, your magazine was going down the tubes and apparently you didn't give a damn. You had alienated every single one of your colleagues. You yourself had completely lost your bearings and were behaving in a way that was more and more self-destructive and absurd.

So you need to understand, Mr Gates, that when one fine morning you are finally discovered blind drunk and smashed up against a tree that you have just driven into at a hundred miles an hour one can only assume it's a case of suicide. Prolonged suicide, Mr Gates. A suicide that has been prepared for and executed for years and years.

Colin *is open-mouthed at this.*

Colin A prolonged suicide? Me?

Doctor S . . . Yes. Using alcohol. The method used by cowards. (*Breaking off the meeting.*) Now, if you'll excuse me. I have other patients to see. (*She goes.*)

Colin *sits down, dumbfounded by what he has just heard.*

The **Magus** *pokes his head on to the stage. He now wears an oriental turban with a moonstone. He makes sure that* **Colin** *is alone, then comes up to him offering his business card.*

Magus The Magus. Clairvoyance to order. ESP on request. I can consult the stars, communicate with your dead relatives, turn tables, interpret tarot cards and the entrails of dead hens. The Magus. Master of Ancient Sciences. Master of the New Millennium. (*Pause.*) Actually, my real name is Jones. Fred Jones of the Mile End Road. I can't help thinking I'm the product of a cosmic mistake. Something took a wrong turning. Either my dad's sperms or my mum's ovaries. Or possibly both. Whatever. My cosmic knowledge is at your command.

Colin *emerges, irritated, from his state of dejection.*

Colin You taking the piss?

Magus Yes. As it happens. A little. But some people like that. Some people even pay me.

Colin Not here, they don't.

Magus Especially here. You would not believe the money I've made here over the last six months. I've made a fortune. The only trouble is I can't spend the money. And it's hard to take it with you. Still. It passes the time.

Colin *hits the walls.*

Colin It stinks!

Magus (*taking this on board*) Come off it, I've got to do something, I've spent the last six months in a coma.

Colin I wasn't talking about you. I was talking about this place. About having to wait!

Magus Wait here, wait there, what's the difference. The difference between a prison and a jail. Here or there there's only one way out, and we don't know where it's leading.

Colin *paces back and forth like a lion in a cage.*

Magus Down there, we all knew we were going to die. But we didn't want to know, that's all. There we all were like passengers in a railway station turning our backs on the trains. The next one won't be for us, we kept thinking, it'll be for him. Or him, or him. Anyone but us. But here we know. We know it's coming, sooner or later, and there's no getting round it. Actually, I rather like it. It makes me greedy. Greedy for life. Able to enjoy it. In this place I can take real pleasure in every moment. It's like a sweet I can unwrap, I can smell, I can slowly savour.

Colin How can you enjoy being here? How do you pass the time?

Magus That's just it, you see. You don't just pass the time. You spend it. Profitably. For one thing, you meet no end of different people. I mean, if you have the opportunity to spend a good few months of intensive care (**Colin** *is shocked at the thought of this.*) then you'll discover that people just keep coming and going. It's fascinating. And there's always time for a nice chat. I mean, look at us, here we are, we're not saying anything that really matters, nothing that's really clever or deep, we're chatting. Just chatting. And spinning the fine and subtle thread of human relationships. Nice, isn't it?

Colin What's the use? I mean, why bother having relationships with people you're never going to see again?

Magus (*somewhat annoyed*) If you insist on a lasting relationship, try talking to a stone. Though you may find it's not reciprocal. And certainly not if you pick on a stone that's as obstinate as you. (*He gets up to leave.*)

Colin (*with a wry smile*) Touché.

Magus (*sitting down again*) You see how life can be amusing. Or rather, you see all the fun you can have in a coma.

Colin *collapses into his chair.*

Colin I'm depressed, that's my trouble. I've always been depressed.

Magus Spoilt child, were we?

Colin What makes you say that?

Magus You don't look at all poor and you don't look at all ugly. You look like a child surrounded by expensive toys. Toys that give him absolutely no pleasure.

Colin Is that meant to be a put-down?

Magus Not at all. I like the idea of the rich being miserable.

Colin I didn't mean to make you feel sorry for me.

Magus (*gently*) It must be terrible to have no appetite. Not to know what it's like to be really hungry. To be full up from the minute you're born, to get kisses even before you've asked for them, it doesn't do much for your will-power. Maybe in the end it's us who are better off, us who never got what we wanted. Maybe what makes the world so good is that it's full of things that we haven't got. Maybe what gives life savour is the fact that most of it is out of reach . . .

Colin (*with an astonished smile*) You've seen right through me.

Magus But on the other hand, the one thing you haven't understood is that in the end it's the same for all of us. It's the same for you with your full belly and it's the same for me with my belly empty. Life is always outside our reach.

Colin I'm sorry?

Magus Because life does not belong to us. (*And he points at the up arrow on the lift.*)

Colin (*slowly*) You mean we don't know what it is we've got until it's gone.

Magus That's always been the problem with paradise. You don't know you're there until you've gone out the exit. And then it's too late to go back.

Jessie *rushes in.*

Jessie (*exasperated*) I just can't believe it. I've got a cabbage instead of a brain. I keep telling myself that this is my chance to think about real things. Important things. Philosophical things. And instead, all I can think about is a stain I can't clean off the wall. Is everyone as daft as I am?

Magus Hard to tell.

Jessie I know my head's not big enough for really big thoughts. And that makes me think I'd rather not be able to think at all. I've a sister like that. Thick as two short planks. In one ear and out the other. Just talks. Talks and talks and talks. Nothing bothers her. Never changes. Just yak yak yak. It's the way to be. Me, I'm only just clever enough to make myself miserable.

Colin *has started to pace about again.*

Colin We're all the same.

Jessie No. Not really clever people. People who've studied. People who know how to think.

Colin And what do they know?

Jessie I don't know. But whatever they know, they know. And when they don't know, they know they don't know. They're not like me. They don't dabble. If I could live my life all over again, that's what I'd be. A philosopher. I'd have a nameplate above my door: Jessie Smith, Doctor of Philosophy. (*She laughs.*)

Colin (*furious*) So what if you are a doctor of philosophy. You're still going to die.

Jessie True. But at least you'll know how to live. (*She goes up to the lift.*) I mean, what do you think there is up there?

Colin Nothing.

Jessie Ever been there?

Colin Course not.

Jessie Then how do you know?

Colin I know we're all going to die. Isn't that good enough to be going on with?

Jessie No, it's not. See, I've never been dead. I don't know what it's like. It's like a shop you can never get into, it's all hearsay. And it may be all wrong anyway, since no one's ever come back. (*To the* **Magus**.) How about you? You've done seances. What do the dead talk about?

Magus This and that.

Jessie For instance?

Magus (*bored*) That they hated their mother-in-law, that they were in love with their secretary, that they'd made a mess of their lives, that they wish they'd taken up knitting. Or learned to play the piano. In other words, crap.

Jessie Is that all?

Magus Unfortunately being dead doesn't make you more intelligent.

Jessie You'd have thought they might have learned something. (*Pause.*) But, I mean, didn't they pass on anything about how they spend their time?

Magus Not a thing.

Jessie Still. I mean, they were talking to you and that means they must exist. I mean, in one sense that means that they weren't really dead.

Magus Possibly.

Jessie What do you mean, possibly? I mean, were they talking to you or weren't they?

Colin (*vehemently*) All he did was make it up!

Jessie Exactly! He used his imagination! That's what the dead use to speak to us with. Our imagination!

Magus You're right. Sometimes I heard voices. Voices from the very back of my mind. But that happens to everybody. That's like the voices we hear in our dreams. That proves nothing.

Jessie All that proves is that you're not really a Magus at all.

Magus (*smiling*) Who knows?

Colin *decides to join in the conversation to stop himself pacing about.*

Colin Be serious. I mean, we all know, really, what's going to happen. I mean, listen, Jessie, tell me, can you remember anything of what happened before you were born?

Jessie No.

Colin See? It'll be the same after you're dead.

Jessie You mean there's nothing?

Colin I mean there's nothing. Fuck all. Absolute zero.

Jessie Wait a minute. I mean in between, in between my before and my afters, there's something. And that something's me! Me existing.

Colin Yes, something. Something's happened. Something inconsequential and useless and stupid that means nothing and should never have happened. A bad mistake.

Jessie (*suspiciously*) You talking about me? Or the world in general?

Colin I'm talking about you, I'm talking about me, I'm talking about him. I'm talking about everybody. It's like being in a football match with a lousy ref that always ends badly and nobody ever asked me if I wanted to join.

Jessie You're just talking like that because you think there's nothing up there.

Colin Obviously. And if I hadn't been so obsessed with the thought that everything's going to come to an end, that everything's going to end up in nothing, then maybe I'd have been better with people. Better with things in general. More attached to them. Able to care about them more. As it was, I'd just be starting on something, and even before I got really involved in it I'd be thinking, 'What's the use?' What's the use of investing time and energy in something that's just going to end up as a piece of shit? Dirt, dust, nothing. And whenever a woman said to me, 'I'm going to love you for ever,' I'd think, 'You liar.'

Jessie What about when you were fucking?

Magus Oh, for heaven's sake. Can't we have a bit of decorum?

Jessie You still want to know. Don't you?

Magus Yes, but still . . .

Jessie Answer the question the Magus won't ask because he's far too well brought-up. What were you thinking of when you –

Magus Shush.

Jessie When you were shush were you still thinking dirt, nothing, dust?

Colin (*laughing*) No, not at all. It was the one thing I was good at. It was the thing I was best at.

Jessie On the other hand, maybe you could't keep it up long enough to get depressed. Maybe you didn't have the time.

Magus Really.

Jessie Lucky for all concerned, really, that you kept forgetting. I mean, forgetting you were dust and dirt, et cetera.

Colin No. That was the trouble. I couldn't forget. I kept thinking about it. I mean, I'd even be walking down the road, looking at people passing. Walking along in their hats and their coats and the fancy shoes, and I'd see them as nothing but a heap of bones. With flesh on their backs that would disappear as easily as their clothes. It was like there was something inside me holding me back from living. From really being alive. And it was death. It was the idea of death. The fact that we're all going to die. And if somebody could have given me a certificate, a certificate that proved there really was life after death, then I'm sure I'd have been a completely different person.

Magus So really what stopped you enjoying life was the thought that it was all going to come to an end?

Colin (*hesitantly*) Suppose so, yes.

Jessie You poor soul. It must be really sad to have got it all so utterly and completely wrong. I mean, there was you, in the middle of life, which you knew about, and thinking it was all shit because of death, which you knew nothing about at all.

Magus It's the dark. It's the dark turning light into darkness.

Jessie So all you've done is taken yourself absolutely nowhere. At last I've found someone as stupid as I am.

Still. Still maybe there really is a garden up there, just like they used to teach us when we were small. And maybe it does have flowers and trees. I'd like it to be a garden. 'Cause then at least I wouldn't have to do any hoovering.

Colin Come off it. There's nothing. Nothing at all! And we all know that. We all know that death's the end of it. The end of everything.

Jessie Oh yeah? So how come, Mister Know-It-All, how come you've ended up here? You never thought that would happen, did you? Where does this place fit into your scheme of things?

For the moment, **Colin** *is stuck for a reply.*

The **Chairman** *enters, grumbling.*

Chairman And now I suppose the doctor's seen everyone here but me.

Magus Listen: no one has spoken to the doctor, but absolutely no one at all. Except for him. It's equality, you see. Equality in action. Everyone is being treated exactly the same. So you have absolutely no reason to believe that you are the victim of some kind of conspiracy or plot.

The **Chairman** *sits down grumpily.*

Chairman I had to leave my room. I just couldn't stand listening to them.

Colin Listening to who?

Chairman My wife. My wife and sons.

Colin (*amazed*) What do you mean? Are they here too?

Magus It's just that when us residents go back to our rooms, we can hear everything that's being said down below round our hospital bed. You just put your hands over your ears and you can hear them.

Jessie You're lucky. Having your family all around you.

Chairman Lucky? You wouldn't say that if you knew the kind of rubbish I have to put up with!

Jessie What do they talk about?

Chairman Money of course. What else would they talk about? They want to sell everything.

Jessie You leaving them something?

Chairman (*offended*) Of course I am! Who do you take me for?

Jessie (*laughing*) See, when I'm in my grave? I'll be taking nothing down with me.

Magus (*laughing*) Me neither!

Jessie I'll have spent it all on food!

Magus Me on drink! (*He laughs.*) I've never been able to bear having money in my pocket. It weighs me down. I just have to spend it. (*Looking at the* **Chairman**.) I just don't have the mindset to become rich. Or talons instead of nails.

Chairman (*aggressively*) You certainly should be making money. You're dishonest enough.

Magus You should know.

Chairman (*irritated*) What?

Magus I've read all about you in the papers. You're famous. For tax evasion.

Chairman It's a lie.

Magus Tax evasion, insider dealing and some very dodgy accounts.

Chairman Journalistic tittle-tattle. Without any foundation whatsoever. And it's a bit rich, coming from you. Fairground fortune teller.

Magus You can call me dishonest if you like. Of course I'm dishonest. It goes with the job. Supposing I was to tell the truth and say, 'No, madam, I cannot see the future in your cards. But given the fact that you are ugly, bad-tempered and fat, and speak badly of every single person you meet, you are most unlikely ever to find true love.' That might be honest, but would it be kind? It's true people pay me, but what are they paying for? The fact that I make them feel better. The fact that when they leave my room they feel a certain pleasure in being alive, they can look forward to their evening and feel hopeful about the next day. You see, in my way, I am always honest. In my way. Always. Except on the odd occasion when I see someone and feel some kind of presentiment, a sense that they are about to die. It happens sometimes. But that I keep very much to myself. I am very ethical, always. Whereas you, Mr Chairman, you use your cloak of respectability to cover all kinds of dirty deals and enrich yourself at everyone else's expense.

Chairman I'm going back to my room. My sons may be spineless and about to waste all my well-earned property but I'd still rather listen to them than the likes of you. Good day. (*He exits.*)

Colin What is he chairman of, exactly?

Magus He is the Chairman of the Board. Has been since the day he was born. He came out of his mother's womb wearing a pinstripe suit and a silk tie, and carrying a briefcase. And the first words he said to his mother were 'Take a letter'. And he's never looked back.

Doctor S . . . *comes back on, followed by the two* **Assistants**.

Jessie Doctor, please. What's happening?

Doctor S . . . I will tell you the minute I know. For the time being your condition is . . . unchanged. (*Crossing the stage to go down the other corridor.*) Excuse me.

Jessie Unchanged . . . (*She drops, discouraged, into a chair.*) That means I'm still not moving, I'm still tied to my bed, I'm still full of drips and tubes, and my little monitor's going bip . . . bip . . . bip . . . And I'm not going anywhere at all.

The **Magus** *gives her a sympathetic pat on the shoulder.*

Magus You'll be all right. Don't give up hope. After all, look at me: I've been here six months.

Jessie (*with utter sincerity*) I just couldn't bear six months of this. They'd have to disconnect me. (*Trying to justify her bluntness to the* **Magus**.) It's not good for me to hang around waiting. I can't think, I haven't the patience for it, I need to be doing something for my brain to work. It's just how I am. If I've nothing to do, I start getting frightened.

Colin *comes up to her and sits next to her, full of sympathy.*

Colin What frightens you?

Jessie I don't know. I feel I'm in the wrong, somehow, and I keep asking myself, 'What right have you got to sit around on your arse all day doing nothing?'

Colin You're not good to yourself.

Jessie Do you know anyone who is?

Colin *and the* **Magus** *genuinely ask themselves before replying.*

Colin No.

Magus No.

Colin (*after a pause*) I bet you were good to your children.

Jessie Yes, well, you got to be really, it's only natural. You got to love them, you can't stop yourself. And I'd have loved a lot of other people if anyone had ever shown any interest. (*Pause.*) It's my own fault, though: I'm not very good with grown-ups. I'm always better with kids. It's just the way they look at you, and they got a smile on their face and this special look in their eyes, and I always know just what to say to them, and what to do with them to make them laugh. But with grown-ups . . . I never know what to say, I feel awkward and I always have this feeling that they're going to realise . . .

Colin Realise what?

Jessie That I'm not very interesting.

She is about to cry. **Colin** *and the* **Magus** *feel great sympathy for her.*

Colin Who told you that you're not interesting?

Jessie Dunno. No one did. Not that I can remember. But then nobody ever told me otherwise. Maybe that's what it is, maybe that's what I've never had. Just people being nice to me. It's not that I've ever fished for compliments.

The **Chairman** *comes back on, holding his portable phone.*

Chairman No, no, no. They want to sell everything and they mustn't. I've absolutely got to put a stop to it.

Colin Why?

Chairman Because this is not the time to sell! It's a bear market. Stocks are down. This is not when you sell. They're going to make me lose money. I simply have to talk to my bank, talk to my broker, but my phone won't work. (*He rings the bell at the reception desk.*) I demand to talk to Doctor S . . ., I must absolutely insist.

Colin (*to* **Jessie**) Are these the kind of profound thoughts you wish you were able to have?

Jessie *bursts out laughing.*

Chairman (*still ringing the bell*) Just because those pretentious little cretins have my blood in their veins doesn't mean they have got the right to lose my money! And anyway, how do I know they're really mine? Little bastards!

Magus Are they stupid?

Chairman Yes!

Magus Very stupid?

Chairman Morons!

Magus They must be yours, then.

Chairman (*annoyed*) What?

The **Chairman** *is so angry he can think of no reply. He keeps hitting the bell.*

Doctor S . . . *appears, followed by her two* **Assistants**. *She crosses the stage without really paying any attention to the residents.*

Chairman Doctor. (*She walks right past him.*) Doctor, I've just called you.

Doctor S . . . (*without looking back at him*) People don't call me.

Chairman But I demand –

Doctor S . . . (*in a tone that allows no room for reply*) There is nothing you can demand. When your time comes, then I will talk to you. But not before.

The **Chairman** *is reduced to silence.* **Doctor S . . .** *has left.*

The other residents quite enjoy the fact that the **Chairman** *has been put in his place.*

The **Magus** *talks to* **Colin** *in a low voice, creating a kind of complicity between the two of them.*

Magus You should talk to the Chairman. He's someone who can explain everything. His arguments are totally sound. Which is another way of saying he's a total cretin.

Colin (*to the* **Chairman**) Do come and join us. (*The* **Chairman**, *to keep face, goes and sits with them.*) Perhaps you'll be able to help us. We're trying to decide what happens after death.

It is obvious that **Colin** *and the* **Magus** *take a malicious pleasure out of making fun of the* **Chairman**.

Chairman You mean you never had a proper religious education? Did no one teach you?

Colin Not a thing.

Chairman Typical. No traditional values, no proper religious education. No standards. Now, as I was saying, and as any child could tell you, what happens is that you go up to heaven and are judged there according to your merits. Ask my grandchildren.

Colin And you really think that's true?

Chairman It's good enough to be going on with.

Colin And it doesn't worry you at all?

Chairman Why should it?

Colin You have an absolutely clear conscience.

Chairman Of course.

Magus And all that creative accounting, don't you think that on Judgement Day . . . ?

Chairman Nothing's ever been proved.

Magus I know, but just the same, do you really think that up there they will really respect the confidentiality of Swiss banks? And they won't mind forty years' worth of insider trading?

Chairman Peccadilloes.

Colin You've forgiven yourself anyway.

Magus Apparently without difficulty.

Chairman God is the real Chairman of the Board. He will understand.

Magus That's the Church. Its great strength is that you can be a practising member and in all sincerity still be immoral as you like. It's all so terribly convenient.

An alarm rings loudly. This frightens everyone, except for **Colin**.

Colin What's going on?

Doctor S . . . *hurries on and starts to study the indicator board at the back of the stage. A red indicator light is flashing.*

Magus One of us is about to leave.

Colin In which direction? Up or down?

Magus No one knows till the very last moment. When they're actually in the lift.

Doctor S . . . *turns to the residents.*

Doctor S . . . Please return to your rooms.

Everyone sighs with relief. The alarm keeps ringing, louder. It is impossible to ignore; it is painful to the ears. At the last minute, just at the entrance to corridor 'A', **Doctor S . . .** *calls* **Jessie** *back.*

Doctor S . . . Mrs Smith, would you mind staying?

The others look at each other in surprise.

The two **Assistants** *enter. They make it clear that the other residents should not stay a second longer.*

Doctor S . . . *goes up to* **Jessie** *who is afraid but who manages a smile.*

Jessie Is it my turn?

Doctor S . . . Yes.

Jessie I hope it's good news.

Doctor S . . . I am not allowed to tell you.

Jessie (*frightened*) No news is good news, I suppose.

Doctor S . . . Let me take you to the lift.

Doctor S . . . *takes her by the arm, helping her enter the lift.*

Jessie Yes, you need to help me, I've got a weak heart. (*Pause.*) Funny, isn't it, to have such a weak heart? It's the one thing I've never really used.

Doctor S . . . Don't be afraid.

Jessie It's not so much tired. More rusty.

Doctor S . . . Goodbye, Mrs Smith.

Jessie Goodbye, Doctor. All the best.

The doors close.

The residents look in to see what will happen to **Jessie**.

After a second or two, the indicator indicates up.

The alarm has stopped.

A moment's distress.

The **Magus**, *the* **Chairman** *and* **Colin** *all go back to their seats, still looking at the lift doors.* **Colin** *is too shocked to speak.*

Magus Poor soul.

Chairman (*worried*) You've been here a long time,

haven't you. Can you tell me, when the first one of the day goes up, does that mean that they all will?

Magus No.

Chairman That's all right, then.

Magus Is that all that matters as far as you're concerned?

Chairman (*thinking about it*) No. I mean, it could be that if the first one goes up, then the next one will go down.

Magus You remind me of my auntie Mabel. She had a passion for reading the obituaries. And every day she found someone of her own age on the list she'd be delighted. 'That's another one gone!' she'd say cheerfully. As if each one of her generation that died left her feeling more alive.

Chairman (*good-humouredly unaware*) You know, it's a funny thing, but I feel exactly the same way myself.

Magus All you think about is yourself.

Chairman (*shrugging his shoulders*) Of course. Who else is worth bothering with?

Magus (*to* **Colin**, *pointing at the* **Chairman**) My dear friend, at last I've found someone who loves himself.

Colin, *in his distress, is feverishly trying to find a way out.*

Colin I can't bear it here.

Doctor S . . . *is watching a new light flashing on the indicator board. She turns to her* **Assistants**.

Doctor S . . . There's someone coming.

Magus Ah, a new arrival. What luck.

Doctor S . . . (*to her* **Assistants**) You stay here while I look for their file.

She goes out.

Colin *is taken aback by this new diversion, stops pacing about and watches the lift.*

The **Magus** *and the* **Chairman** *take their places, as if at the theatre.*

They wait.

The appalling sound of cyclonic wind, the wind we heard when **Colin** *arrived, begins again. It gets louder. It gets deeper. When it is so loud as to be unbearable, the sound suddenly lessens. A little bell goes ding. The lift doors open.*

There's a gorgeous young woman in the lift. She smiles, not at all put out. Her appearance almost has a quality of the supernatural about it, like Botticelli's Venus *coming up out of the sea.*

Colin *is fascinated by her.*

She gracefully gets out of the lift. She smiles at the staff and the residents.

Laura Hello.

The **Magus** *gets up to welcome her.*

Magus Hello. Don't be afraid.

Laura (*bursting into laughter*) What have I got to be afraid of?

Magus Let me introduce you. This is Colin . . .

Laura *looks at him with a certain interest.* **Colin** *looks away abruptly, as if he deliberately wanted to break the spell.*

Magus And this is the Chairman . . . the Chairman of something or other.

Chairman The chairman of three boards and a clearing bank!

Magus (*pretending to be deaf*) Pardon? Did you say a plank?

Chairman A clearing bank!

Magus And I am the Magus.

Laura I am so happy to be here.

The others look astonished.

Chairman You poor, deluded soul, where on earth do you think you are?

Laura (*laughing*) I know where I am because I can walk. I can walk without crutches, without spasms and without pain. And I'm free of catheters, drip tubes, monitors, urine bags . . . (*She does a little dance step.*) I feel like dancing!

Magus (*to the other two*) Poor soul, she must think she's dead.

Doctor S . . . *comes in and smiles at her.*

Doctor S . . . Hello, Laura.

Laura Hello, Doctor S . . .

The residents are amazed. **Colin** *takes a step towards her.*

Colin Do you two know each other?

Doctor S . . . Laura has been a guest here once before.

Laura Almost twice. The first time, just at the moment when I lost consciousness, I left my body behind and was on the revolving staircase. I was light, I was so light, I was like a feather being drawn upwards, upwards to a light I could barely see; but just before I got to the beautiful balustrade of light, that was when I had to go back down again.

Doctor S . . . You just suffered a profound loss of consciousness.

Laura The second time, I was here for three days. And this time . . .

Doctor S . . . We'll see.

Colin *cannot resist giving way to his curiosity.*

Colin Are you seriously ill?

Laura (*without a trace of self-pity*) Good health has never been something I've been good at.

They look at each other. Again, **Colin** *turns away.*

Doctor S . . . Laura, could we speak in your room?

Laura No.

Doctor S . . . I have to tell you something very confidential.

Laura There's nothing very confidential about the state of my health. Ever since I was a child, people have been talking about it. They hold case conferences around my wheelchair, or round my bed, and then they write articles about me in the medical journals. They all seem to find my case terribly interesting. Which must be why I find it so terribly dull. Which is why I never ever want to talk about it.

Doctor S . . . (*insisting*) Laura, please, let's go to your room.

Laura (*gently but firmly*) No. What have you got to tell me? That my heart has almost stopped beating? That it could stop at any moment? That I will die unless I have a transplant? I know that. That my life depends on a stroke of luck, or a random piece of goodwill? That someone has to die very suddenly, very quickly and very tidily so I can steal their heart? I know that too.

Doctor S . . . (*smiling*) You haven't changed.

Laura Why should I get all tragic when I'm talking about my health? That would be unbearable. What has got to be, has got to be.

Doctor S . . . My dear Laura. I'll see you soon.

Chairman (*getting up*) Doctor, is there any possibility of . . .

Doctor S . . . No.

She goes out, followed by her **Assistants**.

Magus Equal treatment for all, Mr Chairman. Why, it's almost socialism.

Chairman I have never been so insulted in my life!

Laura (*turning to* **Colin**) What do you like to do in life?

Colin (*taken aback*) Nothing.

Laura That's not a very helpful reply.

Colin (*cutting himself off*) I'm not a very helpful person.

And he goes off to be by himself in a corner.

She turns to the **Magus** *and the* **Chairman**.

Laura What were you doing before I came in?

Magus Bit of backbiting, bit of gossip, being rude about each other. The usual.

Laura Why not go on?

Magus We don't know you well enough to be rude about you yet.

Laura Maybe I could give you a few ideas.

Magus Go on.

Laura I might shock you.

Magus So much the better.

Laura All right, then: what I would really like would be for someone to flirt with me.

Chairman Don't be ridiculous!

Laura Just a little. Just for a laugh. Would you mind? You see, the thing is that because I'm so ill no one's ever really tried with me. And since we're here and nothing's real, and nothing lasts . . . I thought maybe someone could at least pretend . . .

Colin Pretend to what?

Laura Look, I'll pretend to be normal – see I can move, I can turn round, I can even dance – and you (*To the* **Magus**.) or you (*To the* **Chairman**.) or you (*To* **Colin**.) can pretend to flirt with me. Oh please say yes.

Chairman No.

Laura Just for a laugh.

Magus If you insist. I will attempt to flirt.

Laura Thank you. (*She sits down, delighted.*)

The **Magus** *goes up to* **Colin** *and says to him, very quickly, in a low voice.*

Magus You do it. I get a sense she would much rather it came from you.

Colin I don't want to.

Magus You don't want to?

Colin I can do it with my eyes closed. On automatic pilot. I've done it so many times already it makes me sick to think of doing it again.

Magus It will make her happy.

Colin What's the point?

Magus You mean you can do it to please yourself but when it comes to trying to please someone else you just can't be bothered? Very impressive.

Colin *withdraws into himself without bothering to reply.*

The **Magus** *comes up to* **Laura** *and sits down next to her.*

Magus Very well then, my dear, how do I begin? Do I start with the moon, the stars, the flowers, the birds and the bees, or do I go straight to the nub, so to speak, and start talking of you?

Laura Just start with me.

Magus As you wish.

He clears his throat, looks for something to say, but fails to find a single thing. Embarrassed, he clears his throat again. It is obvious he would love to be able to make a lyrical and eloquent speech, but inspiration evades him. He keeps crossing and recrossing his legs.

The **Chairman** *watches him in quiet amusement;* **Colin** *shrugs his shoulders.*

The **Magus** *tries again for the third time, but once again fails to find inspiration.*

Laura (*conclusively*) You are such a good actor!

Magus (*surprised*) Am I?

Laura You are so good at pretending to be embarrassed.

The **Magus** *shoots a triumphant glance at* **Colin** *and the* **Chairman**. *He has another go at mumbling a compliment but ends up with nothing to say.*

Laura *warmly congratulates him.*

Laura You're so good at it.

Magus (*embarrassed*) I am not pretending.

Laura (*appreciatively*) Yes, it's fantastic.

Magus (*in a low voice, insistently*) I am not pretending!

Laura Yes, I know. I love it. I really do. You see, this is the first time it's happened.

The **Magus** *shoots another look of triumph at the others, who shrug their shoulders.*

Laura Do it again.

The best the **Magus** *can come up with is a terrible cliché.*

Magus I think you're really very pretty.

Laura And I think you're very pretty too.

The **Chairman** *and* **Colin** *burst out laughing in a kind of malicious triumph.*

The **Magus** *furiously turns on them.*

Magus Have you really got no other way of spending your precious time?

Laura *calms him by taking him gently by the hand.*

Laura You're very good at that too.

Magus At what?

Laura At pretending to be stupid. People tell me you're always stupid when you fall in love.

Again, the **Magus** *looks triumphantly at the other two.*

Doctor S . . . *comes in.*

Doctor S . . . Laura, everyone, I would like you all to leave me alone with –

Laura It is absolutely out of the question. The Magus has just made me a proposal of marriage. Haven't you?

Doctor S . . . Laura, I am not joking.

Laura Nor am I. (*Suddenly sad.*) I only wish it were true.

Doctor S . . . I need to talk to Colin.

Colin *is afraid. The others go away, out of respect.*

Laura *obediently heads for corridor 'A'. As she passes* **Colin**, *she cannot stop herself talking to him.*

Laura It is probably just as well you wouldn't play that game with me. Back on earth, I would probably want to fall in love with you.

And then, without giving him the time to react, she goes out to join the **Magus**.

Doctor S . . . Colin, your surgeons are about to operate. The medical team have discovered several internal haemorrhages.

Colin Will I pull through?

Doctor S . . . They are doing all they can. (*Pause.*) But this is a dangerous crisis.

Colin So why are you telling me?

Doctor S . . . So that you know. (*She starts to leave.*)

Colin Thank you very much. Is that really all you have to say.

Doctor S . . . Isn't it enough? (*She leaves.*)

Colin *is left in a state of anguished despair.*

Laura *appears at the entrance to the corridor and looks at him, guessing what he is thinking. She talks to him quite simply, without a* *trace of affectation or flirting.*

Laura Don't be afraid.

Colin I'm trying.

Laura I know.

Colin I'm sorry. I keep thinking I'm the only one.

Laura Suppose you had to travel locked up in a trunk, how would you like the trunk to be? Would you like it lined with sharp nails or lined with silk?

Colin With silk.

Laura There you are, then. Try not to be frightened. Since you don't know where you're going or what's going to happen to you, choose the silk lining. Try to have a bit of trust.

Colin Have you any idea what there is up there?

Laura I just hope.

Colin How can anyone be such a hopeless optimist?

Laura I don't have any choice. I can't make my muscles work and all my energy's got to go somewhere. So it goes into loving. Into loving life, though it doesn't seem to love me. I love death too.

Colin *finds it hard to admit that he finds her attractive.*

Colin Men must find you very attractive.

Laura No. I scare them to death. It's impossible to imagine anyone ever getting seriously attracted to me. Everyone knows I don't have long to live, everyone knows I'll never be able to have any kids. I'm a kind of waxwork. A ghost. Someone with no future. See, down there, people try to live as if they were never to die. And no one has time to love any more. Instead, they invest in relationships. And I'm a very bad investment.

Colin I don't think so.

Laura There was one young man who decided he

wanted to be my lover. He used to phone me, come and see me, send me flowers. He said I was the most important person in his life. I almost believed him. Then a friend of mine told me all about him. How he had a twin sister who died suddenly some years before and he'd never really got over it. I was just a pretext, a substitute for the sister he'd lost and wanted to get back. (*Pause.*) So I refused to let him see me. (*Pause.*) He was devastated.

Colin And then?

Laura Then he found someone normal and married her. And now they're expecting a baby and are about to live happily ever after. I was just part of the grieving process. (*Pause.*) I hate it when people pity me. I hate it. It makes me feel dirty. I don't want pity! (*Pause.*) Perhaps I'm too demanding. Too proud.

The bell starts to ring. The display starts blinking.

Colin *and* **Laura** *start with surprise.*

Doctor S . . . *and her two* **Assistants** *run on. She figures out what is happening and turns to* **Colin**.

Doctor S . . . Colin, your time has come.

Colin *is panic-stricken. Terror roots him to the spot.*

Colin Me?

Doctor S . . . Yes. You. Please come this way.

Colin *does not move. The* **Assistants** *go either side of him and start to lead him towards the lift.* **Doctor S . . .** *puts her hand on his shoulder to try to calm him. But* **Colin** *cannot stand the sound of this ringing or the fact of having to wait. He starts to tremble.*

Colin (*to himself*) I'm going to die. I know it. I'm going to die.

He detaches himself from **Doctor S . . .** *and turns to* **Laura** *as if looking for a way out.*

Colin I'm afraid.

Laura There's no need. Believe me, I know. There's no

need to be afraid.

Colin I'm afraid. Speak to me.

Laura What about?

Colin (*with a kind of feverish haste*) About you. Talk to me about you! Now, quick, while I still have some time. Where do you live?

Laura In a big house beside the sea. A house with windows as big as the sky.

Colin And is there a beach?

Laura A long beach. White sands, blue sea. I love it when they wheel me along the edge of the beach.

Colin What else?

Laura I like to dream. I like music. Music, and the silence all around it.

Colin What else?

Laura I like reading. Reading and reading, about all the lives that I'll never live.

Colin What else?

Laura I'd like . . . I'd like to know what it is to really be in love.

Colin Me too. (*He looks at her a moment and suddenly says:*) You are so gorgeous.

Laura Why tell me that?

The bell keeps ringing but the lift does not come. **Colin** *makes the most of the time he has left.*

Colin Because I thought it the moment I first saw you and I didn't dare find a way of telling you. (*Feverishly.*) From the minute the lift doors opened I thought I'd never seen anyone so amazing. You looked like . . . a pearl from the deep blue sea and I thought, I'm an ugly bastard but who cares, she can be gorgeous for both of us.

Laura Stop it.

Colin Then Doctor S . . . called you Laura, and said something really trite like 'hello' and even that sounded poetic, and I thought, my name's really ridiculous but it doesn't matter because she is Laura and that name's lovely enough for two.

Laura Don't be silly.

Colin Then I saw you standing up to Doctor S . . . and it was like watching a ship in a storm facing up to the worst the world can throw at her, and I thought, I'm just a coward but it doesn't matter because she can be brave for the two of us.

Laura Stop it.

Colin And as soon as I saw how strong you were I also understood how vulnerable you are too, and how your strength comes from that somehow, too, and yet how all of a sudden that strength could suddenly disappear and that maybe you could do with someone to support you. And if I had my life all over again and this time didn't screw it up, I'd gladly hold out both hands to you to help you.

And that's what I couldn't tell you. Right now there are other things I haven't told you and I want to: about how I want to be with you in that great big house beside the sea, how I want to be with you and hear that music and that silence too, and how I so want you to be able to read a little less so you can live a little more.

Laura Don't.

Colin Because all of a sudden right here in front of you I feel this incredible energy, this energy that fills my lungs with air, that fills my body with strength, that makes me want to live and run and feel as if I could move the whole earth, as if I could hold you in my arms and really could give you back your health and we could both live life to the full and not give a damn about death . . . and it's so strange but I'm not afraid any more.

The alarm bell stops ringing. There's a kind of brutal silence.

Colin *and* **Laura** *are shocked and stunned.*

Then **Doctor S . . .** *calmly turns to* **Colin**.

Doctor S . . . It was a false alarm. It's not your time. It happens sometimes. Not often. They are still operating. There must have been a crisis of some kind.

Colin *and* **Laura** *are completely overwhelmed.*

Doctor S . . . I must go.

Colin *and* **Laura** *stay still a moment, as if life has pinned them to the wall.*

Doctor S . . . *feels she should say something but is not quite sure what.*

Doctor S . . . A technical fault. I am so sorry. (*She leaves, thinking she has said what needed to be said.*)

Colin *and* **Laura** *look at each other.*

Colin So sorry! She is so sorry! (*He starts laughing wildly.*)

Laura *is concerned: he seems to have gone a little crazy.*

Laura Colin!

Colin (*hysterically*) So sorry! So terribly sorry! A technical fault!

He is furious. He overturns the armchairs, desperately needing to express the violent rage inside him. He wrecks as much as he can. Then he drops down, his shoulders shaken by sobs.

It's too late. I've said it. It's too late.

Laura (*gently*) Said what?

Colin Said I love you.

Laura (*panic-stricken*) No, you never said that.

Colin Yes I did.

Laura No, you just talked about simple things, about living in a big house beside the sea, listening to music, but not –

Colin Yes. I did. You know, I've said those words so often, like some exercise in a sexual workout, but this time, for the first time, I really meant them, I could feel them coming out of my mouth. They burn.

Laura (*shivering, struggling with her feelings*) You never said that.

Colin I did. I did. And I'll say it again.

They look at each other. He gets up, goes to her and kisses her gently. She shivers. She breaks off to ask:

Laura You don't feel pity for me, do you?

Colin No. Not in the slightest.

They kiss again. She is completely passionate.

Laura (*with her eyes suddenly full of tears*) It's so wrong. It's so wrong! I never used to be afraid. And now I'm terrified.

Colin Terrified of what?

Laura Terrified of losing you.

The **Magus** *comes back in and finds them embracing.*

Magus I'm so sorry.

Colin (*joyfully*) It's really strange. Things are going so well and all of a sudden everyone's so sorry.

Magus Well, I'm shocked. And there was me thinking I'd been so romantic.

All three laugh.

Doctor S . . . *appears.*

Doctor S . . . I need to talk to Colin.

Laura Don't take him away from me.

Doctor S . . . *smiles kindly at* **Laura**.

Laura (*forcefully*) He's staying here now. And so am I. No one wants to get any better.

The **Magus** *gently takes her by the arm.*

Magus It's all right. I know what to do: I'll be the one she confides in. It's the part I always play. Something to do with my manly physique.

They go out. **Doctor S . . .** *comes up to* **Colin**.

Doctor S . . . I know what happened now. Just for a moment, you almost came out of the coma.

Colin Yes. That's exactly what happened. The fog lifted. (*Suddenly.*) And Laura.

Doctor S . . . There is nothing I can tell you.

Colin Down there, what are they thinking?

Doctor S . . . They have to find a new heart to transplant into her. It is her only hope.

Colin Is there much chance of it?

Doctor S . . . 'Chance' is the operative word. Someone must die for her to live. Someone who gets brought to Guy's Hospital. And in the next few hours.

Colin And you don't know if –

Doctor S . . . I never know who will die today or tomorrow.

Colin But you are told?

Doctor S . . . Who is there to tell me?

Colin God. The devil. Destiny. How am I supposed to know? Perhaps there's a great big book somewhere where it's all written down. (*Almost violently.*) What's written in your files?

Doctor S . . . (*holding tightly on to them*) Certain factors.

Colin Oh yes!

Doctor S . . . Factors like your temperament. Your personal history. Your general health. But not the choices you make. (*Suddenly more precise.*) You arrive in the world with a whole range of given parameters, burdened with heredity, a family history, an environment, a village, maybe, or a town; belonging to a country, a language and a particular time. You have so much that makes you different from each other, so much that makes you special, individual and unique. But there's one thing, just one thing you have in common and which makes you all the same. Your freedom. The fact that you're free to wreck your body, to slit your veins, free never to recover from the heartache of lost love, free to let yourselves rot in the past, free to become heroes, free to take all the wrong decisions. Free to ruin your own life or bring your own death much closer. Believe me, there is no great book of destiny. Just a few facts in a file. A few parameters. The only thing that you can't ever predict or calculate are the consequences of your freedom.

Colin What kind of rubbish is that? I mean, look at Laura. Born with a body that just doesn't function. How is she supposed to be able to choose?

Doctor S . . . She could choose to become addicted to suffering. She could choose to sink into depression and death. Instead, she chose to love life, to be joyful, gentle, in love with everything. Her birth left her in shadow; she chose the light. Everyone who has crossed her path remembers her as sunlight.

Colin I love her.

Doctor S . . . *turns down the corridor 'D' and then sympathetically turns back to face* **Colin**.

Doctor S . . . I know.

Colin Isn't it stupid?

Doctor S . . . Stupid to love? Never. (*Pause.*) On the other hand, in all honesty, you need to ask if you really love Laura . . . or whether you've just fallen for her now you know there's no possibility of real commitment and you know it has to end.

Colin *is knocked sideways by this.*

Doctor S . . . I'll go and see her. Leave her to me a moment. (*She exits down corridor 'A'.*)

The **Chairman** *crosses her path and watches her go.*

Chairman Of course the doctor has to go the minute I arrive.

Now it is his turn to drop into an armchair in front of **Colin**. *He suddenly looks bewildered.*

I'm beginning to think I've got everything completely wrong.

Colin (*lost in his thoughts*) Me too.

Chairman You think you've played your cards right and then they're just flung back in your face.

Colin True.

Chairman I've taken the wrong approach.

Colin (*suddenly paying attention*) Now you too? (*Almost amused.*) This hotel's infected with self-doubt. It's a kind of plague.

Chairman My dear young friend, cretins are the only people who never change their minds. And believe me, I've known a few.

Colin I'm sure you have.

Chairman (*ignoring him*) The big mistake I made was letting slip to the doctor that I belonged to the Panthers. The doctor's just the kind of person who'd be desperate to join and would have been turned down. The Panthers aren't going to accept an insignificant little doctor from a clinic like this. Some suburban clinic. And ever since I said the words Panthers club that doctor's had it in for me.

Colin Be serious. I mean, do you really think that the Panthers club has any meaning to anyone here?

Chairman (*without a second's doubt*) I don't know anyone who wouldn't give an arm and a leg to join in.

Colin You do now.

Chairman Do I?

Colin I'd never dream of joining it.

Chairman (*shocked*) What?

Colin It's never even crossed my mind.

Chairman (*suddenly understanding*) I get it! You'd rather join the Rotary!

Colin No, I wouldn't.

Chairman But I am telling you that the doctor turned right against me the minute I said I was a member of the Panthers.

Colin Have you any idea of the responsibilities the doctor has? Guiding human beings towards life or towards death? Helping them accept their fate?

Chairman (*bursting into laughter*) What? Have you swallowed that ridiculous idea of the Magus about the place we're in?

Colin Well . . . yes.

Chairman (*laughing*) A space between heaven and earth where we have to wait until our fate's been decided? Whether we live or we die? According to the direction of the lift? A hotel between two worlds?

Colin Yes.

Chairman (*laughing*) How naive can you be!

Colin But when I arrived, I remember getting the definite impression that you believed it too . . .

Chairman I pretend to. That ridiculous fortune teller believes it. The residents believe it. The doctor lets them all believe it out of sheer convenience. As for me, I'll just keep on pretending. It wouldn't do to cross them.

Colin So according to you, where are we exactly?

Chairman In a lunatic asylum.

Colin I see.

Chairman It's obvious, isn't it. The place is full of lunatics.

Colin (*amused*) So what are you doing here?

Chairman Administrative error. After I fell, the ambulance that brought me here brought me to the wrong place. That's what I keep trying to tell the doctor.

Colin So how come I don't feel any pain from my fractures? And how come Laura can walk quite normally when usually she's confined to a wheelchair?

Chairman Hypnotic auto-suggestion.

Colin And how come when you're in your room you can hear what your family is saying?

Chairman Now that is very strange. You're right there. But there has to be an explanation.

Colin And the explanation is the one that you're denying.

Chairman Now come on, my dear young friend, let's be serious. It is absolutely impossible for such a place to exist. There are no records of it anywhere and it certainly isn't mentioned in the scriptures. Now if, like me, you'd paid any attention to the higher truths of religion you would know perfectly well that after death we go straight to the presence of God.

Colin Well, perhaps God comes at the next stage –

Chairman Ridiculous. It doesn't say so in the Bible.

Colin But if you look around you, at the lift, the reception desk, the –

Chairman It simply does not exist. I can categorically state that none of it exists.

Colin And I suppose I don't exist either?

Chairman I can state that categorically.

Colin But how can you deny the existence of everything that's around you? I am here, you are here, we are both here. How can you possibly explain that? How can you put people and things to one side without even seeing them?

Chairman But my dear sir, that's very easy. That is known as having the courage of one's convictions.

Colin But you must admit there are some things you simply can't explain.

Chairman Of course. But my dear young friend, when things are confusing and bewildering, that is exactly when one has most need of one's convictions.

Colin So at the end of the day your convictions matter more to you than what you see in front of your own eyes?

Chairman Of course. Life is troubled, dark and confusing. That's what belief is for: to be a light to guide our feet. Otherwise what would be the use of it? Your trouble is you think too much.

Colin (*exasperated*) And your trouble is you don't think at all!

Chairman What?

Colin You don't think!

Chairman (*shrugging his shoulders*) What a lout. No wonder you want to join the Rotary.

The **Magus** *and* **Laura** *enter arm in arm. They both look very happy.*

Laura What a shame you weren't here the last time.

Magus Let's hope you're with us for a long long time.

Laura (*looking at* **Colin**) I hope so too.

Colin *gets up. He and* **Laura** *slowly go up to each other and look each other in the eye. This irritates the* **Chairman**, *who leaves. We hear his bedroom door slam.*

Colin Now it's all much harder.

Laura Yes.

Colin I don't really know what to say.

Laura Me neither.

Colin, *aware he is being watched, turns to the* **Magus**.

Colin We're not disturbing you, are we?

Magus Not a bit. Truly. Absolutely not in the slightest. (*He unfolds his newspaper.*) I will make the most of the peace and quiet. I will read my paper.

Laura Leave him. He's a sweetheart.

They look at each other again.

Colin There's no future in this.

Laura The future doesn't matter.

Colin (*tenderly*) You're right.

They look at each other. They touch hands.

Laura There. We've made it. And now there's no need to say a word.

The **Chairman** *charges in, angry as usual, and makes a charge at the* **Magus**. *He tears the newspaper out of his hands.*

Chairman Would you please give me the financial page!

He tears out the page and drops the rest on the ground.

Magus (*ironically*) But of course. Be my guest.

Chairman (*scanning down the columns*) My cretin of an eldest son in claiming oil shares are down! (*He finds the place and exclaims.*) But this is yesterday's paper!

Magus Of course. And it was the same the day before that. It's the one I had when I came here six months ago. I read it every day.

Chairman That's stupid.

Magus Tut tut; you speak out of ignorance . . . I absolutely know this paper by heart and I can assure you that *The Times* of 12 April is the best there has ever been.

Chairman How can you bear always to read the same newspaper?

Magus I can't claim that each time I read it I experience the same feeling of astonished surprise, but on the other hand I am always interested. Always fascinated, for instance, by the story of the poor woman who weighs twenty-four stone, has six children to bring up and has just lost her job because she's a little overweight. What will become of her, I wonder? How will she continue to feed her gorgeous children? And as for you, my dear Chairman, whose party has so disastrously lost the election, how, I ask myself, how are you going to continue to rule the country?

Chairman Oh, that's no problem at all, I can assure you. That's ancient history. It's simply a matter of . . .

Magus No, please don't tell me. If you give me the answer today, it will take away all the joy of asking the same question tomorrow.

Chairman But if you really want to know . . .

Magus If I really wanted to know, I certainly wouldn't be reading the newspaper! I like the suspense. I like the soap opera of life. I like asking myself whatever's going to happen tomorrow, I like imagining that something is actually happening. If I wanted to learn anything, I'd read history books.

Chairman You are completely and utterly mad.

Magus And I suppose you represent the voice of reason? In that case I'm only too glad to be mad.

Chairman What?

Magus What saddens me about you, dear Chairman, is your utter lack of repartee. All you can say when I strike home is 'what?'

Chairman What?

Magus Your replies are so feeble that I have the most awful feeling that one day you won't even notice I'm insulting you.

Chairman What? (*Pulling himself together.*) My opinion is that one should never lose a friend over a witticism.

Magus The trouble is that words tend to be more faithful than friends.

We hear the alarm ringing to announce someone is about to leave.

Doctor S . . . *enters, followed by her* **Assistants**. *They head for the screen.*

Doctor S . . . Mr Chairman, your time has come.

Chairman At last! It was high time to put an end to this scandalous state of affairs.

Doctor S . . . Mr Chairman, you must understand that I have neither the right nor the power to treat you any differently from anyone else; nor have I been in a position to bring forward the occurrence of whatever has to happen.

Chairman (*visibly softened by these apologies*) That's fine. Now everything is sorted out we've no need to talk about it. I was in a hurry; I was pressed for time.

Doctor S . . . I do hope this brief stay and this opportunity for reflection have been of use to you, Mr Chairman.

Chairman (*having a sudden thought*) Yes, it certainly has. I think I shall make a new will.

Doctor S . . . (*without really listening*) Very good.

Chairman I will leave my wife as little as I decently can, disinherit both sons and set up a charitable foundation.

Doctor S . . . (*again without really listening*) I'm delighted to hear it.

Chairman And the foundation will be called the Delbeck foundation, in my honour, and will ensure that I am never forgotten.

Doctor S . . . Would you mind just stepping into this lift, Mr Chairman?

He goes up to her and whispers.

Chairman You know, if you want I can put in a good word for you so you get into the club.

Doctor S . . . What?

Chairman (*with a certain air of self-importance*) The Panthers. They can't possibly turn me down. My building firm is the only one that can mend their lifts.

Doctor S . . . *signals to her* **Assistants** *to help the* **Chairman**.

He maintains his air of self-importance and winks at **Doctor S . . .**

Chairman So? Do you agree? I'll sponsor your application . . .

Magus The doctor prefers the Rotary Club.

Chairman (*beside himself with rage*) I might have known! I might have known! Rotary Club! They're nothing but left-wing terrorists!

The doors begin to close. The **Chairman** *suddenly becomes anxious and starts to protest.*

Chairman But where are you taking me? You've no right to! I'll call the police! Let me out! Let me out! Help!

The doors have closed. We no longer hear the **Chairman***'s cries.*

Everyone intently watches the indicators above the lift to see which way the **Chairman** *will go.*

After a second or so, the arrow indicates 'Down'. The bell stops ringing. We hear the lift going down to earth.

Colin (*outraged*) What?

Magus He's going back to earth! (*To* **Doctor S . . .**.) Tell me I'm wrong! He's not really got the right to go back to life a second time?

Doctor S . . . He has recovered from the shock. The Chairman's health is really excellent.

Magus It would be. He's totally selfish. Best thing for your health. Doctors recommend it.

Doctor S . . . And don't forget he was only knocked down by a bike.

Magus Give me that cyclist's address and I'll buy him a tank.

Colin So you kill Jessie and you resurrect the Chairman.

Doctor S . . . I did? I had nothing to do with it. Death isn't a punishment and it isn't a reward. You all take death to be something personal. That's a ridiculous attitude. Nobody escapes death. To put it in your terms, I haven't yet met anyone who deserved to die.

Colin Oh no? You never met a murderer?

Doctor S . . . They tend to die a violent death. As for the Chairman, his time had not come.

Magus (*with sudden vehemence*) And my daughter. Her time had come, had it?

Colin *and* **Laura** *look at the* **Magus** *with some surprise.*

Doctor S . . . (*going up to him, gently*) You know what I think about that. We have spoken of it before. Whether you're ten years old, twenty years old, or eighty or a hundred, it's always loss of human life. And it is always painful.

Magus (*calming down immediately*) Forgive me.

Doctor S . . . Life is a present that everyone receives. And everyone receives death also. The Chairman is a human being like anyone else.

Magus I try hard to respect everyone's right to their life. I simply find it hard to respect someone who has no respect for anyone else's.

Doctor S . . . *leaves.*

Colin Your daughter? You mean you had a daughter?

Magus (*controlling himself*) Me? No.

Colin *understands he should probe no further.*

Laura *smiles: she understands.*

All three sit down together.

Magus So, dear heart, tell me. How are they getting on down there?

Laura There's nothing more that they can do. It all depends on whether they can find someone to give me a heart.

Colin Aren't you worried?

Laura Why should I be?

Magus You are very strong.

Laura I've no strength in my body. I've had to try to get strength from somewhere.

Colin *takes her hand and kisses her. She takes pleasure in his kiss.*

Laura I'm not that special. It's just I've had to find happiness in little things. I've spent so much time of my life trapped in a bed or a wheelchair that I've really had no other option. I knew happiness was never going to come to me, so I've had to become an expert at finding happiness. There's no way I could ever hope to go for a walk in a garden; so I've had to learn to take pleasure in a single rose. There's no way I could hope to go sunbathing; so I've had to learn to take the same pleasure from a single ray of sunshine. I used to watch it coming through the slats of my venetian blind, and learn to really feel it on my face, on my shoulders and my breasts so that I really missed it when in the end it slid down to the floor. There's no way I can ever travel by boat, so I've had to learn to listen to the sound of the wind and the rain on the roof, and learn to imagine it. That's how I've sailed on all the oceans of the world, that's how I've felt the force of the hurricane, felt my little boat battered by the waves, and then the happiness of the glimpse of slate-grey coast in the peace of the dawn.

Ever watched a kitten playing with a piece of wool? It concentrates on it all its powers of imagination, mind and will, and I've had to learn to do the same. (**Colin** *kisses her again.*) And when I learn to take each moment as it comes, and to narrow my horizons, then I don't think happiness is ever really that far from us. You just have to stay still, to live totally in the present, forget what happened the day before and the thought of what might happen the day after. It's true. If you manage to make yourself very small, installing yourself very securely in the present moment of being in a chair placed in front of the window, you can savour the whole universe. Great happiness is made up of very tiny things. (*She looks at* **Colin**.) Just now, at this moment, you can't imagine how close I am to you. It's as if I'm touching each centimetre of your skin, as if each one of your breaths fills my lungs too, as if I can feel each movement of your limbs and each pulse of your blood. You fill each part of me. And I have never been so happy.

Colin You mean this is making love?

Laura Yes.

They look at each other intensely. The **Magus** *feels like a bit of a voyeur and hides himself behind his newspaper.*

Colin (*intoxicated*) I never knew there could be so much happening in a single second. I never knew each moment could have such possibilities.

Laura A second can carry a whole eternity.

She suddenly doubles up and starts to sob. **Colin** *quickly holds her in his arms. The* **Magus** *stops reading.*

Colin What's wrong?

Laura I don't know . . . all of a sudden, it all became too much for me . . . I am completely drained . . .

Colin Come. Let's go and lie down in my room.

They get up. **Colin** *helps her leave. Her nerves are stretched to breaking point.*

Laura They're going to tear us apart, Colin, it will be terrible, they're going to tear us apart.

Colin (*trying to calm her*) No, they won't. Whatever happens, we'll stay together.

Laura But nothing lasts, Colin, I know. They're going to tear us apart.

Colin Come on.

He takes her by the hand and they leave.

The **Magus** *watches them go.* **Doctor S . . .***'s* **Assistants** *have just come in and they also watch the couple leave.*

The **Magus** *turns to the* **Assistants**.

Magus Tell me, do angels have love stories too?

In reply, the two **Assistants** *look at each other tenderly.*

Magus Well, you lucky sods, at least you won't get bored here. (*Going up to them.*) But how do angels make love?

The two **Angels** *look amazed and mystified*

Magus So there is a justice in the world after all. What about me? Well, no, not often, as it happens, I can't really claim to have been much of a lover. Why not? (*Looking at himself in a mirror.*) Don't have the looks for it, I suppose. (*Astonishment from the* **Angels**.) You don't think so? All this time, I've been living in the wrong dimension. (*Jokingly.*) If you've got a moment or two to spare some time, perhaps we should take this a little further . . .

Doctor S . . . *enters.*

Doctor S . . . I would like to see you.

Magus You have some news for me?

Doctor S . . . Yes.

She sits down near him. She looks a bit depressed. He smiles at her sympathetically.

What I am about to say is outside my remit. According to the regulations, I do not have the right to inform you of this. It's just that you've been here for six months and I . . . I have become attached to you.

Magus All this smells like bad news coming.

Doctor S . . . (*brusquely*) Your condition is not improving.

The medical team is considering switching off your life support.

The **Magus** *looks shocked.*

Doctor S . . . I am very sorry. It's a nasty blow.

Magus You can say that again. To have to face being unplugged, as if one were a hairdryer. (*Pause.*) I hadn't really taken on board that I had fallen so low, that my life just depends on an electrical plug, at the mercy of a cleaner who might unplug me in favour of a floor polisher. (*Pause.*) What are they waiting for?

Doctor S . . . Someone's consent.

Magus Who is there to give their consent?

Doctor S . . . Your nephew. He's your only surviving relative.

Magus Oh, him. That snotty litle shit. You know, it really was quite extraordinary how much mucus used to flow out of his nostrils. Like a lava flow. I hope he remembers all the boxes of chocolate I've brought him. And those jolly Christmas gatherings we used to enjoy together. All those games of beggar my neighbour. I hope he never noticed how much I used to cheat.

Doctor S . . . They can't find him just now. There seems to be no way of contacting him.

Magus (*smiling*) The dear little fellow. He is in the United States to finish his degree. (*Beaming.*) There's an awful lot of United States.

Doctor S . . . Don't give yourself false hopes. They will find him. And you will never come out of your coma.

Magus I know.

She touches his shoulder. He takes her hand. He smiles.

Colin *rushes in.*

Colin Excuse me. A moment. Doctor, there's something I've got to ask you. But I need to know that you'll say yes.

Doctor S . . . (*letting go of the* **Magus***'s hand*) In which case the answer is probably no.

Colin No, wait. Give me a second. And listen. What I'd like is that no matter what happens me and Laura travel in the lift together. Whichever way it goes. Understand? Whether it goes up or down, as long as we're in there together.

Magus Aren't you frightened any more?

Colin There's just one thing frightens me: the thought of losing her.

Magus So you've changed your mind about up there? Do you think there is something now?

Colin Before it seemed to make sense to me to think that life had just come together by accident, that it was just an arbitrary mixture of molecules, all tossed together like some vile soup, which is why it used to make me feel so sick. But now when I look at Laura . . . Could molecules bumping together by accident have created Laura? Could some random combination of chromosomes really be capable of creating Laura's beauty, Laura's smile, Laura's mind?

Doctor S . . . Quite possibly.

Colin No. Now I have a good reason to be an optimist. And that reason is Laura.

Doctor S . . . I am glad that you have started to love life. But aren't you afraid of dying?

Colin (*trembling*) Less.

Doctor S . . . The God who has brought you into being could also make you disappear.

Colin (*hesitantly*) If you can't be around for ever, what's the point in being around at all?

Doctor S . . . Isn't it enough that things just exist? Why do you want them to last?

Colin We can't just have been given this intelligence, this consciousness, just for it all to disappear. That's a rotten joke, that is, that's a poisoned chalice. But the fact that we know, doesn't that count for something? I can't believe consciousness is just like drops of blood on a hunk of flesh. It's got to be consciousness that makes us more than bleeding lumps of meat.

Doctor S . . . This is what the mystics called the razor's edge. The fine line between hope and despair. Are we talking about being conscious of a tragedy? Or conscious of a mystery?

Colin I'll take the risk. Knowing that we're going to die, I'll take it to be a sign.

Magus A sign of what?

Colin A sign that death isn't the end of everything.

Doctor S . . . But everything is still very unclear.

Colin I used to see darkness everywhere. But now I see it as the darkness before the dawn.

Doctor S . . . And you owe all that to Laura?

Colin I mean, what's a miracle? A miracle is something that leads us to have faith. So Laura is that miracle. I know she is.

Doctor S . . . I'm glad.

Colin It's all it takes. One miracle. Now I feel a certain faith. A certain trust, and I want to be able to have hope in something I do not understand. (*Pleading.*) Please let us leave together.

Doctor S . . . I would like to be able to say yes.

Colin Then say yes.

Doctor S . . . But it is not my decision to take. (*Pause.*) I have no authority. None at all.

Colin (*demoralised*) I see . . .

Doctor S . . . What happens to Laura depends on circumstances. I have no control over circumstances.

Colin Of course. Of course. (*He slowly goes back to corridor 'A'.*) I'll go back and see Laura. It's stupid of me to spend so much time apart from her. (*Dazed.*) Thank you. (*He goes.*)

Doctor S . . . *is worn out by this exchange and lets herself fall back on to a chair.*

Magus It's a tough job.

Doctor S . . . *says nothing.*

Magus (*with understanding*) You get to know people, you get to care about them and then, all of a sudden, you have to tell them there's nothing you can do for them.

Doctor S . . . *still says nothing, but smiles at him.*

Magus I like you, Doctor. I didn't at first. I thought you were very hard. I used to get very angry with you for not answering my questions.

Doctor S . . . You didn't want answers. You just wanted me to comfort you with lies.

Magus Yes. With lies. Like the Chairman. And the so-called courage of one's convictions. The refuge of the feeble-minded. Even negative convictions feel better than doubt. I so needed someone to say: this is how it is.

Doctor S . . . And then you learned how to live with hypotheses.

Magus The pleasure you get from a good hypothesis. It's like playing with a soap bubble. And when it bursts, you just blow another one.

Doctor S . . . *is about to leave.*

The **Magus** *gets up suddenly, takes out a card from his pocket and gives it to the doctor.*

Magus Take this. It's my nephew's phone number. I want them to call him so he can give permission to unplug me.

Doctor S . . . It's no use. What will happen will happen. It is not for me to communicate this information.

Magus Doctor, I beg you, we have to move fast. Laura is in the same hospital as I am. It's very simple: all they have to do is pull out a plug, take out a little piece of flesh from inside my chest and take it down in the lift to the floor below.

Doctor S . . . You are asking me to do something that is completely forbidden.

Magus Aren't you sick and tired of seeing people coming and going? Tired of watching them slowly become aware of all they've done wrong and all they might have done right, tired of seeing them possibly develop; the chance of becoming better people and then, all of a sudden, clunk, it's all useless? Aren't you tired of seeing fate working like a lottery? That the only criterion should be randomness? Why doesn't God say anything? Is God in a coma too? Why doesn't He reply? Is He in a state of shock? For hundreds and hundreds of years there's people saying prayers at His bedside. So why doesn't He do something? Or if He's really pissed off somewhere, or if He's never going to wake up, then you take His place. You play God!

Doctor S . . . What you're saying is completely naive. God! Do you really imagine that somehow the universe keeps accounts of your good deeds, that the good are rewarded and the bad are punished, that illness itself is a kind of punishment, that goodness fights off death? Do you really imagine there's that kind of justice? Anything that vaguely resembles justice, even something arbitrary and absurd, even an unjust kind of justice, ruled by gods whose actions are arbitrary or partisan or even ruled completely by chance? Don't you see how absurd it is to imagine some kind of ordering principle, some kind of thinking being, some kind of will that is just like us only somehow a bit higher? No, it's not like that. Life is how it has always been: blind, deaf, profoundly indifferent. The world couldn't give a shit for your courage or your dignity.

Magus What about free will? My free will? What about yours?

Doctor S . . . You are living in the one place in the

whole universe where will counts for nothing at all.

Magus Listen, Doctor. We can only have freedom if we believe in it and make use of it. All right, matter obeys its own laws of entropy and chaos, I know that, but wouldn't you like just once to put a tiny little spanner in the works, and introduce just a tiny little element of will and humanity into the whole gigantic inhuman universe machine?

Doctor S . . . *says nothing.*

Magus It's not that much to ask. Just a tiny little spanner. A little human decision, that's all, the simple opposite of blind chance.

Doctor S . . . *says nothing.*

Magus Besides, Doctor, just imagine: think how delightful to bend the rules . . .

Doctor S . . . Sometimes you say things that are so intelligent. And then I never understand why you can't resist the temptation to add something unbelievably stupid.

Magus Sometimes, when I was a boy, I would climb up to the top of our little apple tree and look up at the sky and feel different. Able to do anything. Superman. And I would say to myself, 'If I really want to, I can hold my breath for ever.' And that's what I would do. And the harder it became, and the redder I got, the stronger I felt. In the end, of course, I had to let go. But I never let go of that feeling. And some days, I would tell myself: 'If I decide not to, I won't ever die.' And that used to seem so easy. Particularly because those days to make it happen I didn't have to do a thing. Later, I finally understood there was no escaping it. It was unavoidable. And that was the first lesson I learned of my long, long stay with you: to accept the unavoidable. And now all I want is for someone to make use of me so that girl can live. I want my heart to beat in place of hers. I want my death to be a gift. A gift for her. So let that, dear Doctor, let that be the second lesson I learn here. To learn to love. To love the unavoidable.

He puts the card in **Doctor S . . .** *'s hand. Then he kisses her: and the kiss seals the bargain.*

She is profoundly moved. She wants to say something in reply; but she is too moved to speak. She slips away.

Laura *and* **Colin** *enter the reception area. The* **Magus** *hides behind his newspaper.*

Laura (*troubled*) No, listen, that's what happens. I know what'll happen when we get back down to earth. We'll forget everything that's happened here. I had forgotten all about my first stay here and only remembered when the lift doors opened. Just imagine if we get back to earth and don't recognise each other.

Colin But we will. I'll recognise you, I know I will.

Laura No. You won't. One day we're going to bump into each other somewhere, in a corridor maybe, or on the street, and you'll just look right through me and you won't even notice I'm there.

Colin No, that's impossible, I'll look for you everywhere.

Laura Me too. But I'd like you to train yourself.

Colin Train myself to what?

Laura I know something not even the doctor knows. Last time I was here I met a man called Juan, who taught me to tango.

Colin (*suddenly jealous*) What?

Laura (*laughing*) Don't worry, he was over eighty. He was so happy to feel himself free of arthritis and supple again that he really wanted to dance. So I was his partner. It was the first time I had ever danced.

Colin And so?

Laura (*suddenly serious*) So listen. When I came back down to earth, I'd forgotten all about the hotel, and all about Juan and all about his tango lessons. But my feet hadn't forgotten. My feet kept trying to do the steps. Even if I didn't know, my feet did. They still knew. Our conscious mind forgets everything that's happened here, but our body has a memory all its own. We must get into training. I want to be sure that our bodies will recognise each other.

With real urgency, she puts **Colin***'s hands round her waist.*

If your hands don't feel that, it isn't me.

Colin I love you.

Laura Smell my hair.

Colin Freshly cut grass. Ripe pears.

Laura If you don't smell that it isn't me.

Colin I love you.

Laura Look into my eyes.

Colin Green and dark-blue threads.

Laura How many?

Colin Oh, I don't know. Thousands . . .

Laura If there's less than a thousand, it isn't me.

Colin I love you.

Laura Kiss me.

They exchange a kiss which makes them shiver.

Colin Don't worry. I'll never forget. I won't. I promise I won't.

She detaches herself from him in exasperation.

Laura I'm a fool. You're going to look for me in hundreds of women who won't be me and when they smile at you – and they all will – you'll speak to them, you'll pay court to them, you'll kiss them. And that is absolutely not what I want. No, we'll have to find something else.

Colin I'll teach you a code. A secret code.

He draws her lovingly towards him. She snuggles up to him. He does exactly what he says he will do.

I kiss your ears: one, two. I kiss your brow: three four. I

kiss your eyes: five, six. I kiss your lips: seven, eight.

Laura *is so charmed by his tenderness that she seems a little drunk.*

Laura Yes. Yes I like that. Let's repeat.

They start again.

You kiss my ears: one, two. You kiss my brow: three four. You kiss my eyes: five, six. You kiss my lips: seven, eight.

They draw apart, intoxicated.

Colin Shall we do it again?

Just at that moment, **Doctor S . . .** *appears, followed by her two* **Assistants**

Doctor S . . . Colin, I have to speak to you. In your room.

Colin Fine. Coming.

Doctor S . . . *passes close to the* **Magus** *and speaks in a low voice to him so that the others cannot hear. The* **Magus** *gets up.*

Doctor S . . . The card happened to fall out of your locker. By the purest chance. A nurse happened to be passing and picked it up.

Magus By the purest chance?

Doctor S . . . The purest chance.

Magus It's amazing what chance gets up to sometimes.

Doctor S . . . Sometimes. (*Pause.*) They're ringing your nephew. He is astonished to hear how ill you are. He is embarrassed not to have known before. He says he is not in favour of people being kept artificially alive. He also says that he used to love you a lot.

Magus Used to . . . ?

The imperfect tense hits the **Magus** *hard and he has a moment of weakness. He sinks back on to the arm of a chair.* **Colin** *leaves with* **Doctor S . . .** *and her* **Assistants**.

Laura (*surprised at how pale the* **Magus** *is looking*) Are you not feeling well?

Magus No, I'm fine. Thank you. Absolutely fine. (*He sits.*)

Laura *sits next to him.*

Magus You know, I used to have a daughter who was rather like you. The same defiant little eyes that always seemed to be laughing at the world. A certain cheekiness in the profile. The same courageous air about her, the look of someone who wasn't going to be defeated by life. The same heavy silky hair that seemed to be overflowing with good health and beauty. Whenever I looked at her I found her so lovely I would say to myself, 'How could you have produced anyone so beautiful?' She had magic powers: every time she entered a room, she made all of life's tediums completely disappear. At that time I was a travelling salesman of some kind, always in a plane, spending nights in identical hotels, customers who were always showing me the door; but at the end of the darkness there was always this little light glowing. My daughter. My beautiful daughter. Then, all of a sudden, business started to pick up and I began landing the most enormous transatlantic contracts. One day, when I was at the far end of the United States, she gave me a ring. Her voice sounded somehow strange: 'Daddy,' she said, 'I'm not well,' and I learned she'd had to go to hospital. But I had to stay the wrong side of the Atlantic. I was making the most extraordinary amount of money and somehow I just couldn't let it go. I was feeling terribly pleased with myself and even though I could hear on the telephone that her voice was getting weaker, I was sure she was so strong, so full of health, that she'd get over it, and we would see each other and she'd be fine again. (*Pause.*) She died. She was twenty years old. It was a virus. One of these new ones they don't yet understand, an implacably destructive war machine that eats away human strength and human flesh, and just leaves you with a shrivelled-up little body in a huge hospital bed. I came too late. Just after.

He can't go on. **Laura** *rests her head on his shoulder.*

Magus I left my work. I learned how to make tables turn

and talk to spirits, and how to look into crystal balls. I wanted her to speak to me. I couldn't bear for her to have just disappeared. But all I found was silence. Then I became the Magus. I started to wear this ridiculous costume that somehow helped me stop crying out in grief. (*Pause.*) It's strange, the memories you have of your own child are somehow locked up in a sanctuary, as if protected by pain: they don't seem to have the same substance as ordinary memories. They don't fade. They can't be changed or touched. (*Pause.*) I did nothing for her.

Laura There was nothing you could do.

Magus I wasn't even there.

Laura You couldn't be.

Magus I still feel guilty. I would have liked to . . . make amends.

Laura You can never make amends.

Magus Yes, I think you can. And I have. I did it one day. For someone else.

Laura Really?

Magus Yes.

Pause.

Laura That must have been a wonderful moment.

Magus (*crying with happiness*) Yes. Yes, it was wonderful.

Laura *goes up to him and speaks with a simple warm directness.*

Laura I really like you. People tend to make fun of you a little. But I really like you.

Magus (*crying and smiling*) Thank you.

She hugs him. He is profoundly moved and a little clumsy in his response.

Just then, **Doctor S . . .** *rushes in, followed by her* **Assistants**. *She is about to leave, as usual, but when she sees* **Laura** *hugging the* **Magus**, *she stops a moment. Then she says gently:*

Doctor S . . . Laura, I'd be grateful if you'd give me a moment or two with the Magus.

Laura Of course, Doctor.

She cheerfully leaves the **Magus**.

See you soon?

Magus (*putting his hand to his heart*) See you soon.

Laura *goes.*

Doctor S . . . *is consulting her illuminated screen. A light is flashing red. The bell starts to ring. She turns to the* **Magus**.

Doctor S . . . Excuse me, but we are already late.

Magus Is this going to happen?

Doctor S . . . Please enter the lift.

She accompanies him to the lift doors, which open.

Magus Doctor, I know you have not the right to tell me this, but is this going to happen?

He is already in the lift.

Doctor S . . . The medical team have decided to transplant your heart into Laura.

Magus Thank you.

Doctor S . . . (*profoundly moved*) Don't say that. No one has ever thanked me. Above all, not going up.

Magus (*just before the doors close*) Thank you.

The lift has closed. We see the 'Up' arrow light up. We hear the tremendous roar of departure. The bell stops ringing.

Doctor S . . . *a little anxious, turns to her two* **Assistants**, *who know she has disobeyed the rules.*

Doctor S . . . I know. I have broken the law.

The bell begins to ring again.

Quick. Go and find Laura.

The two **Assistants** *run off. They return a few seconds later, followed by* **Colin** *and* **Laura**, *hugging each other.*

Doctor S . . . Laura, it's your time.

Laura (*still in* **Colin***'s arms; suddenly frightened*) No, please, not yet.

Doctor S . . . (*looking at her indicator with some alarm*) Please, Laura, there's not a second to be lost.

Laura No, not yet. And where's the Magus? I wanted to say goodbye to the Magus!

Colin *takes this very calmly. He leads* **Laura** *to the lift and, once she's there, passionately embraces her.*

The two **Assistants** *gently separate the two lovers and lead* **Laura** *to the lift.*

Colin Dear love, don't be frightened.

Laura (*feverishly repeating*) One, two: you kiss my ears. Three, four: you kiss my brow. Five, six: you kiss my eyes. Seven, eight: you kiss my lips.

She is alone and frightened in the lift.

The doors close.

Laura (*her cry smothered by the closing doors*) Colin!

Doctor S . . . *and her* **Assistants** *look at the indicator arrows with real anxiety. Suddenly the 'Down' arrow lights up. The lift leaves.*

Colin (*shouting for joy*) Yes! Yes! Yes!

He joyfully kisses **Doctor S . . .** *and her two* **Assistants**, *who don't mind this at all.*

Thank you, Doctor. Thank you for telling me just then what the Magus did. Otherwise I would not have been brave enough to take Laura to the lift. That was the second miracle.

Doctor S . . . (*somewhat embarrassed by the presence of her* **Assistants**) Don't mention it.

She leans against a wall to get her breath back.

Nothing right now is quite following the rules. But tomorrow will be different. (*And she looks at the two* **Angels** *in white who smile enigmatically. She understands what they are saying; pauses a moment and also smiles.*) No, you're right. Tomorrow will be exactly the same. (*She goes back to her indicator and tells* **Colin**.) Soon it will be your turn.

Colin (*gently*) In which direction?

Doctor S . . . I don't know.

Colin (*even more gently*) Doctor, have you really any idea what happens up there?

She is about to reply, but feels a little constrained in the presence of her **Assistants**.

They perceive her feelings. They consult each other and leave.

Doctor S . . . *stays alone with* **Colin**.

Doctor S . . . No.

Colin Not even you?

Doctor S . . . I just know my job. To greet you. To make you wait. Then make sure you get in the lift. (*Pause.*) I know nothing. I just guard the door. (*Pause.*) All I know is that once you go up, you never come down.

Colin Why does everyone call you doctor?

Doctor S . . . That's just how you happened to perceive me. It could change. It depends on the situation. (*Pause.*) You, for instance, took me to be a woman.

Colin Sorry?

Doctor S . . . The Chairman of the Board took me for a man.

Colin (*stupefied*) That's all a bit beyond me!

Doctor S . . . (*with a small knowing smile*) Me too. (*Pause.*) For me, as for you, death is not so much a fact as a mystery.

Colin You know more about this than you're letting on. (*Pause.*) If life is a gift, then who has given it to us?

Doctor S . . . What do you think?

Colin I'm asking you.

Doctor S . . . And I am asking you.

Colin (*hesitantly*) God? Or life itself?

Doctor S . . . All the answers are simply new questions. What if it's God? Or what if it's life itself? What difference does that make? In any case, it means you have a debt to pay.

Colin A debt?

Doctor S . . . Someone's given you a present. You have to accept it.

Colin Of course.

Doctor S . . . Then look after it.

Colin Yes.

Doctor S . . . And then pass it on, this present, give life something in return: children, perhaps, or actions of some kind, works of art maybe, or simply love . . .

Colin Yes. Yes, you're right. (*Thoughtfully.*) And maybe, at the very end, when our time's up, when the present is about to be used up, maybe we will eventually have earned it . . .

Doctor S . . . (*mysteriously*) Maybe . . .

Colin So you really don't know what death is?

Doctor S . . . The worst thing that could happen to that question would be for it to get a reply.

The bell starts ringing.

It's your turn now.

The two **Assistants** *reappear.*

The lift doors open. **Colin** *obediently heads towards them.*

Colin It's strange. Even if I'm going to die just now, I still feel . . . very calm.

Doctor S . . . Don't be afraid.

Colin No. But now I'm not so sure. Maybe I'm just less afraid of something I know nothing of.

Doctor S . . . Trust is like a little flame. It may not light anything, but it does help keep you warm.

Colin *enters the lift, but once there, all of a sudden, he is seized by anxiety.*

Colin Doctor, if Laura and me do meet back on earth, do you think we will recognise each other?

Doctor S . . . I think so. As soon as you leave the lift, you'll forget everything. But on earth we still keep an unconscious memory of what has happened beyond earth. It's a profound memory, hidden in the depths of the soul: but it is revived when two people look at each other for the first time. It makes them recognise each other. It's called love at first sight.

The doors close on **Colin**.

Doctor S . . . *and her two* **Assistants** *look up to see which arrow is going to light up. But the light gets brighter and brighter until it is a dazzling white, a blinding white, as if the whole stage were dissolving in the light, before we have been able to discover if* **Colin** *died or went back down to earth.*

Lightning Source UK Ltd.
Milton Keynes UK
05 March 2010

150959UK00007B/1/P